THE CROOKED PATH TO A CHARMED LIFE

A CLAIRVOYANT MEDIUM'S JOURNEY TO
EMBRACING HER SPIRITUAL GIFTS

BERNADETTE GOLD

The Crooked Path To A Charmed Life

A Clairvoyant Medium's Journey To Embracing Her Spiritual Gifts

Publisher: Sarcastic Queen Press

ISBN: 978-1-7379566-1-7

CONTENTS

The Crooked Path To A Charmed Life   v

1. 1992 The Vision That Changed Everything   1
2. Unexpected Adversity   24
3. Tragedy Strikes Again   30
4. Radical Healing   37
5. Sent To Paradise   43
6. Hiding In The Tower   50
7. Finding My Spirit Animal   57
8. Crashing Into Adulting   65
9. Finding The Love Of My Life   76
10. Blindly Moving Forward   88
11. Returning Home   98
12. A Cry For Help   103
13. Creating A Magical Life   112
14. Living In A Postcard   129
15. Spiritual Puberty   135
16. Horsing Around   139
17. Falling Into My Purpose   144
18. The Middle Of Nowhere   150
19. Hidden Darkness   162
20. I'm Not Your Mom   168
21. Spiritual Battles   177
22. In Comes Dad, Out Goes Hubby   183
23. I Choose To Live   200
24. Miracle In The Desert   207
25. Fulfilling My Promise To Teach   229
26. Finding Alignment   237
27. Protection And Alignment   248
28. 4Th Dimension Spiritual Hierarchy   255
29. Continuing The Journey   263
30. Completion, Endings & New Beginnings   275

Afterword 283
Acknowledgments 285
Bernadette's Bio 287

THE CROOKED PATH TO A CHARMED LIFE

PREFACE

Years ago, Spirit prompted me to write a memoir, an account of my life as I journeyed through the unseen realms. Born a clairvoyant, clairaudient, medium, and empath, I've always been able to see angels and spirits, hear their voices, receive teachings, and connect to God. Although these are great blessings and sacred gifts, there have been times in my life when they have been burdens, weighing heavily on my mind and heart. As I sit to write, I am filled with resistance to unearth personal stories, feelings, and memories long since buried.

With a sense of vulnerability, tinged with fear, I am sharing events and incidents directed by Spirit, trusting it will help those who read it. Please understand, while I refer to God a lot, I am NOT referring to the religious God. The Tao Te Ching calls it "The Nameless, that if named loses all meaning or The Mother of 10,000 Things." You can call it Universe, Source, Father/Mother,

Infinite Creator; to me it's all the same. One God, One Creation. After years of religious deprogramming, I can call upon God, Spirit, Universe, Creator, instantly connecting to All That Is.

It's been a blessing to witness miracles and manifestations that are nothing short of awe-inspiring, even to me. I've agonized over feelings of not belonging anywhere on this planet throughout my life. Feeling much of the time as if I'm alive by some mistake. As a result, I've struggled with depression, anxiety, and even ideas of suicide. I hope that my journey will help you to understand your journey and heal your wounds.

The retelling of my life from my perspective is by no means meant to be taken as fact. Perception, beliefs, and experiences create a filter of our worldview, making it very personal. I don't believe that my account of events is 100% accurate except to me—it is my vision of events, how these events affected me and still affect me that I relate them.

In the year 2000, I began giving psychic readings professionally. Since then, I have walked with angels by my side, filled with every emotion available in the human experience. If not for the support of God, my guides, angels, and The Holy Spirit, I would not be here today. Although I've struggled to understand my purpose on this planet and in this lifetime, I am finally at a place where I am not only empowered to stand in my truth but to share it with others. I've spent a good deal of my life running from the responsibility of my psychic gifts and soul's obvious path. The funny thing about rejecting your soul plan is that no matter how hard you try to get away from it, it follows you relentlessly.

EVERYTHING CHANGED when I finally submitted my life to be a vessel of service to God's Divine plan. What people see now is a woman transformed by years of the work I've done with the angels and Spirit in addition to a steady course of deep internal self-reflection. It is only because of their unceasing support and guidance that I am not only alive but thriving. I hope that others struggling the way I have in the past can find solace in knowing they are not alone. The Holy Spirit and God's Angelic army are here for us, to assist in the human journey and guide us to our highest good. Though painful at times, there is such beauty in life and all its experiences. This time we live in is a pivotal time in history. God is calling many people forward into the light of service. Some are called to have visions, give messages, or heal; others to anchor the light of love, joy, peace, compassion, and kindness. No matter what our Spiritual Gifts are, God has chosen each of us for a specific task that we agreed to before our birth and assigned Angels to help us each step of the way.

My prayer for everyone is that we all come to know God the way I do, each in our way. I pray that everyone can feel the true Spirit of God in their life, guiding, directing, and loving them. It is my deepest hope that sharing my story inspires others to fulfill their purpose in a powerful way that spreads love and compassion. I pray Spirit to guide us all to the light of God—a light truly unfathomable from our narrow Human perspective.

There have been many characters in my life who have taught me many lessons. I am not a victim but a seeker of truth and a perpetual student in this world. Names have been changed to protect the privacy and anonymity of the people included in the book. My search for understanding has taken me many places and through many challenges, yet I never walked alone. This connection to God has blessed me with an amazing journey with the Angels and Spirit.

1

1992 THE VISION THAT CHANGED
EVERYTHING

In 1992, I lived with my one-year-old daughter and her father in a small town in Eastern Washington, where I began an intense study of the bible.

So many strange things were occurring in my life during that time, both good and evil. It was a farming community with a vegetable processing plant in the center of town. Migrant workers came seasonally to preserve vegetables. Farmers grew acres of wheat. The tone was mellow, small-town America. I certainly thought it was a harmless place at first glance.

When my daughter Brindi was just a few months old, she was hospitalized at Seattle Children's Hospital. Unable to hold her formula down, she was diagnosed with infant gastroesophageal reflux. In addition, the lower esophageal sphincter (or LES), a muscle that separates the esophagus from the stomach, wasn't fully developed. In the room next door was a young family with an infant daughter that had a heart condition. The other Mom and I hit it off instantly, keeping each other company while our babies were being poked, tested, and treated for their ailments.

My new friend referred my husband to a job in a small town of migrants and farmers where she lived. It was an opportunity we seized when Brindi recovered. Moving east, we settled into a lovely old blue Victorian, surrounded by apple trees, horse pastures, and beautiful meadows just outside of town.

Born and raised in Southern California, I was a city girl through and through; I lived in Seattle through junior high and high school, returning to California after graduation. Shortly before Brindi was born, I moved back to the Seattle area to be near family. Although I trained horses, knowing the dirty work involved in farm work, I was ill-prepared for the education I was about to receive.

Once settled in our new home, the rancher's wife decided she would school me in the ways of the farm. These duties extended beyond anything even remotely familiar to me. We were required to attend church with her and her husband, and I had to allow her to teach me the "sound habits and traditions of a good Christian woman." Within days of our arrival, she taught me how to pluck a chicken, bake bread, preserve tomatoes and measure the "proper portions" to feed our husbands and farm hands. Without warning, my life was thrown into a flurry of change and expectations. I was exhausted from raising a one-year-old and doing my best to adjust to my new life. I had little time to pay attention to a lot of small things happening around me. I found myself thrust into a surreal world of spirits, both benevolent and malevolent, inside and outside of our home. Noises, unseen voices, and spooky chanting all began to fill the house at various times of the night and day. I was utterly overwhelmed, scared, and confused.

I gradually made a couple of friends while attending the Assembly of God church in town. Then, I cautiously began asking questions about the area, the house we lived in, and the town's history. I wanted to get information that would help me make sense of what was happening to me. Unfortunately, my husband didn't seem concerned, believing I was just "freaking out" from living so far out in the "sticks."

It's important to note that I can recall seeing angels, having friends no one else could see, and feeling protected by unseen allies throughout my whole life. Seeing spirits wasn't new to me, but the initiation I was entering was something I could never have imagined. Being raised in a Catholic family turned Christian, talking about spirits, ghosts, or anything else that frightened us was unacceptable. Entering Catholic school in Kindergarten, I realized that the nuns didn't really "know" God or his Spirit. It was always better to keep my visions and unseen allies a secret. My unseen friends comforted me, played with me, and often gave me a heads-up on how best to protect myself and my relationship with them. They cautioned me about sharing with others what I saw and experienced. Living with an emotionally unstable mother made it even harder to speak about any of my human feelings.

Much of my life as a child was about surviving and avoiding trouble. I did everything I could to avoid attention, to keep from getting spanked either at home or at school. I trusted my friends in Spirit far more than I trusted the humans who appeared to be so ignorant of so much.

Things got increasingly intense as the weeks in the farmhouse passed. Bats would circle our house and dive bomb us as we walked in and out. Voices from beyond would haunt me while I was in the kitchen. The entire upstairs of the house was always cold and eerie. I hated going up to the sitting and reading room we had on the third floor. Dark and scary, it always felt as if someone or something was watching, waiting for an opportunity to attack.

I continued my research into the town and the history behind it. There was an attitude of blatant racism and limited thinking that I'd never quite experienced before. Growing up in California and Seattle, both melting pots of culture, there weren't such biased, hateful beliefs about the color of one's skin. Nor had I ever been exposed to the religious dogma of the Assembly of God church. I began to pray earnestly for assistance and answers, realizing there was so much I didn't know.

The more I prayed, the more lucid my dreams became, creating an awareness that I was dreaming while still asleep. Soon I began having waking dreams or visions with scenes that played out like holographic images full of sound, color, and smell. Clairvoyance and clairaudience both intensified as I continued to seek help from the heavenly realms.

Religious dogma intensified too. Ordinary things like wearing makeup, cutting my hair, and not wearing nylons were considered "sinful" in the church. Members of the congregation were quick to chastise and criticize me. Not attending church wasn't an option, an unstated rule; even if you didn't fully believe in God, you were expected to attend.

Sitting through sermons at church every Wednesday evening and Sunday morning, I began experiencing strange things with my hearing. It was as if my hearing was shutting down, replaced by loud, high-pitched ringing. My ears wouldn't stop ringing no matter how hard I tried to clear them. I felt like I was being pulled into a soundproof tunnel, totally disorienting me until the Pastor concluded the service. However, once he stepped off the podium, my hearing and balance always returned to normal.

Eventually, I began to notice glowing colors, dark shadows, and shapes around some of the people in the church. At the same time, the dreams and messages I was receiving from Spirt were getting more precise, sustaining me through all the turmoil. One Sunday morning, when a visiting minister was preaching, not only did my hearing close off, but I very clearly heard: "she is not of God." I remember looking around to see if someone was sitting close by trying to talk to me, but everyone was distracted, mesmerized by this minister's teaching. Dark orbs began bouncing around the church, crawling along the floor and walls like beetles, unsettling me to the core.

One of my friends at church began meeting with me to talk and pray together. Fran was much older than me, but a welcome relief to a growing feeling of isolation and alienation. She had lived in town her whole life and was aware of the eerie feelings constantly in the air. We talked daily, and she would answer all my questions frankly and honestly. My new friend was a huge relief and blessing in my life. I confided in her, sharing everything that was happening, and she was eager to listen, never put off, and always supportive through it all. Fran was the first person I'd ever known who believed me and didn't think I was crazy when I shared my dreams and the messages from the Angels. She was fascinated that I had so much information about a place I had just moved to.

Fran's desire to get closer to God was growing, and though she didn't have experience with the higher realms, she was open to exploring communication from Spirit and the Angels. A compassionate warrior at church, she prayed for many people and offered her time in contemplation to help others. When I told her about the dark orbs, she would simply say it makes sense. I never knew what that meant to her, but it was comforting for me to hear.

My husband's job was growing difficult for him while I continued dealing with the crazy phenomena alone. The rancher and his wife were demanding, far beyond the scope of his responsibilities. He decided to quit. That meant we would have to vacate the house immediately. We rented a small one-bedroom in town, close to Fran. My husband got a new job with Schwann's delivery, including an hour commute. Fran and I continued to share and study the Bible as things on the new home front were quiet and peaceful—at least for a while. I remember feeling strange the first time I saw the house but dismissed it as the town's eerie feel, not the home itself.

As the weeks wore on, I slept less and less. I studied and talked to Spirit in my free time when Brindi played or slept. I would sleep an hour here or there between reading and writing notes every day. My life became surreal. The lines between physical and non-physical were hard to discern. The waking visions were more regular and my dreams more lucid. I was fascinated by the insights downloaded into my consciousness with clarity and ease. I asked God to direct me to a teacher who could make all this more accessible and faster.

One day while praying, I heard, "You aren't going to have a teacher; we will teach you. You are to remain incorruptible in your understanding." This voice told me that I would become very transparent in how I lived my life. I was to live "above reproach," which meant I wouldn't be caught off guard by someone's accusations or finding fault in me. I was instructed to live an authentic life, not perfect but transparent; if called into question, I'd have nothing to hide.

With my spiritual initiation well underway, the peace in our little blue house was suddenly interrupted by something I couldn't see. A root cellar located outside the kitchen door on the back of the property scared me to death. Anytime I was in the kitchen, I could feel dark, heavy energy that seemed to pulse in the direction of that cellar. I avoided the root cellar, but that didn't stop whatever was living in there from coming into the house. One day while doing dishes, Brindi was fussy, playing under the kitchen table. It was a cheap table, with plastic covers over the screws connecting the legs. Brindi had been a little agitated, sticking close to me as I cleaned. Then, when I turned my back to put a dish away, I heard a blood-curdling scream. I looked down to see she'd somehow gotten her fingers caught in one of the plastic screw covers. I panicked, struggling to free her little fingers while trying to comfort her, without success.

Eventually, I called the Fire Department for help. When they arrived, they had no idea how she had gotten her fingers stuck yet, stuck she was. They put dish soap over her fingers as they cut the plastic cover to free her hand. Although she looked frightened as she clung to my leg, I was grateful she was okay. I thanked the crew as they were leaving, listening to them go on and on about how bizarre it was for her to get stuck. I wasn't as shocked as they were, of course, as the supernatural incidents were spiraling out of control. I didn't mention that to them, though, since I was already considered a bit weird by certain community factions. Fran was the only person I could talk to, but she was busy dealing with her own crisis at home. In tandem, the deeper I got into subtle and spiritual realms, the more supernatural events were happening to both of us.

Days went by after Brindi's episode without any more strange events, but my dreams were a constant transmission source. I was having a hard time keeping pace in my journals. Then, one snowy afternoon, sitting in the living room reading the bible, the most detailed vision began unfolding before me. I was half asleep, half awake. I found myself in a meadow filled with the brightest colors, the beauty surrounding me far beyond the most beautiful meadow I'd ever seen. In this vision, an Angel appeared and began to speak with me as we walked through these fields of wildflowers and grass. He introduced himself as Archangel Uriel. Requesting that I listen carefully to what I was told and shown. Uriel instructed me to write down and keep the record, stating that someday it would make sense.

As Uriel and I walked effortlessly through the meadow, I noticed that it wasn't hot or cold. There was no wind or no clouds. Instead, it was colorful, alive, and vibrant. He told me there was important work to do, that I was being "prepared" for new experiences. He explained things were changing for me, and while life would be challenging, I would always be protected.

Suddenly the scene changed, the light meadow faded, and we stood between rows of tall evergreens. Darkness filled the sky with thick fog that had a feeling of weight to it. Hundreds, if not thousands of people began running toward us as if we were invisible. At first, I didn't realize what they were running for or from. Then I saw it. To the left of me, at the far edge of the clearing, I could see the darkness chasing people, enveloping everything and everyone in its path. The trees, the people, even the grass all turned to nothingness. It was as if this massive gloom was devouring any living thing. People were trying very hard to outrun it without any direction. They just ran.

I found myself with Archangel Uriel at a barrier made of turnstiles, like those found at Disneyland. Heaven was the other side of the turnstile, looking just like the lush fields where Uriel and I began the vision. Each person trying to cross into the light had to be counted by the turnstiles, wreaking havoc as everyone panicked. There was a total disregard for others. The crowd was trampling older people, children, and the sick as everyone ran. I was very confused by what I was seeing, but Uriel spoke to me without uttering a word of concern, "In the end, you have a big job," he said. "When the darkness moves in, you will help save them and guide them. Do everything you can to get them into the light, to safety."

Just as Uriel spoke those words, he vanished, and another man appeared, yelling at me to help throw people over the turnstiles. I tried to calm the masses and grab the weakest, oldest and youngest, lifting them over the barriers. Once in the light, strength, vitality, and health returned to each person; they were radiating love. This man and I were running back and forth, trying to save and direct as many as we could. The darkness continued to close in, snuffing out anyone in its path; those caught up vanished. Finally, the man and I jumped over the barriers ourselves, just as the dark clouds reached the turnstiles.

Once safely on the other side, I found myself in the meadow again, greeted this time by a few other Angels, Daniel from the bible, and Archangel Uriel. They smiled at me as Uriel and Daniel guided me to a river. Uriel explained we were at the river of life. The water mesmerized me, flowing freely, a color, unlike anything I'd ever seen. It was crystal clear, living, and pulsing, as though it had a heartbeat. Daniel directed me to drink from the river using my cupped hands. I instantly felt calmer, more energized, and alive. Uriel asked me what my favorite food was. Since being pregnant, there was only one answer: strawberry- banana milkshakes. Instantly the scene changed; we now stood before a hillside of wild strawberries. Uriel told me to take a bite. My mouth exploded with the juiciest, most luscious strawberry I'd ever tasted, mimicking a smooth, strawberry-banana milkshake. He seemed amused by my reaction, explaining that in Heaven, anything you think about or want, anywhere you want to be, brings it right to you.

Daniel shared stories about his time on earth and his challenges as a Spiritual Warrior. Both gave me a lot to consider and an excellent education about the times to come. They informed me that I was a Spiritual Warrior who could help those suffering and battle against dark forces. They forewarned of a time when the darkness would rise to overtake the ones in the light. It was unclear how that would play out, but I knew these Angels would be there to assist me at the right time.

My head was spinning with so many questions, and yet I felt no fear. Instead, I had a "knowing" that what I witnessed was indeed real. As we said our farewells, I heard a voice speak out. "In the days of darkness when evil is on the rise, you shall rise to save the lost, weak, and broken-hearted." As I type these words, chills cover my body, and tears are streaming down my face. That vision of saving the people from darkness repeated nightly for over a month. It was the last dream each night, the clarity so embedded, it feels like it happened yesterday. It took me many years to understand what Spirit showed me and how I would fulfill my "job."

It was a 45-minute commute to shop for groceries in a larger neighboring town. I babysat my friend's toddlers one day, so they joined Brindi and me for a casual drive to Walla Walla. I was a bit tired by the time we arrived. The three girls fell asleep within minutes as we made the trek home. I was singing to the radio, cruising down the country roads, yet somehow fell asleep at the wheel. Right before I woke up, I saw a beautiful, ethereal set of wings spread wide over my entire body, as I heard Psalms 91 spoken loudly in a male voice, "He will cover you with his feathers, and under his wings, you will find refuge; his faithfulness will be your shield and rampart."

Twenty miles had passed before my eyes popped open at a stop sign, ten minutes from home. As the car came to a sudden stop, I became fully conscious and heard another voice say almost audibly, "roll down the windows." I did so quickly as I struggled to make sense of what was happening. Since I was close to home, I made a beeline for my house, got the kids out, and ran inside. I was afraid to tell my friend what had happened when she picked up her kids. I shared the whole story with my husband, though, when he got home from work. The very next day, he took the car in and explained to the mechanic what happened. They checked my exhaust system and confirmed it had a horrible carbon monoxide leak. They repaired it immediately. We were thankful no one was hurt.

After sitting with the events of the drive, I was in awe. Winding, country roads with ditches on either side were not easy to navigate awake. How was I able to stay on the road for over 20 minutes without wrecking the car? As I questioned everything that happened, the vision of the wings appeared in my mind's eye. I felt a surge of peace and knew it was divine protection that saved me that day and even drove my car while we were all passed out. Did I mention it was a 5-speed stick shift? Not exactly a vehicle that can in any way drive itself.

Study and spiritual warfare were the main focus; raising Brindi consumed the rest of my time. It seemed the more I understood about what was happening in the church and town, the more spiritual attacks occurred in our everyday lives. One day, Fran and I walked around town and circled the church to pray against the threatening darkness. I heard a loud voice yell, "Jump in the ditch," and felt a shove from behind me in broad daylight. I grabbed Fran's arm and pulled her into the ditch with me. As we stumbled, a loud, yellow Dodge Charger came speeding down the road right for us. Even though we were safely entrenched, we were still sprayed with gravel as he sped away. Had we not been warned by some unseen protector, I don't doubt that we would both be dead. Unfortunately, we weren't able to see the driver, obscured by black tinted windows. We'd never seen that car before in our little town and never saw it again. Not long after that day, all hell broke loose—in Fran's home and ours.

Seeking more answers, Fran and I discovered a large witch coven conducting black magic ceremonies almost nightly. Not only were these women performing rituals, but they just happened to be the wives of the local politicians, churchgoers to boot. Their meetings took place well past midnight inside the town hall offices, down in the basement. One night, Fran and I observed hundreds of bats circling the courthouse while we listened to chanting in what sounded like Latin permeate the building inside and out. I hated going downtown, feeling a heavy dread of darkness every time I drove in that vicinity. Unfortunately, Fran lived only blocks away from the hub. Huddled in, she would call to tell me what was happening as we both committed to pray for divine light to enter the scene.

Documenting all the messages and revelations I was receiving was exhausting but exhilarating. Meanwhile, visited frequently by the visiting woman pastor, our church was becoming more bizarre by the day. Her energy was infiltrating the way everything felt, from the pastor's home to the services themselves. I was subjected to several weeks of her "prophesying," tolerating her dirty looks cast my way. In one service, she pointed right at me with her skinny finger and judgmental tone, raising the hair on the back of my neck.

Once home, Spirit instructed me to deliver a message to the church elders that would shine a light on the recent changes in the congregation's lives. Unfortunately, none of the changes had been for the better. I had no idea what the message was, but Spirit assured me that the words would come if I were willing to give my voice to God. Unsure of myself, standing before this group of elders and the Pastor, it was apparent they were very resistant to hearing any messages from me. They had branded me a "witch who listened to demons." They asked, "why would God use you to speak to us?"

Immediately my mouth began to move and what came out surprised me as much as them: "God used a jackass to speak to the

Apostle Paul; he can surely use me."

It took everything I had not to laugh, but the reprimand continued as Spirit spoke to each member in a very personal way. I don't remember much of what was said, but I remember the shock on each person's face as I spoke each of their 'sins' in vivid detail. Things I had no way of knowing were brought into the light and exposed.

Just before Spirit began calling these folks on the carpet through me, they used my cigarette smoking as a sure sign that I was a 'sinner.' Spirit replied, "where does the bible say, thou shalt not smoke?" Spirit proceeded to recite the sins as listed in the bible, word for word. It was quite a show! In the end, as the elders refused to listen, Spirit whispered, "leave and don't look back." At 26 years old, this was the first time Spirit guided me to deliver this kind of message, and I hoped it was my last. It was the official public debut of my natural-born gifts: clairvoyance, clairaudience, and claircognizance.

That winter, the roads became challenging to navigate as the snow blanketed our little Eastern Washington town. After being kicked out of the church, I spent a lot of time at home alone. On a rare night, returning from a dinner out, we pulled up to the house, admiring the lovely winter landscape enveloped in freshly fallen snow. Appreciation turned to horror when I saw a prominent, dark figure running away toward the backyard and the root cellar from the corner of the house. Instantly struck with terror and dread, stomach in knots, I turned to my husband, who saw it too.

We quickly got Brindi out of her car seat, grabbing a flashlight from the trunk, making our way toward the front door. There was an obvious path of footprints in the snow leading to the back of the house. Once inside, I ran frantically through the house, turning all the lights on, filled with a sense of dread; I placed her safely in the playpen. We headed outside, following the tracks, noticing these were NOT human footprints or shoe prints. Instead, there were three long talon-looking, skinny toes and a heel resembling large chicken feet. Completely terrified, we both saw the figure again as it ran straight to the damned root cellar. Neither one of us was willing to go down there. Convinced this was no person, we returned to the house uncertain of what to do, trying to forget what happened.

The following day I was alone in the house with Brindi sitting on the sofa studying; I began to sense heavy energy all around us. I had just read a few of the Psalms and felt at peace when a heaviness filled the room. I reached for Brindi, who was on the floor in front of me. In a split second, her little body lifted into the air as she flew toward the front of the woodstove, where a fire was burning hotly. Her hands touched the front of the stove before she immediately fell to the floor. I grabbed her quickly, took both her hands into mine, and watched as tiny blisters began to form. I was desperate, but more than that, I was pissed. I called out to Archangels Michael, Raphael, and Uriel for healing. As I prayed for protection and healing over her, her hands miraculously returned to a normal color, and her crying ceased. In awe, I knew this was Divine intervention.

I turned my attention to the "thing" that caused this horrible attack. The angels led me to bind it, using the name of "Jesus Christ," also invoking the power of the Holy Spirit throughout the house. Immediately the thick, heavy energy lifted, replaced by a lighter feeling of safety.

For the first time in a long time, I felt an overwhelming peace. I hugged my baby until she and I both fell asleep on the couch. Later that night, when her Dad got home, I relayed what happened. Convinced it was no longer safe to stay in this strange, dark little town, we decided to move back to Western Washington. As we began making the arrangements to leave, money was tight, and groceries were running low, although we had a few packages left in a meat freezer locker in town from the quarter cow that was a part of my husband's benefits on the farm. Confident we only had two big pieces of meat left in the locker, I prayed that it would feed us for the time we had left before leaving for Seattle.

By now, I had experienced Divine providence and the power of manifestation many times. Not thinking about anything other than cleaning the locker out and closing our account, I opened it. I was shocked by what I saw. Instead of just two remaining chunks of meat, the locker was almost completely full. Steaks, roasts, and a couple of pounds of ground beef were inside. I ran to the front of the store and asked the owner if anyone had been in our locker. He assured me that since it was our lock, no one else could access it. When I told him I was closing the locker and our account because we were moving, he happily handed me a cardboard box to pack the meat as I signed off on our contract. I must have been glowing as I loaded that meat into the box. He asked if I was happy we were moving. With a look, I'm sure, of sheer joy on my face, I didn't want to say too much. I just nodded, packed the car, and made a swift getaway.

Once home, I unloaded all the meat into our freezer, leaving out a steak for dinner. I dropped to my knees and thanked God for multiplying the meat. I had no idea it was even possible for such a thing to happen. I then recalled how Jesus fed thousands with just a couple of loaves of bread. Finally, my husband arrived home to a lovely steak dinner with potatoes. As I relayed the events of the day, we both felt grateful, in awe, delighted and full. The abundance of meat in our locker was the perfect amount to keep us well fed until moving day, which, thankfully, seemed to arrive quickly. Finally, I could get my life back, reconnect with family and friends, leaving the darkness behind.

Looking back at my initiation into the subtle realms of light and dark, people asked me later why I didn't clear that little house before moving. The fact was I was young, ill-equipped to clear a house of evil, and wasn't instructed to do so by Spirit. Our time there was about awakening my gifts and learning how to recognize the forces of light and dark. There was so much dense, heavy gloom there that I'm not sure I could have cleared it, with or without guidance by Spirit. When we left the house, we left the energy as it was before moving in.

I never recommend clearing a property without proper tools and training. Depending on the strength of the dark entity or energy, you can make things worse by attempting it. It's always wise to have someone skilled and experienced perform rituals for cleansing the space. I wish I could say that the effects of our encounters didn't impact my family in the long run; I'm sorry to say it did.

Once back in Seattle, I had a chance to breathe and review the teachings and revelations of our Eastern Washington escapades. I recalled Spirit's disclosures about a particular group of entities affecting the town, the people, and the churches. My angels and guides explained that it was a legion of them operating as one. They intended to cause division, sexual immorality, addiction, and ultimately loss of faith. Their targets were those who have faith in God/Source Energy, who are kind, loving, and innocent. Children seemed to be their priority, intending to strip them early of their innocence and faith. Because there are many spirits to the legion, it quickly absorbs energy from the victims of the attacks.

Psalms 91 was given to me to pray daily, to strengthen my connection and faith. This legion of spirits—which I will not name-seemed to be growing in size and influence. It was not by coincidence that I found a pastor in Seattle who was given the same information. I stumbled upon his church one day and attended a service where he exposed the legion's name and what it was here to accomplish. His church had been exposed to it by the same "prophetess" visiting minister who brought it to our church in the small eastern town. It ripped through his congregation, ending several marriages, inflicting great hardship among its members. Like my friend Fran's family, several children suffered sexual molestation during the spiritual attacks on his church.

Approaching the pastor after the service, I explained what we had gone through and the revelations, warfare, events. Since I was very young and even younger-looking, his attitude was one of dismissal. For whatever reason, he didn't seem interested in talking to me further or extending any help in understanding the events we lived through. We decided it would be better to leave the church and put it all behind us.

Unfortunately, triggers were ignited within my husband when we began discussing the events amongst ourselves and a couple of friends. My husband suddenly began to distance himself from our daughter and me. He began working later and later at night, no longer communicating with me. Money was tight, and some of it seemed to be missing from our bank account. One day while out buying groceries, our card was declined. I checked the bank balance, realizing my husband had taken $100 out of the ATM without telling me. When I confronted him about it, he denied it. I matched the ATM with an address he had serviced through his work receipts, located right across the street from a job he did. He wouldn't tell me what he used the money for. It was weeks later before I managed to put it all together. My husband had started drinking and partying every night at local clubs.

Within months of returning to the Seattle area, we were at odds; repressed memories of childhood sexual abuse began to surface in my husband. Something was wrong; we were not getting closer but moving further apart. His mood swings, angry outbursts, and lies were scaring me. I sought advice from pastors in the Assembly of God Church, not knowing where else to turn—advised that I was to submit to my husband, no matter what was happening. Using scripture to inform me that "as God is the head of the church, your husband is in charge of you." Confusion turned to anger as I listened to instructions that would leave me in an abusive situation. "Is this what God wants? Is this the God I have followed, loved, and been guided by all these years?" My head was swimming, my body gripped by tension, unable to breathe. It didn't make sense! How can a loving God expect me to stay in fear and abuse?

Yelling at this "god" of the church, I refused to submit. The energy behind this religious god didn't come close to what I felt when receiving guidance from Spirit. Controlling, devoid of love, compassion, and kindness; "If this is "god, I refuse to have any part in it." Sadly, this is the same religious god that was held over me as a child, making me feel as if I was inherently wrong. So that was it;

I decided to break ties with the church. Instead, I listened to my feelings, following my discernment. If I was sinning by leaving my husband, then so be it.

Feeling helpless, I started to pull away. My hair at the time was almost to my waist, which my husband loved, and for that reason, I cut it all off into a pixie cut, hoping he wouldn't want to touch me. As the hair fell to the floor, I felt like I was cutting away my past. When he arrived home, he was shocked at my appearance, but it worked! He no longer wanted to touch me, and his anger grew, so did the distance between us. We separated within weeks, beginning the process of divorce.

For months things were quiet on the spiritual front. I was busy working multiple jobs to support Brindi and myself. The past seemed like a distant memory that never really happened. I was still studying and journaling a lot, but I certainly wasn't focused on demons, angels, religion, or what we lived through. It was a nice breather and the break I needed before the next set of lessons appeared. Unable to reconcile the God I knew and the religious god, I pushed aside all references to "god," I stopped praying, journaling, and meditating.

Brindi had been super close to her Dad before our separation. She missed him greatly since he refused to see her for months on end. He had moved to Portland to stay with his Mom, refusing to visit or stay in touch with his little girl. He was unreachable, secretive, and unresponsive. While I felt guilty for leaving, I knew I couldn't live the way we were anymore. I couldn't dwell on the past; I had to focus on what was before us. Working as a waitress to pay the bills, I kept busy, too tired to overthink or get stuck in my head.

While waiting on an older customer with dementia named Ody, I received a call from his daughter, his caretaker. She wanted to know if Ody was eating breakfast there. He had wandered off alone; she couldn't figure out where else he would go. But, of course, he was eating his oatmeal at his regular table. So, she asked that I keep an eye on him until she could come to pick him up. That was easy for me because he was such a sweet, quiet man.

Weeks passed, Ody showed up accompanied by a man in his forties that slightly resembled him. It was a pleasure to serve them both. The man introduced himself as Ody Junior. He asked if I had waited on his Dad when he went missing and thanked me for watching over him. We began a conversation about energy and the Universe. He asked if I would be willing to read a book. Ody Jr. left me with a copy of "The Celestine Prophecy." He said he was visiting his family and would be returning soon to discuss. I dove right into the book, discovering I loved it. I sat down with Ody Junior later to review its many spiritual insights. He asked, "If you could do anything for fun, what would it be?"

That was a no-brainer. I would record some songs I wrote and make a demo, fulfilling a dream I nurtured for a while. In a whirlwind, we exchanged contacts. Before I could wrap my head around what was happening, Ody Jr. wired me ten thousand dollars to record my demo and take voice lessons, saying it was all in the name of fun. He said, "no matter what comes of this, just promise you will have fun."

I had already written several songs that were candidates for the studio, but I felt like something new inside me wanted to come out. So, I wrote a few new songs in an altered state, or rather a channeling state, that seemed to flow just magically. Two of those songs were chosen as demos. "Sandcastle Dreams" was written for Brindi at a time I was dreaming of sandy beaches. Later I would realize how prophetic it would be.

Sandcastle Dreams (c)1994

Verse:
Feeling like the world was over, nothing left for me,
Tears in my eyes, turned to my little girl and whispered
Oh Brindi...
Mommy feels like life is choking me,
What should I do now?
And then she turned and answered me—

Chorus:
Let's go walk along the sandy shore, waves crashing at
*   our feet.*
Wind blowing through our hair, birds flying on the
*   breeze.*
Then we'll build sandcastles by the sea,
Building our hopes and dreams.
Nothing to stand in our way,
Our dreams eternally free......

Verse:
Twenty years have passed since our first visit to the
*   beach,*
Walking hand in hand, just you and me
Now you're all grown up, you've gotta be strong
Life's hard sometimes I know
When you feel like your choking,

Call on me and...

Chorus:
We'll walk along the sandy shore, waves crashing at our
  feet.
Wind blowing through our hair, birds flying on the
  breeze.
Then we'll build sandcastles by the sea,
Building our hopes and dreams.
Nothing to stand in our way,
Our dreams eternally free......

Life had changed radically after separating from my daughter's father. We moved into a beautiful townhouse with a close friend. While we had a lot of fun, Brindi missed her Dad a lot, and there wasn't a way to get around her desire to see him. Her Dad had moved back to the area, so I called, asking him if he would please take her. Finally, he agreed, making Brindi very happy. It just so happened to be the night I recorded the demo in a middle-of-the-night session block.

After a couple of months working with a producer and one of the best vocal coaches in the business, we recorded my songs. After a very exhilarating studio adventure, I went home to sleep, knowing I fulfilled my end of the deal: I'd had fun. Amazed by the whole experience, I floated along on cloud nine as I began to understand the principles of conscious manifestation. My joy was intense as I basked in the feeling of singing and recording my songs. I didn't have a single warning about how our lives were about to change again.

2

────────

UNEXPECTED ADVERSITY

Without divulging the horrible details, Brindi began showing signs that something was very wrong just days after the recording studio. She wouldn't go to the bathroom at daycare and withdrew from me. She shared some things with my sister while I was at work. What Brindi described to her was shocking, with unimaginable details of an event that happened while visiting her Dad. I immediately took Brindi—who was only three at the time—to the Sexual Assault Center at Children's Hospital. Shaking with fear, we waited as she was interviewed and examined. Her symptoms and rapidly changing, unexplained behavior spoke of definite signs of molestation. So many things flooded my mind and body. The counselors told me not to show emotions or cry in front of Brindi, instructing me to display as much strength as possible so it wouldn't alarm her.

As the days passed, I felt everything from anger to disbelief. I wasn't sure what to believe. I didn't want to think that my little girl was violated, robbed of her innocence. As reality set in, the emotional pressure kept building. I ran a hot bath, where I could cry, away from the peering eyes of my daughter. I sat in the tub praying, crying, and pleading with God. I didn't know what to think. I couldn't pull myself out of the sadness, depression, and darkness. Then, tears flowing with my head buried in my hands, I heard her sweet, innocent voice say, "Don't cry, Mommy, I will tell them he didn't hurt me."

At that moment, everything became real. My worst fears were confirmed. I knew I couldn't let my child see me upset, so I quickly got out of the tub, climbed in bed with her, and told her we were going to tell the truth. I reassured her that everything would work out, secretly wishing I could believe what I was saying.

"How could this be happening to us?" Overwhelmed by sadness that gave way to anxiety and severe depression, the days that followed were painful. I constantly had panic attacks. I discovered the statistics showed two in five children would be sexually assaulted every year. Unable to relax, going to the park was impossible. Instead, I found myself counting kids in groups of five, wondering which two would become victims. My mind was a war zone and my body a mess. Then, while waitressing at a posh French restaurant, a busload of five-year-old kids came in for a manners class. I lost it! My boss had no sympathy, leaving me no choice but to quit on the spot. Unable to breathe, I headed to the ER with chest pains, where they prescribed Ativan to calm the panic attacks. Everything else was a blur. I felt numb, buried my pain, and did my best to do everything I had to do each day.

I wish I could say that the justice system protected my daughter and me. Because she was so young, Brindi was considered "preverbal," which eliminated her as a credible witness. The female investigator interviewed my husband first before speaking to us. She was convinced that he didn't fit the profile of an abuser or predator. He convinced her that the accusations came from me to get custody in the divorce. While no charges were filed, I was blessed with free legal representation in the divorce and custody case. Through all the pain, confusion, and sadness, Susan, my lawyer, protected us as best she could in the family court system. She filed a motion for a permanent no-contact order, with the condition that a Sexual Deviance evaluation would have to be completed by Brindi's father in addition to counseling before visitation would resume.

Before awarding sole custody, the judge asked my ex if he understood the allegations, the restrictions, and motions, asking if he had anything to say. He shook his head side to side, refusing to speak. Dread filled my body. If I were innocent, I would defend myself, fight for my child, doing whatever it took to stay in her life. Upon his refusal to speak, the judge granted the motions, giving me sole custody. After that, we were free to move on with our lives.

Waiting for the divorce and custody case to be resolved took months. I searched for answers from God, looked for affordable or free counseling, and tried my best to simply deal with life. I was on prescription anti-anxiety medication, including Zoloft, for depression. Nothing felt right, and I wasn't finding the help I needed. None of the churches would offer to counsel if I was not a member. There were long waiting lists for free counseling services throughout the county. I finally found a Baptist church nearby with an ad in the Yellow Pages that listed "Spiritual Counseling." I called on a whim, explaining to the pastor what had happened and how confused, angry, and desperate I was to find answers. Pastor Al immediately set an appointment for me, invited me to speak with him, emerging as an earth angel —a true Divine instrument of compassion.

Pastor Al and I met weekly to talk about God, my life, and my shaky faith. I was outraged and kept asking why God would allow this to happen. He patiently listened, gave me scriptures to consider, saying, "Sometimes we don't know the reason, but God always has a plan." He never tried talking me out of my anger or rage. He didn't judge me for cursing or challenging his teachings. Instead, he exuded such faith and love for me, but most of all for God. He eased my mind, disagreeing with the advice to submit to the abuse received by the pastor at the Christian church. So maybe the God I knew wasn't the same religious god taught about in some churches. Regardless, I wasn't comfortable referring to my God as god anymore, so I started calling out to "Source."

I will never forget that man or the help he offered me in a time of crisis. His kindness and patience were exactly what I needed to get through the trauma. Pastor Al listened, provided guidance, prayer, and parables that fed my Spirit even though I didn't recognize it at the time. I had all but given up on praying when none of my calls to the angels resulted in answers. I heard nothing even though I desperately begged to have them appear and speak to me. It seemed my visions were gone. Considering my anger and depression, I figured God just didn't care anymore. There were no more magical synchronicities, no more clear visions, and no guidance.
Overtaken by the circumstances, I had forgotten all I learned about spiritual battles, warfare, and the attacks by the legion of spirits we encountered in Eastern Washington.

While it took many years of healing, I finally realized that even though God is there and angels are present, we can't feel them in moments of depression. Vibrationally, we have to raise our frequency to experience them. Access to the higher realms is difficult, if not impossible, when in a lower vibrational state.

As the months passed, I began thinking of moving away, leaving the clouds of Seattle for something new. I kept having recurring dreams about living in Colorado with Brindi and what I presumed was a baby boy that was mine. Colorado was cold, and I had no desire to move there and no idea why I was dreaming about it. Yet each morning I woke from a dream about it, I heard, "you have five years." Uncertain about the "five-year warning," I was determined to leave Seattle. I felt alone and didn't want to be in the area with such painful memories. I needed a fresh start and to put distance from the traumatic events. Since most of my family couldn't handle the court proceedings or my distress, I was left alone to forge a path of healing. When I received my tax refund, we packed up and headed for California. I had no family or ties in San Diego, making it the perfect place to start over. Since singing created my daughter's trauma, I put songwriting and singing in a box. Messages from music executives about publishing my songs were left unanswered. It would be more than 12 years before I felt like singing or writing songs again.

Twenty-three years later, while gathering old journals to tell this story, I stumbled upon both Ody and Pastor Al's business cards. It's so amazing how the Universe brings things to me when I need them. Googling "Pastor Al," I found he had moved to a different state, heading another church. So, I sent tithe along with a thank you note to Pastor Al's current church and sent a thank you to Ody after finding them both on the internet. I believe in paying it back and paying it forward whenever possible.

3

TRAGEDY STRIKES AGAIN

The moving truck was packed, my car in tow; on the night of April 18th, 1995, my Dad, Brindi, and I began our trek to California. I had no job, no place to live, with just enough money to start our lives over in a new city. Getting a fresh start and leaving behind the memories of all that had happened was appealing. I'd driven to California with my Dad often in earlier years. No stopping except for gas and potty breaks; he was a road warrior! We shared a lot of conversation. He told me how he and my Uncle Pete talked about getting cows in Oklahoma and becoming ranchers. I laughed, knowing neither had any experience with livestock, let alone farming. We talked about everything except Brindi's abuse.

Arriving in Northern California by the morning of April 19, 1995, we began hearing reports on the radio that disturbed us. At first, all we heard was some sort of tragedy had happened in Oklahoma City. But, within thirty minutes, it became clear that whatever happened occurred at the Alfred P. Murrah Federal Building. Dismayed by the news of a bomb going off in Oklahoma City, we listened intently to the radio broadcasts. Uncle Pete had just moved to Oklahoma City to take a job at H.U.D. a month before. He and his wife were still living in an extended stay hotel. We pulled over at the first rest area to use the phone booth (*this was before cell phones were in use*). Dad called the extended stay in Oklahoma City only to get a busy signal. He tried for five more minutes, to no avail. Finally, we decided to go on to the next rest area and try again.

After several hours and many stops, Dad finally got through to Peter's wife. The news was unsettling. Peter wasn't feeling good that morning before work but went in anyway. He hadn't been located, nor had he made contact. The bomb went off somewhere close to 9 am; things were still chaotic hours later. We were several hours from arriving in Orange County when Dad decided to drop me, the moving truck, and Brindi off at my Mom's house and hop a flight home to Seattle. From there, he would jump on a flight to Oklahoma City. Pete was missing, and Dad needed to be there to help in whatever way possible. Plans drastically changed, and I was on my own now.

After dropping Dad at the airport, I drove the moving truck to San Diego, found an apartment and a job all in one day. Moving day was a bit of a comedy. I'm 5'2" yet pretty strong for my petite size. I emptied everything I could into our apartment alone. I carried the bed on my back, taking small steps before giving up and dragging it on the sidewalk. Leaving the loveseat hanging off the back of the truck, I was exhausted, ready to give up. How was I supposed to move it alone? I sat at the back of the open truck and prayed. I pleaded, "God, PLEASE send someone to help." It seemed impossible since several people drove or walked past for hours without offering a hand.

Finally, snuffing out the cigarette I was furiously puffing, I turned and was greeted by a lovely man who walked right up and asked if I needed help. I was so grateful for his offer I started crying. Although he may have thought I was nuts, I didn't care. We carried the loveseat into the apartment, and I was finally home. The man quietly left with a nod as I thanked him again. To this day, I don't know who the man was or if he lived at the complex. I never saw him again. I will always wonder if he was an angel. It certainly made me wish I had asked for help sooner. Either way, my prayers were answered rather quickly.

Trying to stay in touch with my Dad to get updates on the search and rescue efforts became pointless. Instead, I focused my attention on setting up our new home and getting Brindi into counseling at Children's hospital. My brother and Pete's children flew out to OKC to support the rescue efforts and wait. It took nearly two weeks for his body to be recovered and for the waiting to come to an end. Then, sadly, my Uncle Pete's remains were found; it was time to make arrangements to put his body to rest.

It seemed like world events were mirroring the circumstances I was personally reacting to. I had never noticed or paid attention to how my life was a microcosm reflection of world events and energies. For example, the terror of the Oklahoma City bombing and the trauma it caused for so many was reflected in my circumstances. With the revelation of Brindi's abuse, it felt like a bomb had gone off; I felt like my whole world was leveled; nothing remained but dust. I had to start over from scratch, somehow relieving this heavy burden. I had to heal both myself and my baby girl.

Somehow our family recovered, and we were all forced to move forward beyond the tragedies that struck. Yet, in the midst of it all, I received an unexpected blessing. I met my Uncle Pete's stepson Grant at a Memorial service held in Los Angeles in his honor. Grant and I became instant friends within weeks of the move to San Diego. He lived in Los Angeles, and through all the events of the family memorial, we bonded. It wasn't long before Grant became an essential part of my life and healing. He was an excellent male role model for Brindi. Before long, Uncle Grant was someone she looked up to, someone she loved.

Grant and I were in our 20s, doing our best to find joy, creating adventures in confusing times. Whether we were out on the weekends partying, in Vegas gambling, or camping, we always had a way of having fun. He was non-threatening to me since he was family. He was a safe person to share my thoughts and feelings with, able to handle my truth. While we laughed a lot, he was always there when I had breakdowns. I will forever be grateful for his companionship and tireless efforts to deal with me during a dark, stormy period of life.

Grant had an incredible imagination. He was open-minded, making it easier for me to share things I was studying with him. We played with Astral Travel, concepts of aliens, and all sorts of out-of-the-box thinking. But mainly, he taught me how to play again and cut loose. For the first time in my life, I was able just to be me. I didn't have to filter, prove or be anything. It was liberating. Everyone needs a Grant in their lives.

Entirely focused on creating a new life, I put traditional religion behind me. I focused instead on praying, meditating, and studying whatever I could get my hands on. Some books appeared on my path with little clue of where they originated. I was hungry for understanding and eager to feed my soul. I studied psychology, the brain, metaphysics, philosophy, and the order of the Universe. I learned about the Angels and the hierarchy of the spirit world. I even learned to channel consciously. I studied the bible but with different eyes, different ears, and a deeper level of understanding. It was becoming easier to use "God" instead of calling upon "Universe or Source."

It seemed the tragedies in my life opened more of my gifts because they created more questions. Out of necessity, I began to pray more, journal daily and approached life with more spiritual hunger. Thankfully there was no demonic or evil activity for months. I was relieved that it all seemed to stop when we left Seattle. I focused on building a new life while my Spiritual life was unfolding on its own. Familiar spirit guides returned with gentle communication as I navigated a new level of understanding.

One of the first tasks I accomplished when we settled in San Diego was registering Brindi for services at the Children's Hospital Sexual Assault Center. She began a series of counseling sessions with a beautiful soul named Ginger. Ginger taught her how to articulate her feelings. I attended the 'parents of victims' support group. Within months Brindi graduated from the program. There is only so much counseling you can do for a small child that experienced molestation. Ginger said she would have to go back into counseling when things began to surface in her late teens or early twenties. With that behind her, I enrolled Brindi in kindergarten, and life moved forward.

To say I was angry at the destruction of our lives is an understatement. My daughter's abuse brought up my past abuse. I hadn't processed through the pain of my childhood. With her abuse, I felt utterly betrayed by life, even by God. Nothing made sense. I felt a massive void within me. As the trauma of Brindi's abuse was fading, I found myself in an all too familiar state. While I looked okay on the outside, there was a storm brewing inside me. Depression and anxiety surfaced as I went through Brindi's ordeal. With the molest fading into the past, I found myself sinking fast. The shock from all the trauma we experienced faded, and the adrenaline needed to get through it had worn off. But a dark ocean of unexpressed emotions, rage, fear, and a sea of confusion began to stir within me.

Somehow, I was getting through each day at work, paying bills, and caring for my daughter. I stopped praying, meditating, and studying as my life got busier; I jumped into my life in San Diego, trying as hard as I could to run from the past. Weekends were spent with Grant, partying and riding motorcycles, and whatever adventures we could find. I would lie in bed sobbing in between parties, dancing and trying to find anything to quiet my mind and emotions. I was doing everything I could to numb my pain. I became an expert at hiding my turmoil with the various men I dated, colleagues, and even friends. I was great at portraying the perfect picture of what everyone expected of me. I'm not saying I didn't have fun. I did, thanks to Grant and a couple of friends. It was the moments alone when all activity stopped that life was hellish and seemingly unbearable.

Grant would listen without judgment to an endless cycle of communicating my depressed moods whenever I hit bottom. I spun through several short-lived, dysfunctional relationships.

Most of the men I dated looked great on paper and were physically attractive, but something was missing. I had buried so much of myself; none of them knew who I was. I was living in survival mode. Superficial, materialism was my focus, anything but facing myself and the dark emotions always lurking under the surface. In my opinion, men were not to be trusted. I felt none were good enough to meet my daughter. Yet, she wanted a "Dad" to replace the one she lost.

One day as I was pumping gas, she accompanied me to the register. This handsome man walked up behind us, and she asked, "Will you marry my Mom and be my Dad?" I was so embarrassed as I quickly apologized and hurried out of the store. I realized I should probably get serious about healing and find a real relationship. To heal enough to find a relationship, I had to figure out my life. That meant revisiting my childhood wounds, facing the very things I was doing my best to avoid.

Journal entry December 18, 1997

Depression is my constant companion. I've been in bed or on the couch for several days with little motivation to get up. I've watched movies, read books, and slept. My thoughts are overwhelming and ranging from love to doubts to repulsion. I am reminded of my shortcomings and weaknesses. Of my longing to be loved. Of dreams that come and go. I've questioned life, and the meaning of it. Everything has been questioned. I'm sad and have no real reason to be. I'm tired of living such a meaningless life. No horses, singing, dancing, nothing. Laughter only comes when I drink. My existence seems futile. I don't know why it has to seem so bleak. Darkness follows my every step. Blackness engulfs my every breath. I am uncertain of everything....

4

RADICAL HEALING

Knowing I needed to heal myself, I dove into my childhood. Youngest of three children, I was raised by my Dad for most of my childhood. I didn't have a great relationship with my Mom. After years of battling mental health issues, suicide attempts, doctors administered shock treatments and psychotherapy. Serving in Vietnam, then a Marine Corps Drill Instructor in San Diego, Dad was gone a lot during the first five years of my life. We had a live-in housekeeper, Dicey, since Mom couldn't take care of us by herself. Dicey, a sweet, older German lady who ran a tight ship, was great at getting us to school and caring for our basic needs, but without affection. As a result, I spent a lot of time by myself before entering kindergarten at a Catholic School in Anaheim, CA. I was never really alone, though. My "imaginary" friends always surrounded me.

There were no happy memories of my Mom when I was a child. I remember being afraid of her, not liking her energy at all. I learned to be as invisible as possible to avoid her yelling rants and physical abuse. Growing up in a volatile environment, showing emotions was not safe. My maternal grandparents constantly argued, yelled, and screamed. Crying was not allowed no matter what. I remember being told repeatedly, "You have no reason to cry; if you don't stop, I will get the belt and give you a reason." Emotions and self-expression were something I could ONLY do in secret. I felt everything profoundly but had no outlet to express what I felt. I had no one to talk to either; the authority figures and caretakers in my life were not 'safe' to confide in.

While visiting my grandparents one day with my Mom, I was sent to a dark guest closet as punishment because I was crying. My grandfather locked me in the "bowling ball" closet. Squished between bowling balls and shoes, I had to stay until I stopped crying. I could hear the adults sitting around the table talking. That punishment didn't make me stop crying; it made it worse. Emotionally exhausted and scared, I eventually fell asleep.

Not being seen, feeling unimportant, and even forgotten was normalized. Hours after I was locked in the closet, my grandfather woke me up. He was holding back laughter as he grabbed my arm to pull me out of the closet, "I hope you learned your lesson," he said coldly. When I finally emerged from the guest room, I learned that everyone had left and gone out to eat. No one noticed they had forgotten me. It wasn't until they returned home that someone remembered I was still in the closet. There were no apologies, and no one checked to see if I was alright. All the adults, including my Mom, made excuses about leaving a five-year-old home alone. They blamed me for missing out on dinner. I went home with my Mom without being fed or offered dinner, hungry and hurt. The only thing I learned was that crying was a punishable offense. From then on, I didn't cry in front of other people.

I recall trying to understand and make sense of why my Mom seemed to hate me so much. After yet another verbal assault by her, I prayed to God to help me understand what I had done. Receiving nothing from my prayers and feeling completely alone, I prayed that God would make me blind so I wouldn't have to see the hatred played out in front of me. I told God I understood that I would still feel things and see things in the other realms, but I couldn't deal with seeing people being mean to each other anymore. I didn't understand the repercussions of that prayer until I was 16 years old. I was given prescription eyeglasses in first grade and did everything to destroy every pair I received. My parents eventually stopped buying new ones. The kids in school called me names like "four-eyed freak." All the names couldn't have hurt as bad as watching the evil adults did to one another.

Without glasses, my eyesight slowly declined. Finally, when I turned 16, I went to the eye doctor for contacts; the doctor informed my Dad that my vision was 20/-400. That meant what people saw at 400 feet distance; I could only see at 20 feet. He also explained at the rate of decline I was having, my eyesight would either continue to worsen until I was blind or plateau when I hit 18. As we drove home, the reality hit me hard as I saw the day I prayed to be made blind in vision. In that instant, I asked forgiveness for begging to be made blind. I didn't ask for my eyesight to be fully restored; I just asked that it stop declining. I reasoned that although the horror I witnessed was hard to deal with, there was also a lot of beauty to see in the world when I looked for it.

When I turned 18, my eyesight was rated 20/-450 in each eye, remaining the same since that day. Although I can't see without the aid of glasses or contacts other than what is directly an arms distance away, I can see. The lesson I learned about prayer, belief, and God's abiding love to give us what we ask began to sink in. I was more careful about asking for things without thinking of the long-term effects.

Between the ages of 4-5, I suffered recurring bloody noses. Heat and activity would start nosebleeds that lasted for hours. A few nosebleeds resulted in emergency room visits to get the blood vessel in my nose cauterized. The doctor said my blood vessels were close to the surface, and eventually, I would grow out of it. Unfortunately, I couldn't control it. The nosebleeds made my Mom very angry. I remember having to lie on her lap while she squeezed my nose for a long time while having to listen to her displeasure and anger. Usually, my Dad was the one that pinched my nose until the bleeding stopped, but on a few occasions, he wasn't around. I prayed it would stop bleeding so she wouldn't have to take care of me. I clenched my fists, trying to keep my tears away. I knew if I cried, she would be furious. I just wanted to disappear.

Since the age of the internet, I came across a few interesting articles while was piecing together spiritual meanings of disease and illness. One by Louise Hay discusses how nose bleeds are related to feeling unseen. She says it's a need for recognition. Feeling unrecognized and unnoticed, it's crying out for love. In other articles, others believe that nosebleeds are a side effect of spiritual experience. They can also occur to people who have an inherited ability to have paranormal or spiritual experiences. It can also be caused by the sudden changes in blood pressure caused by intense spiritual experience. As the emotions are extremely high during a spiritual experience, the emotions can cause the blood pressure to rise extremely fast. That itself is dangerous, and the sudden rise may cause hemorrhaging.

To this day, I'm not sure what caused those nose bleeds, but both explanations resonate. As I grew up, the nosebleeds stopped. The body's wisdom is a beautiful mystery, communicating or manifesting our thoughts, feelings, and unconscious beliefs.

Mom never said, "I love you," and never expressed care or concern for me. I thought there must be something wrong with me since my own mother didn't love me. As the years went by, every time I was around her, that's the feeling I had. Weakness, sickness, or any emotions were cause for violence from her. So, I tried my best to be healthy, strong, and non-emotional.

One weekend, we visited Mom's boyfriend at a marina where he was restoring his boat. Walking a long plank up to the deck, I was terrified of falling into the water. Once aboard, I realized I had to use the bathroom. Afraid to tell her, as she constantly got angry at my tiny, inconvenient bladder. Trying to hold it in for what seemed an eternity, I told my Mom I needed help getting off the boat. She repeatedly told me to walk down the plank and find the portable potty. No matter how hard I tried, I couldn't make my six-year-old self walk that plank alone. So instead, I shivered in the corner, unable to hold it any longer. Finally, terrified but soaked, I whispered in her ear that I hadn't made it down the plank. She went red, grabbing a beach towel to wrap around my waist. Then, gripping me firmly by the ear, she tugged me down the plank, forcing me inside the car. As we drove away, she screamed uncontrollably, blaming me for ruining her day. I sat quietly in the back seat, choking back the tears, afraid of further punishment.

Many years later, Mom was diagnosed with bipolar disorder. As a child, those labels are meaningless. I carried the abuse, blame, shame, and guilt well into my adulthood. Understanding the "why" behind her behavior helped, but more inner work was necessary to reprogram the patterns locked into my body, psyche, and behavior.

5

SENT TO PARADISE

Constantino, who was nicknamed "Uncle Goose," was one of my favorite uncles from Hawaii. He was visiting California when I was still in pre-school. Uncle Goose was confined to a wheelchair after becoming paralyzed from a fall from an airplane wing. Uncle Goose, my mother's uncle, was always very sweet, fun, and joyful. His energy made me smile, unlike the energy of my Grandparents or parents. He had a great sense of humor, and he loved joking and playing. While I don't recall much of the events that led to his departure, I remember feeling good with him. I didn't know that my parents were planning on a divorce. So, without Dicey around to take care of me, my Mom and grandparents decided to send me to Hawaii with him.

Uncle Goose lived in a basement-style, one-room apartment at the end of the Honolulu Airport. As planes took off and landed, it created a loud, unsettling environment. While I loved him, I wasn't sure what was happening or why I was there. I was scared at the constant noise. Even worse, I felt abandoned. As a five-year-old, I thought I had done something wrong. Neither my brother nor sister were banished, just me. No one talked to me about the trip, how long I'd be there or why I was there.

After a few days spent in Honolulu with Uncle Goose, the adults realized he couldn't care for me. My Great Grandpa Zoilo lived on a little farm on Oahu in a tiny North Shore town called Kahuku. My uncle and aunt, who lived in Honolulu, picked me up from Uncle Goose and delivered me to the little farm.

Kahuku is beautiful to this day, located just a short distance from Turtle Bay. It was a sugar mill town filled with locals that worked there. Back in the early 70s, it was very rural. Great Grandpa didn't have indoor plumbing or electricity. I hadn't met him before, but he was to be my caretaker for several months. Grandpa Zoilo was a short, tan Filipino who spoke little English; I followed him around with little communication. He had chickens and small black puppies. I vaguely remember my time with him except for how I felt and what filled my days. One of the first things I was told was not to name the chickens or the puppies. That didn't make sense as a child, so of course, I gave them all names. They were my new friends in a lonely, strange place.

Feeding the chickens was fun, and the puppies and chickens followed me around when I played outside. Using the outhouse at night was terrifying to me. I quickly learned how to "hold it" so I wouldn't have to go out at night. If I did, I knew the chickens and dogs were out there.

Thankfully the weather in Hawaii was pleasant. The property wasn't far from the shoreline. It was beautiful and peaceful. If it weren't for the circumstances, feeling abandoned and punished, I probably would have enjoyed it. Angels were with me, yet I don't remember much of what they said. I was afraid I was sent away because of them. Their presence was undoubtedly felt and seen but more at a distance to respect my fears that communicating with them is what landed me in exile.

Finding ways to get through the day, I made friends with all the animals. I fondly remember Great Grandpa gave me sugar canes as a treat. He was always busy doing something as I followed quietly behind him on command. One night we attended a big "party." Kids were running around, men gathered in a circle, and a lot of yelling, joking, and storytelling.

Great Grandpa disappeared with one of the roosters before grabbing my hand and taking me to the circle where a noisy crowd gathered. Before I could make sense of what was happening, I witnessed my first cockfight in horror. The rooster, who was my friend, got mutilated by another rooster. No one seemed bothered by it except me. I was screaming and crying while Great Grandpa laughed at me. Cockfights were a pastime for him and the locals, but to me, it was traumatizing. I cried myself to sleep that night, no longer trusting the only person that seemed to be looking out for me.

Aside from the loss of my rooster friend, puppies were disappearing as well. Only three remained. Trying to make sense of what was happening around me without anyone to talk to was pointless. I just needed to behave, play with my animal friends and stay out of Grandpa's way.

I have questioned the rationale and sanity of my family when I look back on that time. What the hell were they thinking of sending a child to live with a person with paraplegia? When that didn't work, who felt an older man who didn't speak English could care for a child he never met? Was I in trouble? Was I abandoned? Why didn't my brother and sister get sent away? So many questions, but no one bothered to answer them.

I was very young, and that whole time is very foggy in my memory. Recalling those pivotal events is both funny to me and heartbreaking. As a mother, I have no idea what the hell the adults were thinking. Thankfully I had a great imagination, and my imaginary friends watched over me. I asked my parents a few years back about it, and they were less than helpful. Mom said she believes she was having a breakdown, and Dad was in San Diego training Marine Corps recruits. Astonishingly, I am not a complete mental and emotional basket case. I tried regression therapy, but I could not remember all the details of this time and different traumatic events. Sometimes the human brain stores that stuff away where it's inaccessible.

My time there finally ended after what seemed like forever, but it was only about six months when my grandparents showed up and took me home to California. Arriving home while still having no explanation of what I just lived through, everything was changing. My parents were getting divorced, and we would live in a small two-bedroom apartment with my Mom. After Hawaii, I was afraid to cry, laugh, or even speak. I retreated within myself, fearful of what would happen next. I used telepathy a lot to talk to my guides, angels, and God. Sometimes I had entire conversations in the privacy of my mind with someone I could feel but couldn't see. The skill of telepathy has been a gift that continues to serve me.

In 2014, I returned to Oahu to visit my cousin and my past. Kahuku is still small but quaint. The Kahuku country club has replaced

Grandpa's home, a little-known golf course where mostly locals play. It's gorgeous there, but in my 5-year-old brain, it's dark, scary, and lonely. In some ways, that was a reprieve from the craziness of my mother's moods. It was a chance to see a faraway land and meet new relatives. Had I known why I was there, it may have had a far different feeling. It was, however, just another experience that led me to believe I was in the way and that nobody could love me.

While visiting in 2014, my cousin Bernee explained that black dogs are a delicacy in the Philippines, much to my horror. She laughed as she put the pieces together of my time with my Great Grandpa. When I told her about how the puppies just disappeared one by one, she explained the old ways. As I searched my memory, I couldn't remember going to a market with him. We ate eggs from the chickens; I remember that, but not actual grocery shopping. I know we didn't have big meals at all. Bananas, fruit, and eggs were most of my meals. I have no animosity towards my Great Grandpa. He was kind and tolerant. I probably wouldn't have known if he corrected me as we didn't speak the same language. He smiled a lot, worked hard, and let me tag along, which was better than how my mother treated me. He remarried when he was 72, taking a 22-year-old Filipino as a wife. They had two children younger than me that are my Great Uncles. He lived a full life in his little piece of paradise. All my cousins speak fondly of the time they spent in Kahuku; I wish I had had the same experience as them.

Now that my parents were divorced, life became all about survival. There was no time for being a kid. Thankfully, divorce meant Catholic School was no longer affordable. I hated going to Catholic School. The teachers were nuns; they were mean, impatient, and far from loving. I seemed to be the target of my teacher in kindergarten. I can barely remember school, except I spent a lot of time in the corner after being hit with the paddle or ruler. Physical, mental, and emotional abuse was all I knew from the authority figures in my life.

Angels, spirits, and animals were my only allies. I hated the world I lived in, where I constantly felt hurt and sad. I prayed and prayed that God would send someone to save me. No one showed up. I prayed that I could sleep and wake up in heaven with my spirit friends. Somehow, I survived; I owe that to my allies in the subtle realms.

Music was important to my Mom, so at 5-years old, I learned to play acoustic guitar; she had a sweet young woman from Argentina teach me to read music and play. I loved playing music, and I loved her. She treated me like I was special. I looked forward to the lessons. She stopped charging my Mom because she knew we couldn't afford much. During one Christmas holiday, just before my birthday, she was leaving for a visit to Argentina. She gave me a present and promised to bring me another one when she returned. Mom hated the way she was with me and how I wasn't afraid of her. She interrogated me about my feelings for her, forbidding me to see her again. Happy I had the songs she taught me until I was heartbroken when my brother broke my guitar.

Through all of these events, I learned I was NOT to speak of what I could see. Early in life, bombarded by messages to keep my sensitivities and "gifts" to myself were given. The priest from our church visited as I sat on the floor watching cartoons. Angels made it clear that I needed to listen to the conversation between Mom and the priest, but I was to stare at the television as if I couldn't hear them. From that visit on, I kept all my unseen friends a secret. They were with me through all the terror, silently holding me in love. I quickly learned that to the world and the church; these "gifts" were considered evil. From then on, anytime I heard or saw spirits when people were around, I either stared off in the distance or looked at my feet to avoid attention.

6

HIDING IN THE TOWER

In the first year or so after the divorce, we lived with my Mom. She was going through a bit of an identity crisis, out late singing in piano bars and dating. My brother, sister, and I kept the house clean, taking care of ourselves. There was very little food in the apartment. We were able to keep pet mice and my pet rat "Chim Chim" hidden and undetected in our room for months, that is, until she came home from work unexpectedly, in the middle of the day, catching us while we sat on the steps playing with them. She made us give them to our neighbor as food for his pet boa constrictor. From that day forward, I hated snakes and wasn't too fond of her either.

During one of our weekend visits with Dad, he walked in on my sister, serving us chicken that was still raw. He dumped the chicken and took us out to eat. He didn't know that we had stolen bread and some other food from a convenience store nearby. I'm pretty sure the owner knew, but he didn't stop us. I thank God for him whenever I think about those days. I was this thin, short, Asian kid with a loaf of bread tucked under my shirt.... Yeah, he knew.

In third grade, Dad secretly remarried and took custody of us. I wish I could say life got easier. It didn't. My sister moved back with my Mom, leaving my brother and me with Dad. My stepmother was far from friendly, even worse when Dad wasn't around. She loved telling me how my Mom didn't love me and didn't care about me. She refused to buy me new clothes. Instead, I had to wear hand-me-downs from my stepsister.

'Step-monster,' as I called her, would threaten me constantly. I was not allowed to tell my Dad what was happening. She said I would be sent away if I did. During the holidays, her parents were visiting from out of town when I learned she had the same rule about crying as my Mom and grandparents. I said or did something that earned a face slap hard enough to turn my cheek red and bring tears to my eyes. She threatened if I didn't stop the tears and make the handprint on my face go away, I would go to bed hungry. She sent me to the bathroom to wash my face with cold water, demanding I stop crying. I did as I was told and went downstairs for dinner when called. My long hair hid my face as I sat quietly and ate dinner, making no eye contact, staring down at the lima beans I loathed on my plate. I was disgusted at her cruelty and shocked that no one noticed how withdrawn or sad I looked, not even my Dad. Inside I was crumbling.

I was not allowed to excel at anything, nor was I allowed to do anything unless my stepsister did it. Unfortunately, I excelled at gymnastics, dance, baton, and playing instruments. The dance school we attended promoted me to the talent unit team. Step-monster refused to let me participate unless my stepsister was able to do it too. Thankfully the school allowed it, as I enjoyed the reprieve from the volatility at home. Being promoted to the talent unit felt good and meant someone liked something I did. It felt great to be rewarded and accepted by adults for once. Gymnastics and dance gave me an outlet for my suppressed emotions. Yet, the message to stay quiet, invisible, and unassuming continued. Believing that I was worthless became ingrained in me.

Playing instruments was the only creative, emotional outlet accepted in our home. My stepsister had a piano, so I got to learn how to play. Although, I wasn't allowed to practice or excel at it. I chose to play violin in music class at school. Of course, my stepsister wanted to play that too, so I eventually gave it up for the Cello. I hated the Cello. It was too big, and I didn't like the feel of it. I wanted a guitar, but it was pointless to ask for one since I couldn't make noise or enjoy anything. Eventually, I just sang when I was alone and rehearsed melodies in my head. I began to see my mind as a 'safe' place, calling it my attic, thinking of it as a tower in a castle that imprisoned me, yet kept me safe from attack. It became the only place safe from the threat of having someone steal my creativity, talents, and dreams.

As the tension between me and the step-monster grew, I yearned to live with my sister and Mom. My sister convinced me to run away from home, telling me that Mom would pick me up. So one day, I filled my backpack and took it to school. Before the dismissal bell rang, the Principal's office summoned me, where the step-monster was waiting. According to her, my Mom's lawyer called to inform them that I was planning to run away, but she didn't want me. Step-monster angrily told me how Mom chose to give up custody of us since we were in the way of her singing career. Every chance she got, she reminded me that my Mom never wanted me. She relayed a story about Mom's pregnancy with me. She blatantly told me, at eight months pregnant, Mom attempted an abortion of sorts. Step-monster said that Mom set her dress on fire and stood under a scalding hot shower pointed right on her stomach, all efforts to get rid of me before I was born. While those attempts didn't work, her mental stability came into question. Step-monster wanted me to know how "lucky" I was that she was willing to "allow" me to live with her and my Dad. After the attempted runaway, I didn't see my Mom again for months. It wasn't until Dad and the step-monster separated that I saw her again. I remained quiet around her, avoiding any eye contact, afraid I'd burst into tears.

Some moments in childhood were memorable and heartwarming. In 5th grade, a group of latch-key kids from our neighborhood were home for the summer. We were left to our own devices during the day while our parents were at work. We decided to go to the local convenience store, about a mile or two from our street one day. There were about 7 or 8 of us who made the trek to get candy from the store. On the way, I noticed a dead cat on the sidewalk. Immediately I was struck by how sad it would be to die without anyone noticing. Being the pack leader, I sent some of the kids back to our houses to get a wagon, explaining we had a duty to bury this cat. Some of us stayed to guard the dead cat I named Crystal. I announced we would have a funeral for her and bury her properly. We gathered dandelions to hold during our funeral procession while we waited for the wagon. After we loaded Crystal into the wagon, we went to the store to get our candy, with Crystal in tow, not thinking anything of the sight we must have been. Imagine a group of elementary kids lined up single file behind a red wagon, holding dandelions, heads bowed, in silence and reverence.

Once home, we found a spot to bury her, behind the planter beds in our front yard, right outside our living room window. As the self-appointed minister, I led some prayers as the rest of the kids bowed their heads and said their "Amens." I made up a story of how she was sad, alone, and left for dead on the sidewalk. I asked God to take her to Heaven and that she rest in peace. We dug a hole about a foot deep. We had no idea what we were doing. We wrapped Crystal in a trash bag, put her in the hole, covered her with dirt, and left the dandelions.

As fate would have it, our family was leaving for vacation to Hawaii for a week. After the burial, none of us thought about it again until we returned from vacation. Saturday, we resumed the weekly chores, including yard work. My Dad mowed the lawn and began trimming the edges. He grumbled about something smelling like it died. My brother and I were both in on the smell and knew what he was referring to. He found the source of the smell and told us to go into the house. Once he unearthed the cat, he was furious. My brother and I huddled together, whispering about getting in trouble when my Dad told us to take the dog for a walk. We overheard him telling my stepMom that the troubled kid across the street, a teenage girl none of us talked to, had buried a dead cat in our yard. Immediately my brother and I ran to the park with the dog. We knew the animal control was coming to pick up the cat, but what scared us was how angry my Dad was. We decided not to tell the truth about the cat and hoped none of the others would squeal to their parents. After alerting the neighborhood kids, we made a deal that none of us would tell the truth about the dead cat.

For years Dad would tell that story of how angry he was at the "damned troubled kid across the street." One night around the kitchen table when I turned 18, I couldn't take it anymore. I confessed the truth and couldn't help but laugh at the shock on Dad's face. He was laughing too, but then questioned how we could let him tell that story all those years and not tell the truth. I told him I was an adult now and knew I couldn't get beat for it, so why not set the record straight. It was the first of many confessions to come.

It wasn't unusual for me to bring home stray dogs I'd find on the way home from school. They wouldn't let us have a dog, so I would do my best to bring it home anytime I saw a lost dog. Blackie was a cute poodle mix that happily followed me home. We wanted to keep him so bad, but it was a stray, and Dad wouldn't have it. Later, after animal control came for Blackie, Dad conceded and bought a Cockapoo we named Toby. Toby was instantly my best friend. I told him all my fears, worries, read books to him, and cuddled him. He was the only affection I had at home. Things were becoming volatile between my step-monster and Dad. Toby kept me calm. When they fought, I was always in the garage with him, hanging out in his bed. Sometimes, I would carry whole conversations on with Toby. At times I swear, he understood. His eyes would acknowledge that he was listening. He would agree with me when I told him how scared I was. Anytime I needed reassurance, he would climb on my lap or lick me. He was the only living being at the time I could relate to and felt safe with.

Animals are reliant on humans to care for them. They don't have a choice. They are often helpless victims of abuse too. Like me, they are sensitive to energy and intentions that are unspoken. Sensitives always feel better with an animal because their energy is pure. In a world where I felt unloved, Toby made sure I felt loved. I believe God sends animals to us as teachers of how to love unconditionally. They teach us about natural connection, living in the moment, telepathy, and intuition. Toby was my furry angel.

Somehow, I learned to deal with the circumstances life had thrown my way; it had become somewhat bearable. I was finding things I liked doing and was good at, like skating. As the arguments between my Dad and his wife escalated, my brother and I made up code words to replace the word 'divorce' secretly, hoping it was happening. Then, finally, it happened, ushering in even more changes.

Just as I began 7th grade, they separated and began divorce proceedings. Unfortunately, the step-monster was having an affair with my Dad's best friend, a man they worked with. Dad needed a new start far from the betrayal he experienced. So, Dad, my brother, Toby, and I moved to the Seattle area, leaving behind everything we knew, including the shaky relationship and visits with Mom.

7

FINDING MY SPIRIT ANIMAL

In Junior High, I had a fascination with everything horse-related. Our quasi-grandparents, who were family friends, had Shetland ponies they let us ride as a small kid. As a result, I always wanted to ride. I even wrote stories about horses. As a Sagittarius and Chinese Horse, it's no surprise I was attracted to the strength, courage, power, and freedom embodied by horses. Once my Dad received his divorce settlement, he bought my brother a dirt bike, and I was given horseback riding lessons.

I was in my element when I was finally able to learn how to ride English and jump. At the barn, I felt in tune with the horses. My instructor said I was a natural. Being with horses made me feel at ease, peaceful, and connected to God. I could forget everything going on at home or school while I spent time at the barn. It was the beginning of healing for me. It gave me a sense of self, connection, and acceptance I hadn't felt before.

I bonded instantly with one horse, in particular, a retired race-horse named Royale. He was for sale, although I had no hopes of buying him. He had been abused and was afraid of everyone but me. Anytime I came to the barn, Royale lit up, calling out, excited to see me. I could feel all his fears, knowing what he needed and how to treat him. The barn owners were happy to let me take care of him. He and I would communicate telepathically. When I rode him, I would think of what I wanted to do, and he would do it. I would think turn left, and he'd turn left or think halt, he would stop. He taught me so much about my psychic gifts, my ability to sense, and how to be in sync when I relaxed. For the first time in my life, I didn't feel awkward about having psychic gifts. I believed that with animals, I could secretly use my gifts to communicate. It helped me, and I like to think it helped them too.

Horses made me feel accepted, like I was good at something. I was excelling at riding, and the horses trusted me. I was working for my lessons and didn't even think that I would lose the ability to ride. The barn was 40 minutes from home but, Dad was dating a woman near the stables at the time, so it wasn't out of his way to take me. I spent every weekend at the barn, leaving Toby home alone, locked in the garage. He began tearing things up while we were gone. Finally, Dad decided he needed more attention, so he gave Toby to his girlfriend without asking me.

Toby wasn't even with them for a month before he ran away from home. I was furious! I made up a story in my head that he was coming to find me. I knew something terrible had happened to him, knowing I would never see him again. It was easier to believe he was on his way home. Eventually, I added details to the story that he encountered a deer and got trampled. I didn't want to think of him getting hit by a car. I had an active imagination which served me well getting through life.

Toby was gone. It was like he didn't matter, but he was my family and my friend. I was grieving and depressed. Not only that, Dad had broken up with his girlfriend, so trips to the barn were no longer convenient, I had to quit. I lost my joy and everything I loved in a matter of months. I constantly journaled, writing poems, songs, and all my dark thoughts. I was lonely again and began to believe that everything I loved would be taken away. Somehow, I had to learn not to love or need love. I felt an all too familiar feeling like I had no control over anything. So, I created a little secret hiding spot in my closet. There I kept my journals, poetry, and a blanket. Anytime I got sad, I hid in there with my bed lamp and wrote. It was the only place I could shed tears and let myself express my feelings.

Mom was living her life in California while I was in rainy Seattle. Sometimes I fantasized about how she would finally love and accept me. I thought that day arrived when she asked my brother and me to move in with her and her new husband. My brother jumped at the chance. Eventually, I agreed with the promise of a horse. I hadn't seen her for a couple of years, so the first greeting at the airport should have been great. The first thing she said while giving me a half-ass hug was, "Wow, you gained weight. Don't you look healthy?" I had given up gymnastics due to back problems and my newly formed "boobs." At that point, my body was chang-ing, as was everything else. That ONE comment started a cycle of anorexia and bulimia, lasting well into my twenties.

When I was around her in a group, it was super confusing. She talked about me like she cared, but her treatment was different.

She was heavily involved in her church. I remember one day, while she lit into me over something, the phone rang. She answered and went from screaming at me to talking sweetly. As soon as her call finished, she went right back to screaming. I was shocked as thoughts raced through my head, "You liar. You are full of shit. You hypocrite!" My head was spinning, my emotions were flying, and all I wanted to do was get away from her.

When I arrived, Mom set me up with her friend, a horse owner, with a horse named "Crystal." I got to ride a few times, but the promise of my own horse never materialized. Instead, she had bought me a beautiful rose-colored comforter for my room. It was one of the first pretty things I received as a gift. Although I had high hopes for a happy life, those hopes came crashing down quickly.

Attending church on Sunday was a must for our family. Mom sang one morning while talking about excerpts in a book she wrote about her "Christian journey." She stood in front of the whole church, telling them how happy she was now that I was living with her. Then, she told a story about an attempted suicide in November 1966. Quickly doing the math in my head, I froze. I was born in December 1966, which meant the stories the step-monster told me were true. Thoughts raced through my mind, "She didn't love me. She never wanted me. She wanted me dead." I bolted out of the church toward home as quickly as my feet, dressed in one-inch heels, would carry me. I called my Dad and asked if I could move back with him. Mom was furious that I left the church. She gave me no explanation about why she chose to share that story before ever having a conversation with me about it. How could the God I knew condone this? How could my mother know the God I knew and act like this? I was devastated, angry at God, and disgusted with so-called "Christianity."

Within days I was on a plane back to Seattle. I asked if I could take the comforter she bought as my birthday gift, she said "no." I wouldn't get that comforter back for over 30 years, and only after she had gifted it to my niece. When I received it as a hand-me-down, it was worn, faded, and falling apart. I have it to this day as a reminder of everything I've come through. Receiving gifts became something I dreaded because of that. I believed gifts had strings attached, that gifts were a tool to hurt me. It took a couple of decades to accept gifts from others without questioning the intent.

Once at home in Seattle, I immersed myself in my studies, books, and boys. I was becoming self-conscious about my body. Without gymnastics, I needed to find a way to stay thin. Depression made me lose my appetite and set the tone for destructive habits of not eating. With Mom's comments about my weight, I began to see myself as fat. I was a tiny, framed girl, only weighing around 100 pounds, but I saw fat every time I looked in the mirror. I hated my body and how I looked. I wanted to be small with no boobs and no hips. I had this image in my head that if my body were perfect, maybe my Mom would finally love me, accept me, and approve of me. Boys seemed to like my appearance, but I didn't see it when I looked in the mirror. The skinnier I got, the more I hid my body from everyone by wearing baggy clothes. If I had to get undressed in the locker room, I waited until everyone was busy and snuck into a bathroom stall to change.

Anorexia and bulimia made me feel in control of something. It seemed like everything in my life was controlled by everyone else.

I could quietly starve myself for days on end and feel like I had some personal power. It was a personal triumph in some ways, and in other ways, it made me feel "lighter," like I was less weighted. Hiding an eating disorder wasn't that hard. Dad was barely home, so when he was around, I ate in front of him. After the dishes were done, I ran to the bathroom, turned on the shower, and stuck my finger down my throat.

High school was overwhelming on every level, but I found ways to make it work. I hated the cliques but carved out a small group of friends a grade above mine. We all had friends in cliques, but we weren't in one. Drinking on weekends and smoking pot became my new way to cope with life. I quickly learned that when I was high or drunk, I didn't feel the same. I didn't feel great, but I didn't hurt as badly. Numbing my pain by self-medicating, not eating or purging food became my coping mechanisms.

At sixteen, life was bearable but not happy. I had a steady boyfriend I loved, and I thought he loved me too. He did stupid things I forgave, like breaking up with me right before a holiday, so he didn't have to buy me a present and getting back together with me after. I coped with the dysfunction; it was familiar to my upbringing. I felt like I could deal with things easier since at least he loved me. Until he didn't, he broke up with me when he met another girl. Without warning, I was alone, rejected, and abandoned. It was too much to handle. I broke. I had two bottles of pain pills from my doctor for back pain I had never taken. No one was there for me to talk to, so I did what I learned from my mother. I wrote a suicide note and swallowed both bottles of pills.

Turning off my bedroom lamp, I closed my eyes, cried, and fell asleep. I prayed for forgiveness and asked to go to heaven. I felt my body get farther and farther away. I felt light. I passed through a tunnel of light, thinking I am finally free. Just as I was ready to step out of the tunnel, I heard a voice say, "You have to go back. You can't leave yet". My eyes popped open. Barely conscious, I somehow made it to the bathroom. Six hours had passed since I swallowed the pills, and here I was in the bathroom throwing up whole pills. They weren't even the slightest digested. I was quietly sobbing as I made my way back to my room. In a daze, I was shocked by an angry father. He was holding my note and yelling, "What did you do?"

Sobbing, I told him I had thrown the pills up, but he wasn't satisfied. The next thing I know, he is on the phone with poison control, furiously writing notes. They told him to make me drink a gallon of milk. I hated milk, and he expected me to drink the whole gallon. I quietly cried and did as I was told. He finally let me go to my room. Before I made it to my room, I was running for the toilet to throw up the entire gallon of milk.

Talking and processing problems wasn't something we ever did. But, ironically, the next afternoon, an after-school special was playing on television about a kid who tried to commit suicide. Dad was listening to it while he was in the kitchen. He came in, looked at the TV, and said, "Why would he want to do something stupid like that?" I quickly shut off the television, ran to my room, closed the door, and hid in my closet. Then, shutting out the world, I wrote about the darkness that enveloped my soul.

Somehow, I made it through those years living with my Dad. He was preoccupied with his life, dating, and working. He did the best he could, but I knew he wasn't happy either. Many times, Dad traveled out of town with his girlfriend, leaving me home alone. It was during those years I learned to hate holidays, especially Christmas. He decided to spend Christmas with his girlfriend's family the year I decided never to celebrate again. I woke up on Christmas morning to an empty house, a small tree on the coffee table holding a card and a small gift. It felt like a lame gesture that left me feeling unloved and abandoned again. I couldn't wait to turn 18 and move out to have my own life, far beyond the crappy life I was living.

Moving out and becoming an adult was all I could fantasize about. I had a great G.P.A., so sovereignty wasn't too far away. During the final months of my junior year in high school, I realized I only needed a few credits to graduate. All my friends were in the class of '84, but I had an entire school year ahead of me, alone. The school principal had me write an essay on why I should be allowed to graduate early. I didn't want to get stuck in school for another year. I didn't want to have to take needless electives either, so I wrote the essay.

On my 18th birthday, I had enough credits to get my diploma, school let out for winter break, and without any celebration, I graduated. While I had to wait until June of 1985 to get my official diploma, I was free. Immediately, I packed my little green Volkswagen bug with a plan to temporarily move to my Mom's house in Laguna Niguel, CA, until I got a job. I hadn't thought it through, other than just getting back to the sun in California.

8

———

CRASHING INTO ADULTING

Within weeks of arriving in Southern California, the stress began building. I started partying with some coworkers in their mid-twenties. But, staying up all night and drinking wasn't helping my depression. The relationship with Mom was stressful, constantly feeling judged and not good enough. She bible thumped continuously, telling me I needed to be "saved." My sister lived in Huntington Beach with her new baby and husband. I called her on a Friday when I had lost hope of a decent future. Sharing my thoughts of just wanting to die, she told me to check myself into a mental hospital voluntarily. I looked up to her, so I did.

Unsure of what to expect at a mental hospital, I thought I'd be with kids my age. I was 18, but I looked like I was 12. Due to policy, the hospital explained they had to admit me to the adult ward that Friday evening. In short order, I was registered as a patient and escorted to a shared room. I hadn't eaten that day but wasn't hungry after the whirlwind of activity. Before my sister left, she handed me a pack of Marlboro Lights, saying I should smoke them because I would need them. She wasn't wrong.

Since I was on a 72-hour suicide watch, all my personal belongings were taken from me, except the cigarettes and lighter. I entered my room to find an Asian woman on the other bed. In my estimation, she was close to my Mom's age. She didn't say hello or even look up from the book she was reading. The nurse who escorted me to my room told me I could smoke outside if I needed to. She just left me there without taking me on a tour of the ward. I slowly walked through the T.V. room where many patients were drugged, unresponsive, or babbling incoherently. Immediately I was struck by a heavy weight of dark emotions, ranging from sadness to rage.

Eerie, the room felt thick yet sterile. What had I done? I wanted to run out of there so badly, but now I was stuck for the next few days. I began to have an anxiety attack, quickly going outside to make use of the Marlboro Lights. It took me a few puffs to stop coughing since I wasn't a smoker. Thankfully, it was quiet outside, the energy was lighter, and I was left alone. Hours passed before sunset; I finally went inside to sleep.

Waking up in the mental hospital Saturday morning with no clue where the cafeteria was or what time meals were served, I made my way out to the smoker's haven. Bored, I tried going into the T.V. room a few times, but the patients scared me. Finally, I laid down to take a nap to try and forget where I was. The psychiatrist was off until Monday, so as far as I knew, I was to sit until "suicide watch" was over. My Asian roommate was reading the bible aloud, sounding quite irritated. Some of the things I heard her say reminded me too much of my Mom. I couldn't take it. I went back out to the smoker's picnic table, where I stayed the whole day. As I sat and smoked, my mind was filled with things like, "You're not crazy; these people are crazy." I was so terrified of the craziness that I deemed myself sane. I couldn't wait to see the doctor to get out of that place and go home.

Starving, tired, and chilled, I made my way inside around dinner time. I still hadn't been told about meals or shown where the cafeteria was. Rather than chase a nurse down, I went to my bed. I laid down for a few minutes before a nurse and two big dudes, dressed in white, barged into the room. They grabbed me, one by each arm, and walked through another doorway. Next thing you know, I'm in a "solitary confinement" room in the teen ward. I was screaming, panicked, unsure what was happening or why. They stripped and cavity searched me, looking for something. I felt violated and threatened. No one bothered explaining what was happening. They just kept yelling at me to cooperate. I hadn't been eating much; my weight had dropped to 80 pounds. Struggling with these men as hard as I could, wasn't working. I went limp, collapsing on the rubber mattress.

Finally, they left my room. All I heard as the door closed and locked was that I would stay in solitary for the night. There was just a rubber bed, no pillow, blanket, or sheets. Outside my room, I could see young, teenage faces looking through the small window like I was an animal in a cage. Everyone wanted to know who got stuck in solitary. I rolled over, back to the window, and cried. Somehow, I found myself caught in a nightmare. I had come to get help. I wanted so badly for someone to tell me what to do to feel better. I wanted someone to tell me what was wrong with me. I had hoped this hospital stay would be my salvation. But laying there feeling violated, raped, and betrayed, I knew this wasn't the solution. I had no way to call my sister, and no one else knew I was here. I prayed God would just let me die and go to heaven before I finally drifted off to sleep.

Morning arrived with a nurse opening the door to solitary confinement. She said I was being put back in my room. She explained that a spoon went missing in the cafeteria the night before, and my roommate accused me of taking it. I was furious as I broke into tears. I told her I hadn't been shown the cafeteria and hadn't eaten since Friday night. She then informed me the spoon was found a few hours earlier, under my roommate's bed. I wanted to slap the nurse in the face; instead, I asked for my smokes and ran out to the smoking table. For the next half hour, I chain-smoked, trying to stop the tears. Anger eventually took over. I marched to the Nurse's station, demanding to get released. The nurses said I couldn't leave since I was under suicide watch. I begged, pleading that I was a voluntary admission. Nothing swayed them. I was to wait until the Psychiatrist saw me in the morning. Defeated again, I walked outside to the only place I could be alone, the smoker table. My head was spinning, my emotions ragged, my body drained.

Monday finally arrived, and with it, a visit with the Psychiatrist. No one had apologized for the cavity search or solitary confinement. I demanded as calmly as I could to be released. He looked shocked that I hadn't eaten for days. I told him, after being there, I knew I wasn't that bad off. I wasn't crazy. It was clear that my roommate, who reminded me so much of my mother I was trying to escape, had problems, not me. He said if I left, it would be A.M.A. (against medical advice) since they hadn't treated me. I told him I would find a counselor just to let me go home. He signed my discharge papers A.M.A., and within hours I was out.

When I got into my car to leave, all I wanted to do was go to the beach. Thankfully it was close to my Mom's house, so I made my way there. As an empath, the ocean was the only place I felt somewhat at peace. The following week, I began counseling with a nice woman. She encouraged me to find a room to rent and leave my Mom's house. Within weeks, I was living on my own for the first time. I traded a secretary job for waitressing, which afforded a decent lifestyle. I began making new friends and having fun for the first time in forever. I continued in counseling for as long as I could afford, maybe three months. Then, the counselor said one magical thing to me that changed my perspective. "If you met your Mom on the street and she treated you the way she does now, would you go to lunch with her? Would you be friends with her?"

"No way," I said.

Then she held my hand, looking directly into my eyes, and said, "Then why do you think you have to now?" I sat for a moment and contemplated that question. Then, finally, light bulbs went off in my head. I didn't "have to" do anything with her anymore. She was never a mother to me; why pretend any different. It was the first time I had permission to stay away from her.

I found a great deal in the paper as a first-time renter, sharing a house with a lifeguard and a Medical student. We all had busy schedules and kept to ourselves for the most part. The lifeguard and I became friends, our rooms right next to each other at the front of the house. The walkway to the front door was dark, the porch light constantly burned out, so we gave up replacing it. Instead, I started leaving my bedroom window unlocked, entering and exiting through it. Life was calming down a little as I got comfortable being on my own.

One night, hanging out with a friend, I sat on my bed and mentioned how the house felt a little strange. There was no living room furniture, and none of us ever went into the kitchen. He said there was nothing odd about that. I explained the light bulb issue on the porch and how I hated going to the bathroom at night, it always felt like someone was watching me. The other room next to mine was empty when I moved in, aside from a mirror I took for my room. Although the medical student in charge of the house advertised, no one would rent that room out. I told my friend about waking up feeling like someone was staring at me, and the heavy mirror gave me the creeps. He laughed at me, telling me to put it back and stop letting my imagination get the best of me. At the time, the Freeway Killer had just murdered someone miles from our house. He told me I was paranoid. Just then, the doorbell rang with the pizza delivery. Startled, we both went to the door to get the pizza.

Returning to my room, pizza in hand, I stood in the doorway with my mouth open wide, unable to take a step. My friend nudged me forward and asked why I was so afraid. The borrowed mirror was now in front of my dressing table, leaning against it. Before we left the room, it was on top of the table, with several picture frames in front of it. No one else was home, so how the hell did that mirror end up leaning against the front of the table, on the floor, without any of my picture frames knocked over. I was frantic and shaking. He was a little freaked out too. We stared at the mirror, the table, and the picture frames, trying to figure out how it fell off the dressing table without a sound or without knocking any pictures over. Finally, he grabbed the big mirror, put it back in the vacant room next door, and slammed the door. He calmed me down as we ate our pizza and watched a movie.

Without reason, I hated being in the living room or walking past the bedroom next to mine. I tried to avoid it as much as possible, but I had to use the front door now that a serial killer was on the loose. The Freeway Killer had entered his victim's home through an open window. All the women in the area were terrified, including me. Thankfully the lease expired, my roommates were moving, and I could leave the spooky house for good. I found another room for rent, reasonably close.

When I returned to the house to retrieve my security deposit, I found the landlord painting the living room. I asked if he had ever felt anything weird in the house. I told him what happened, saying it probably sounded crazy. He admitted that a man had died in the vacant room just before we rented the house. He said his wife hated that place too, and she always felt like someone was watching her. In some ways, it was a relief to know I wasn't crazy, but it freaked me out in other ways. Was it some angry ghost? Was it mad I took the mirror? I was happy never to have to return to the house again. Since suppressing my psychic gifts at a young age, I didn't want anything to do with the supernatural.

Not long after moving, I stopped getting counseling. Work was going well, and I was out on my own; I even had a boyfriend. While he was moving back east, I felt good and had hope for the future. Financially stable, I began to search for a horse to lease. I knew I couldn't afford to buy one, but I could afford to lease one. Within a couple of weeks, I came across an ad in the paper to lease a quarter horse. For whatever reason, I couldn't let that ad go. A woman police officer was looking for someone to take care of him. She seemed super nice on the phone, so we arranged to meet me at the stables to meet her horse, Quincy. I fell in love with him the minute I set eyes on him. She gave me very little info except that he was the grandson of a famous quarter horse named Sir Quincy's Dan. Quincy's full name was Sir Quincy's Dunn. She warned he was a little hyper but just needed someone to ride him. I jumped at the chance to lease him, paying just his boarding fees.

Two weeks after I signed the lease, I only had the opportunity to ride him twice. We had been caught in a cycle of rain, causing flooding in the arena. All I could do was sit in his stall and pet him. The first day it dried out, I was struck with a strong desire to ride even though it was a workday. Impulsively, I called in sick to work and headed to the barn. After being cooped up for two weeks, Quincy was ready to run. I turned him out into the arena to burn some energy before riding. No one else was at the stables aside from the laborers who cleaned stalls and fed. I quickly bridled him, not bothering to use a saddle, and hopped on bareback. It felt good to be on him. The time we had spent together in his stall, bonding, was good for us. He seemed to trust and like me.

We cruised in the arena at a trot when Quincy spooked at something downhill in the brush on the riverbed side. Quincy bolted in a panic at a full-blown gallop. I was barely holding on, trying desperately to stop him. I tried to pull his face into the wooden railing of the arena to slow him down. Before I knew what was happening, I slipped between him and the fence, hitting the base of my skull on the railing as I went down. In his panic to get to safety, Quincy stepped on my left hip. I wasn't sure what had happened. All I knew, I was on the ground with Quincy's face dripping blood on me. When I tried to get up, I instantly went unconscious.

I regained consciousness with a crowd of EMTs talking to me and a small group of onlookers that weren't there before. I remember watching the resident horse trainer grab Quincy and return him to his stall. The EMTs were trying to assess how badly I was hurt. They noticed the hoof print in my Levi's, the pocket ripped out, and the blood that Quincy had dripped over me. I remember them cutting my clothes off in the dirt to see if I was bleeding internally and sliding a board under me while stabilizing my neck with a brace. I don't remember much from there aside from waking up in the trauma unit of the hospital.

Lesson number 1: don't call in sick to work if you plan to do something dangerous.

Lesson 2: If you do go riding on a horse you barely know, use a saddle!

I suffered from a fractured skull and hip (left Ileac crest), with bruising down my hip, thigh, and back along with a severe concussion. The doctors wanted to put a metal pin in my hip to make sure it healed properly. I was totally against having metal in my body. I denied the surgery and asked when I could go home. They kept me for a week, trying to convince me that I would never walk the same without the surgery. Donna, Quincy's owner, came to see me after hearing what happened. She apologized profusely, explaining he was abused and had broken her leg the year before. She offered to sign his papers over for free if I still wanted to ride, as long as I agreed not to sue her. Suing was not even on my mind. I was overjoyed at the chance to own him, so I said yes. She signed over the ownership papers and left me the lock to his tack shed, relinquishing all his gear. I was ecstatic! When my doctor checked on me that evening, I asked when I could ride again. He blandly replied, "When you can walk again, you can ride again."

The doctor seemed surprised I still wanted to ride and wasn't sure I would walk without the surgery. Within a few days, I was released from the hospital with crutches and a prescription for Physical Therapy.

On my way home from the hospital, I went to visit Quincy. He was visibly depressed. He had stitches from the cuts on his nose, but the wound hadn't healed totally. A few people told me he hadn't been the same since that day. The trainer explained that it was common for mountain lions to come up the hill towards the arena. The consensus was that a mountain lion spooked him the day of the accident. She was surprised I wasn't upset at him for the accident. I told her I thought he could be a great horse once he trusted someone. She agreed and said she was happy he found his proper owner in me. I entered Quincy's stall. He had his eyes on me the whole time, waiting and watching from the rear of the pen. Crutches and all, I stood, staring at him, talking to him in my head, telling him I was happy to see him. I sent him images of me petting him; within seconds, he walked over, lowered his head, waiting for me to rub between his ears. From that moment on, we were best friends.

Walking took some time to master; the nerves in my left hip were shot, leaving my hip and thigh numb. After about a month, I was able to walk without the crutches. Within two months, I was back at the stables, ready to ride. Quincy had earned the label "trouble horse." Everyone was afraid of him. He was intelligent, big, and very fast. He had the reputation of dumping his riders whenever he had the chance. After hearing about the accident, a stunt trainer took me under his wing and began teaching me how to train and work with troubled horses. Both Quincy and I were recovering abuse victims. I was committed to helping him overcome his fears and past; without realizing it, he was helping me too.

Within six months, Quincy became a well-trained athlete. He had transformed from a scary, nut job horse to an athlete. We began showing both English and Western in local, "C" rated shows. He was winning every class, gaining a lot of envy from other horse owners. We would play tag in the arena when he was turned out, free to run. I would run down the center of the arena, Quincy giving me a head start. As soon as I hit the middle, he would gallop past me, cutting me off so I would run right into him. Then he would prance off as if he won the game. We played like that daily for hours. No one could believe this was the same horse that broke my hip. We became so close, I could show up to see him during feeding time, and he would lay down next to me instead of eating. He showed me how to be brave, strong, and, more importantly, how to forgive and trust.

Quincy taught me countless lessons during our time together. The most important lesson I learned from him was that no matter how abused or how much people distrust you, there is always hope and the possibility of healing. Given the right amount of time, love, and patience, anyone can change. He also taught me to have fun, to play like a child, something I never learned. He showed me that physical wounds take time to heal and leave scars. Emotional wounds are hard to see, but the scars are visible if you look closely at the behavior. Emotional scars can heal but can be cut open without the proper care and attention. I had a lot of emotional scars and unhealed emotional wounds from childhood. Quincy's love and our relationship started the journey of healing that would take years to complete.

9

FINDING THE LOVE OF MY LIFE

In the middle of healing my broken hip, I had ended a relationship with a guy who joined the Marine Corps. Having a relationship wasn't his priority since he had plans for Officer Candidate
School. I didn't care, though, I had Quincy, and nothing was more
important to me than him. My ex-boyfriend left for boot camp; I
started working for his friend, selling financial products. Superbowl weekend, my new boss hosted a pre-game party. He asked
me to attend. Being a friend of my ex-boyfriend, he wanted me to
have some fun. He was worried I wasn't over the breakup. I agreed
to go.

Football wasn't my thing, but the party was fun. There were only a
few people I knew, so I planned on leaving early. One of my
coworkers introduced me to a couple of Marines as I made my way
through the crowd of people. I didn't think anything of it. As the
night wore on, I was getting bored. I made my way to the bath-

room, thinking I would leave right after. When I came out of the bathroom, this short guy was standing right outside the door. He startled me, asking if I was leaving. He re-introduced himself as Robbie. I told him I was bored and was going home. He followed me to the front door and out to my car. We ended up talking for quite some time, sitting on the hood of my car while I smoked. It was getting late, and I was tired, so I told him I had to go. He asked for my phone number and if he could take me out. I quickly jotted my number down on a business card and left.

Superbowl Sunday arrived, the perfect day to ride Quincy. Most people would be home watching the game. As I was getting ready to leave for the stables, the phone rang. Robbie called, asking if we could hang out. I explained I was heading to the stables to see my horse. He asked if he could meet me there. While I was riding in the arena, Robbie approached, waving hello. He didn't know anything about horses, but he seemed to like Quincy. We brushed Quincy down, put him back in his stall, and went out to eat. Robbie was easy to talk to; he was super sweet, kind, and innocent. He mentioned he had a messed-up childhood with a troubled mother, but he didn't get into details. We began spending a lot of time together. At the time, I was renting a room from a woman who believed aliens were visiting her. She loved to talk, telling me stories of alien abductions. She was quite the storyteller. I spent hours after work listening to strange stories about aliens, grateful it wasn't ghosts. She liked me and loved Robbie. For the most part, she left us alone when he visited.

Back in the 80s, Dana Point, California, was the party place to live. My best friend Debbie and I rented an apartment there for six months. My best friend from high school, Christa, was living nearby in San Diego. She had met a Marine from Oceanside, who she eventually married. Robbie and I were going strong when he asked me to do a contract marriage so he could live with me. Unfortunately, his best friend was trying to do the same thing at the time, to get off base. I was pissed he would even suggest it. It took us some time to get over that one but paled in comparison to what came next.

Completely in love, barely adults, Robbie and I faced a difficult decision. Late on my period, we went to Planned Parenthood for a pregnancy test. Within minutes, the nurse returned, confirming a positive pregnancy result. Happy at first, the joy drained away when Robbie told me he wasn't ready to have a child. As a Virgo, he wanted everything to be perfect before starting a family. We weren't married, and on his salary, things would be rough. What was I supposed to do? I couldn't raise a child on my own, and I didn't want to lose him. We spent a week discussing the options. Then Robbie promised that we would get married, once stable, we could start our family. Reluctantly, I agreed to have an abortion and wait until we were married to have a baby. We called to schedule the procedure for the following week.

Arriving at the clinic, protestors holding signs lined the parking lot. Hiding my head under a jacket, we rushed to the door. Once inside, I questioned Robbie to make sure we were making the right decision. He reassured me, painting a picture of a future with at least two kids. On the way home, still drugged from the anesthesia, I quietly cried, staring out the car window, filled with sorrow, grieving the baby I would never meet. Rob was sad, feeling guilty, unsure of how to comfort me. We spent the night on the couch watching movies I couldn't track, lost in my mind, silently praying to God for forgiveness.

Months later, Robbie invited me to meet him in Vegas the following week. His squadron was doing training exercises at a nearby Air Force base. So, Friday, I left work, drove the 3 hours to Vegas, meeting up with Rob in the lobby. We checked into a hotel, went to see the sights, and went looking for a restaurant. All through dinner, he looked nervous, squirming in his chair like he had a secret. Although questioning him about it, he said he wasn't used to being around so many people, I understood. As we made our way back to the hotel, we detoured to see the pool at the Tropicana. Robbie motioned for me to sit on a patio chair. Like a gentleman, he pulled the chair out for me, then dropped on a knee. Before I could process what was happening, a black ring box appeared in his hand. Through tears, apologizing for not being ready to have a child, proclaiming his undying love for me, he asked if I would marry him. I wrapped my arms around him; with tears streaming down my face, I whispered, "yes, I want to be your wife." Robbie stood us up, swung me around in his arms, then stopped to place a solitaire on my finger.

Still wanting my Mom to be proud, I called her when we got home from Vegas, sharing the news of our engagement. But she was determined to control every aspect of the wedding and the guest list. Within weeks, there were 100 strangers invited to our wedding. Neither one of us wanted a big wedding, preferring something small and private. Mom wouldn't listen as I tried to impress upon her how tight our budget was. Arguing with her was annoying; the wedding was getting out of control. Even though I had a dress waiting at the bridal shop, Robbie and I decided to secretly elope before the wedding costs put us in the poor house. We drove to the mountains in Northern California, to a small chapel in Lake Arrowhead, officially becoming husband and wife.

Waiting a few days after tying the knot, we called my Mom to cancel all the wedding plans. Although Mom was furious, we hid our giggles as we listened to her rant on the phone, knowing we did the right thing. Next, we slowly notified our friends and family. Some asked if the reason we eloped was due to pregnancy; it wasn't. But that question triggered a cascade of grief and guilt, ruining the happy news.

Robbie and I married at the young age of 19. He was in the Marine Corps air wing, working as a hydraulic mechanic on the F-18s. Robbie was traveling a lot with the air wing. While we both loved each other, life was getting in the way of our happily ever after. I was getting used to him being gone for weeks at a time. No matter where he went, he wrote me love letters. When he was gone, I focused my energy on Quincy. His squadron went to Egypt for a month to train with international forces. For the safety of the crew and pilots, I never knew the exact day he would return. Quincy was boarded off-base at a stable nearby. After riding and bathing him, I hand-walked him to dry. Robbie had been gone nearly a month. I hadn't received any letters that week. As I approached Quincy's stall to put him away, I heard someone yell out my name. Looking in the direction of the voice, I saw Robbie, still dressed in desert fatigues, running toward me. We stood next to Quincy in a tight embrace, only broken by horse slobber. Quincy was happy to see Rob too.

When he was home, we enjoyed spending time together with our dog Max. Sometimes we hung out at the beach, while Robbie surfed with his friend, I'd read a good book, sunbathing. One of our favorite activities was exploring the trails; I rode Quincy while he rode his mountain bike ahead of us. Friday nights were drive-in movie date nights with our dog. Eventually, we got a puppy named Shadow. We took turns with each dog in our lap at the drive-in. So, life was feeling pretty good. Besides the counselor I used to see, Robbie was the first person I opened up to about my childhood and painful past. I had so much pain hidden away. He never judged me; he just loved me and listened. We did everything together, calling ourselves the "wonder twins" from a cartoon.

Everyone loved Robbie, including my Mom. Dad respected that he was a Marine, stationed at the same base Dad was. Robbie was handsome, but most of all, he was polite, respectful, and kind. Mom was constantly praising and complimenting him. I couldn't figure out why she treated him so well when she seemed to hate me so much. He was a self-proclaimed Atheist but never mentioned that to her. Every time we spent time with her, I felt jealous, confused, and angry, resulting in projections onto him.

Riddled with pelvic pain episodes for months, I ended up in the hospital with an infection. Endometriosis caused ruptured cysts, and ongoing pain was a constant battle. During one of my hospital stays, my Mom came to visit. I remember her leaning over my bed, telling me to get up, get better and stop ruining my husband's military career. But I would later find out, she was projecting. She had been the cause of my Dad's military career being cut short. Robbie was furious with her. He called her away from my bed, sending her from the hospital. For once, I didn't have to defend myself alone.

Having a baby and being a mother was all I wanted since the abortion. I was obsessed with getting pregnant. After two laparoscopies to remove ruptured cysts, the doctors told me I would have trouble conceiving. Just a year into our marriage, the promise to have a family seemed impossible. In my grief, I projected all of my sorrow onto Robbie. I blamed him, wanting to punish him for losing the chance to have a family. I blamed myself for what I had done. He knew I was devastated and felt horrible about the prognosis. In an attempt to find a solution, he suggested adoption. Knowing how unloved I felt as a child, the idea of offering an unwanted child a loving home felt good. Unable to let go of the desire to have "his" baby, I was glad to have options at least.

Our relationship was intense, romantic, and, as you can imagine, sometimes emotionally volatile. We loved each other fiercely. Unfortunately, we fought and argued fiercely too. We were good at making up, though. No matter how mad Rob would be, he never called me a name. I wish I could say the same. He was good at saying that I was "behaving" a certain way rather than saying I was this or that. I knew he loved me, and I loved him. Robbie was so happy and proud that I was his wife. He wanted to take me home to meet his grandparents, who raised him.

Christmas was coming, so we booked a flight to Maryland to spend time with his grandparents and brother Stan. Although he and his Dad weren't speaking much, I talked him into giving him a chance too. He wanted his grandparents to like me and for me to see his family home.

Listening to his stories about growing up, he expressed how much he hated that his family used to own funeral homes. Dead bodies frightened him because of the strange supernatural events he had experienced at a young age. He didn't want to talk about it anymore; the subject dropped. Instead, he told me all about his childhood adventures. Thankfully, they lived in an ordinary house on the river, not a funeral home.

Stan picked us up at the airport, stopping at a Denny's on the way to the house. I noticed heads turning as others stared at us as we walked to our table holding hands. Immediately feeling dread, threatened, I asked Rob what was happening. He explained that people viewed us as a "mixed couple," which wasn't a common sight there. I tried to ignore the stares and eat; I lost my appetite. An old, familiar feeling overtook me, and I wished I could be invisible.

Sitting down for a meal with Robbie's grandparents was a little unnerving. I could feel some disapproval but didn't know what to make of it. At one point, as the food was going around the table, his Grandmother began asking me questions about myself. She then announced surprisingly, "I had a black friend once; she was our maid." I had no idea how to handle that, and I had never experienced blatant racism before. Call me naïve, but I didn't get it; I was just a mixed-race Filipino/Portuguese with parents from Hawaii. As dinner went on, they asked if we were going to have children. Robbie explained we were thinking of adopting since I was having trouble conceiving. His grandmother was not pleased.

After dinner, I overheard a heated talk between Rob and his Grandmother. Voices were getting louder; it was apparent she was furious with him. He had made it clear that we would adopt any baby we wanted, Asian, black, Mexican; it didn't matter. Then, she began yelling about how our marriage was wrong, saying God wouldn't let us have a baby because I wasn't "white," and it wasn't "right." I was in shock, scared, and angry all at the same time. I grabbed our suitcase and began packing my clothes. I wanted to get as far away from this house as I could. Robbie didn't argue with her; instead, he came to the room and helped me pack. Unable to get a flight home, we ended up at his Dad's house, where we spent Christmas with his brother.

Returning home from that trip changed our relationship. I was angry that Robbie didn't stand up to his Grandmother. She threatened to disinherit him just for being married to me. I could not comprehend how he could stand up to my Mom, but he couldn't do it with his grandmother. Our relationship began to fill with arguments. We tried marriage counseling, but even in our sessions, we would end up in a fight. Robbie and I promised we would never go to bed angry. Then, one weekend, an argument broke out on a Friday night. We stayed up all night fighting, refusing to sleep until we resolved it. By midafternoon we had forgotten what we were arguing about, laughing at how silly we were being. We spent the rest of the weekend watching movies, napping, and staying home.

Rob and I talked many times about adopting, but we never applied. Our marriage was rocky. We both were suffering from depression, neither one of us seeking professional help. Military life was making things worse, so we decided it would be better to end his military career once his contract expired. Looking back, I wish we had tried harder to find professional help. Robbie loved being a Marine; he would have stayed until retirement if it weren't for our troubled marriage.

Once out of the Marine Corps, we moved to Washington State to be close to my family. After what happened in Maryland, I couldn't bear to live there; Home to Boeing, Washington was the only place we thought we could make it financially. Robbie had a hard time finding work; Boeing had laid off hundreds of employees before our arrival. His depression worsened, and so did mine. I was angry at him for so many things, and I was desperate to feel better.

Washington turned out to be a disastrous move. Neither one of us was happy, both deeply depressed, unsuccessfully trying to cope. Before moving, I worked at a Private Investigation firm. I loved my job, my boss, and my coworkers. So, when we first arrived in Seattle, I went to work for another Private Investigator. Chuck was an intense man on a mission to find kids in Canada kidnapped by one parent in a divorce, hidden on tribal land. There were only three of us that worked in the office. Chuck's girlfriend handled the paperwork, accompanying him on occasion when he made trips to Canada. I was assigned surveillance cases, mostly spying on cheating spouses.

Doing process serving work and surveillance did not interest me. I spent too much time alone, which meant I had too much time to think. Money was tight too; Robbie couldn't get a job that paid much. Alone in the office with Chuck, he invited me into his office and closed the door. He noticed I was rubbing my back and asked why. Sharing the story about the horse accident, I explained I still had back issues. He offered a chiropractic adjustment to my back, which wasn't too strange; I watched him adjust his girlfriend plenty of times. I agreed and made my way to the couch where he was sitting. Chuck told me to get undressed. Since he didn't have access to x-rays, he needed to view my skeletal structure. Uncomfortable, I undressed while listening to him drone on about his "special talent" for back adjustments. To relax for the adjustment, he poured me a glass of whisky, which I chugged back. Before the glass was on the table, he pushed me onto the couch, holding me down as he pulled his pants down to rape me.

Frozen in shock and fear, I drove home in tears. Rushing through the front door, I ran to the bathroom, stripped off my clothes, and sat on the floor of the tub, under the hot water, sobbing. Robbie pulled the shower curtain slowly to the side, shut off the water, wrapped me in a towel, and walked to the bed. Facing me, he laid down and asked what happened. Trying to catch my breath, making him promise not to do anything, I blurted out the details. Knowing Chuck had friends in the police department, I told Robbie I wouldn't file a police report. He held me tight until I fell asleep; we never talked about it again. Within days, I was cocktail waitressing at a country-western bar.

Drinking nightly became my way of suppressing my emotions. I felt stupid and convinced myself God was punishing me for the choices I'd made. Years had passed without any significant interaction or sign that the angels were around. "Maybe they were only supposed to help me get through my childhood," I thought. I wished they could help me now, but I thought I was too far gone for them to save me. I hated my life, I felt dirty, empty, and I took it out on Robbie. I did everything I could to push him away. We loved each other, but we didn't have the tools or emotional maturity to repair our broken lives or marriage. We had no children, no assets, so we filed a non-contested divorce. While I pushed Robbie away, I secretly wanted him to fight for me and refuse to leave. He didn't. Instead, he moved back to California for a job, and I remained in Washington for another year. Before he left, we told each other if we weren't married and both available when we were

30, we would try again. I thought it was possible. I believed we just needed time to grow and heal. Eventually, he moved back to Maryland, heartbroken. I convinced myself it was better for him that I was out of his life. At least I wouldn't be responsible for a lost inheritance.

10

BLINDLY MOVING FORWARD

Making a living as a cocktail waitress wasn't working, and the nightly drinking was making my depression worst. So, I went job hunting and landed a job as a salesperson at a Ford dealership. I was a natural salesperson. I was quickly able to read the energy and emotions of the customers. Within a few months, I earned Salesperson of the month, and a smooth $10,000, taking the award from one of the other guys at the dealership. The guy was impressed, and he immediately pursued a romantic relationship with me. Staying busy, I was doing everything I could to move on with life and get out of depression. For a while, it worked.

With the new relationship, things seemed to be going okay. Little did I know, life was going to take another nasty turn. Selling cars was fun. I found it easy relating to customers and their wants. But, as an empath, I had a bit of an unfair advantage. Not to say there weren't things I didn't like, there were. We were pushing customers into leases that didn't seem financially sound. I had many a bad dream when my lease enrollment numbers went up. But it was my job, so I did it well, closing many deals a month. Once my sales numbers increased, so did the attention from the managers. Paul, the sales manager, prioritized my deals when customers were in my booth. That didn't go over well with any of the salespeople.

My new boyfriend, Randy, was starting to get jealous of Paul's attention. Paul wasn't willing to tolerate being treated as a subordinate, and he coaxed Randy to find another job. Randy went to work at the Acura dealership across the street, increasingly suspicious, accusing me of cheating on him. Randy could see me from his new dealership when I was on the lot outside, and he made sure I knew it too. I did my best to ignore his controlling behavior, chalking it up to insecurity, but it continued to progress.

While out with friends having a drink at a local Sports Bar on a Friday night, Randy showed up, uninvited. He was agitated, angry, and crazed as he approached the table. He grabbed me off my barstool, dragged me outside, and started yelling at me, telling me to go home. I refused to listen to him tell me what to do; suddenly, I found myself on the ground. Unsure what had happened, I watched as a couple of guys walked him to his car. Someone grabbed my arm and helped me up. Within a few minutes, the police arrived. They asked what happened, took a report, and got me a bag of ice for my swollen face. Then, they asked if they could escort me to my apartment close by to be sure I got home safely. I agreed. As we pulled up to my apartment, Randy was parked outside. The police turned on their lights, putting a spotlight on his car. They instructed me to stay in my car while they placed him under arrest for assault. The police told me he would be "slapped" with a restraining order, explaining how dangerous the situation was.

Domestic abuse, stalking, and assault were not things I could ignore. The police suggested I do whatever I could to disappear. Late that night, I called my Dad and explained what was happening. He came the following day, helping me pack my stuff and put it in storage. The apartment manager let me out of the lease. I was on my way back to California before the boyfriend's arraignment on Monday. Everything happened so quickly I barely had time to think. I arranged to have a horse transport company haul my thoroughbred Batista to California. Since I had friends who ran the Marine Corps base stables, they were more than willing to let me stable him there. The transport company was told about the situation and instructed not to divulge any information no matter who asked.

Arriving in California safely, I rented a room in a townhouse with two other girls near the Marine Corps base. I immediately got a job selling new client services for a Hair Salon in Beverly Hills. It was good money and allowed me to get on my feet quickly. I got the call to meet the shipper at the stables to take Batista to his new barn stall. I was excited to have my horse back. One of the stable hands, James, was there to greet me when I arrived. It was good to see a familiar face. He was always friendly when Rob and I kept Quincy there. Quincy was still boarded there but had a new owner. I sold him to a young girl I gave lessons to before moving away. He was in the barn near Batista's new stall. Seeing Quincy again was incredible. He looked healthy and happy, but James told me his behavior was not as good as when I owned him. We prepared Batista's new stall with fresh bedding while we waited for his arrival.

As the semi-truck pulled in, I felt something strange in the pit of my stomach, like something was off. I couldn't put my finger on it but, the hair on the back of my neck was standing up too. Batista was the last horse delivered; he had the whole trailer to himself. As he walked down the ramp, he saw me and started trotting in place to reach me. He looked great and was moving well as I turned him out to run in the arena. Before I moved to Washington, I had rescued Batista from the racetrack, and this stable had been his home. By the looks of his playful bucking in the arena, he was happy to be back in the sun.

After a good brushing, I put him in his barn stall and prepared to leave. As I popped my head into the office to say goodbye, that strange feeling hit me again. James walked me out to my car when I saw a familiar car parked next to it. Randy was sitting on the back of his dealership Acura; it hit me; he must have followed the horse transport. I was shocked, scared, and didn't know what to do. James noticed the look on my face; he knew something wasn't right. Randy approached us, casually saying hello. Without thinking, I blurted out that I had a copy of the restraining order from Washington, and he needed to leave. James threatened to call the Military Police to remove him. Randy immediately turned around, got in his Acura, and left.

James had me get in my car and wait for him. He told his boss he needed to leave. Jumping in his old Chevy truck, James followed me home, walked me into the townhouse to ensure my ex hadn't followed me. He offered to get some take-out and stay for a while until I felt safe. I was grateful I didn't have to be alone. As the night wore on, he told me how much he liked me but that I was married to Robbie. He said everyone was shocked we had divorced because they knew how much we loved each other. I told him what had happened, and he understood as he too had recently divorced. We stayed up talking late into the night; he fell asleep on my couch.

I followed him to the stables the following day. It was a great day catching up with old friends, seeing Quincy, and spending time with Batista. There was no sign of my ex all day while I hung out in a familiar place, surrounded by the comforting smells of horses and hay. As the sun went down, James asked if I wanted him to follow me home again. I hadn't thought about the incident all day. Suddenly dread and fear set in. I agreed to let him follow me. We made it back to my townhouse safely. Days passed with no signs of my ex, yet I knew inside it wasn't over.

While working on campus at UC Irvine, I started feeling queasy. I noticed hives developing on my arms, and I couldn't stay on my feet. I called my boss to tell him I needed to go to the hospital, thinking I must have eaten something wrong. After going through triage, a nurse asked if I could be pregnant. I couldn't remember my last period, so she ordered a pregnancy test. They administered a dose of Benadryl to relieve the hives. When the doctor came in, he looked worried. He announced the need to do an ultrasound immediately because I was pregnant, and they wanted to be sure there wasn't anything wrong.

Waiting for the results of the ultrasound seemed an eternity. When the doctor returned, he asked if I had family nearby, I wanted to call. "To announce a pregnancy?" I thought. He further explained that I had an ectopic pregnancy, and they needed to remove it ASAP. If left alone, the pregnancy would cause my fallopian tube to burst. I called my Dad in Seattle from a payphone in the waiting room to let him know I was being taken into surgery shortly. I didn't want James to worry that my ex found me, so he was my next call. As if the shock of emergency surgery wasn't enough, in struts Randy. He must have been following me because he knew what was going on. He was sure the baby was his. He started telling me not to have the baby removed, saying he and his family would raise the baby if I died. Everything he said was insane; I had to get away from him. I ran back to the ER, found the doctor, briefly explaining the events in Washington, the restraining order, and that Randy was in the waiting room. When the doctor went to the waiting room to tell him to leave, he was already gone. The surgery was uneventful; I was discharged the following day, James arrived to follow me home.

Barely able to track my feelings; so much had happened so quickly. I was on high alert, unable to process the ectopic pregnancy. Still childless, I couldn't handle the doctor's prognosis that I would probably never carry a baby to full term. James stayed with me that whole day. We went to the grocery store to get some food for dinner. Just as we were coming out of the store, my stomach dropped. I spotted Randy reaching into the trunk of his Acura. I was hoping he wouldn't see me. I was wrong. He closed the trunk, turned around, and pulled out a gun. Pointing it at us, he was in tears, saying, "If I can't have you, no one can."

I pleaded with him to calm down, telling him I wasn't with James or anyone else. Everything seemed to be moving in slow motion. My heart was beating out of my chest, tears spilling down my face. I could hear Police sirens in the distance; he must have heard them as well. He jumped in his car and drove away. James grabbed me, pushing me into his truck, just as the police arrived. Someone had seen what was happening and called the police. I was a little relieved but still shook up. The police took a report and a copy of the restraining order, telling me to go home. The officer followed us to make sure my Randy wasn't waiting there. Once we were safely inside the townhouse, the police let us know they would put out an alert to find him. They told us that they probably wouldn't be able to locate him without a license plate number. Later, I received a call from the Sheriff saying they called his work in Washington. Someone must have known he was in California because I got a call from my old manager Paul telling me he was back in Washington a few weeks later. Finally, I could breathe again.

Amid crisis, I spent weeks with James, which quickly turned into a whirlwind romance. Within months he was talking about commitment and marriage. Marriage was the last thing on my mind; I was lost and confused, completely disconnected from myself. Sitting at dinner one night, sipping a glass of wine, he shared his fears that I'd leave him. Then, out of nowhere, he asked if I would marry him. Thinking I could somehow get out of it in the upcoming weeks, I agreed. Before I knew what was happening, still buzzed from the wine, we were standing in front of an Egalitarian Minister. I felt something wasn't right about the minister as I signed the Confidential Marriage License. He was a little scary, noticing his thumbnails painted black, both very long and pointy. He had long, dark hair tied back in a ponytail. My stomach was upset, my nerves shot, and I didn't know what else to do but sign the papers and said, "I do."

Immediately I felt like I had made a colossal mistake. I didn't want to be married again; I wasn't in love with him like Robbie. I had to find a way to get out of it, to annul the marriage. James moved in and was very happy I was his wife. In the back of my mind, I thought of all the ways to leave. I wasn't in the best position to move again. Filled with guilt, I began justifying the marriage. He was nice to me, and he had saved me from my ex. Finally, I gave up and just accepted the marriage. Within two months, I found out I was pregnant again. This time, it wasn't in my tubes; I was going to be a mother. Now that I was pregnant, I believed God was blessing me. After struggling to have a baby with Robbie unsuccessfully, I was finally pregnant. I settled into my marriage, awaiting the birth of my baby.

Four months into my pregnancy, I was barely showing. I attended my OB appointments in my riding boots and riding pants. Unphased, the doctor would check me and ask how the horse was. The pregnancy was progressing just fine; the endometriosis symptoms had stopped due to the pregnancy. I had gained ten pounds even though I wasn't showing much. Still weighing under 100 pounds, the doctor told me to eat a little more. I was riding every day and still showing at local hunter/jumper shows.

Dressed in a long-sleeve show jacket, riding helmet, and black boots, I started feeling funny as I waited for my turn in the show ring. The horse show was running a couple of hours behind by late in the afternoon. Before entering my equitation class, I leaned over and told James I wasn't feeling well, but I'd ride this class, and then we should probably go home. I made it two laps before I felt a clenching in my stomach. Something wasn't right., I yelled for James to open my exit gate as I approached. Going through the gate, James quickly followed me as I rode to an open area. I slid off Batista, laid on a picnic table, and told him something was wrong. He handed my horse to one of the younger kids I gave lessons to and asked her to put him away. He carried me to the car and took me to the emergency room.

Once at the emergency room, I was given an ultrasound, blood tests, and an IV fluid bag. During the ultrasound, the technician asked what I was doing when I started feeling bad. I told her I was at a horse show, waiting for my class. She was upset with me. She told me how stupid it was and how dangerous it was for a pregnant woman. I tried to convince her she was wrong. After all, my doctor knew I was riding. He told me I could continue since I had done it before pregnancy, my body should be able to handle it. Her arguments continued with fears of getting kicked or thrown off the horse. Looking back, she was probably right. At the time, I felt defensive, judged unfairly. When the doctor came in, he announced I was severely dehydrated and went into premature labor. He gave me a shot to stop the early labor and ordered bed rest. Due to the previous ectopic pregnancy, he recommended I stop riding and only do low activities. With the nurse's scolding and bed rest ordered, I needed to make a decision. As she put it, either choose your baby or your horse; of course, I chose the baby. Within a week, Batista was sold.

James was the only one earning a salary, and money was super tight. We decided it would be easier to be near family when the baby was born. So, we packed up and moved to Washington, just down the street from my sister. She was also pregnant but due six months before me. Thirty hours, two epidurals, and five shots of statol later, my baby girl was born strong and healthy. After so much had happened, I finally had my own little family. I vowed to be the exact opposite of my mother, promising to love her and make sure she had everything she ever needed.

James had bounced around at a couple of jobs after we moved to Washington. My Dad had helped us a lot by giving us a truck, but money was still super tight. Brindi was growing. At three months old, Brindi began having issues with holding down her milk. I would feed her, but she would projectile vomit most of her meal when laid down. One night, she was very fussy, unable to hold down her breastmilk. Our pediatrician referred us to Children's Hospital emergency room in Seattle. Unsure what was causing it, they admitted her to run further tests. Watching her strapped to a board while they ran an MRI was heartbreaking. After a week in the hospital, several tests, and switching formulas multiple times, they diagnosed her with Gastroesophageal reflux. They sent us home with a wedge, a foam triangle to wrap under her so that she could sleep upright. We had to mix baby cereal and formula to weigh it down in her stomach. Assured by the doctors, it would eventually resolve as she got a little older, but we had to help her food stay down until then. I was to pin her into the wedge when she slept so that the formula would stay down. I met the family during our hospital that would lead us to Eastern Washington, where James worked on the farm.

As Brindi got older, the reflux resolved. Opening the book with the story of my spiritual initiation in Eastern Washington, you already know how that marriage ended. As things settled down after the divorce, I found myself thinking about Robbie again.

11

RETURNING HOME

Before returning to California, on my 28th birthday, I reached out to Robbie. I thought about him a lot but was afraid to talk to him after everything we had gone through. Now a Mom, I had grown up a lot since our divorce, yet I still felt empty, like something was missing. We made small talk, catching up on the last few years. He was happy I finally had a child. I asked him if he remembered our promise about getting back together if we were both still single at 30. He became quiet before announcing he had met someone. I told him I was happy for him. I let him know I was moving back to California and if he ever needed anything to look me up. He wished me a happy birthday, and we hung up. Still missing him, I accepted the ending. I wrote in my journal, releasing the sadness as much as possible. It would be the last conversation we would have for over a decade.

As I spoke at the beginning of the book, during our move back to California, the Oklahoma bombing happened. My uncle's stepson

Grant and I met through that tragedy, becoming fast friends, confidants, and family. We partied a lot, met new friends, spent every weekend together, somehow putting the terrors behind me. Yet, I would soon find out I was suppressing my fears, anger, and sadness.

Something besides the endless partying with Grant and my new friends started to happen at this time. My interest in metaphysics and spirituality began to grow. Books began to appear in my life that interested me and helped open my mind to new spiritual concepts. The Seth material by Jane Roberts was one of the many books I began studying. In addition, quantum physics and expanded ideas of the nature of reality fascinated me. I started journaling again, and memories of the big vision returned.

Dating was challenging since I measured everyone I met to the standard set by Robbie. Of course, I distrusted men so gravely; they never had a chance. I remembered how I felt about him, so others had to meet that ideal. No one could hold a candle to him. My heart still belonged to Robbie, but he had moved on, and I had to as well. I ran through a few different relationships in San Diego, nothing lasting longer than six months.

Determined to find love, I wanted to create a relationship that lasted over six months. I started dating Drake, an entrepreneur, training to become a commercial pilot. I loved him, yet it felt lonely, always being put last on his list. We lasted six months and then some. While sitting in his office one day, I asked him where I fit in his life. His response was, "in-between flights, baby." He must have seen the shock on my face as he followed that up with, "you won't leave me; you love me." He was right, I did love him, but I was unwilling to accept such blatant devaluing. Without another word, I ran to my car in tears, driving away. That night in La Jolla, while out singing Karaoke, a guy sitting at a table reading a book caught my eye. Bryan Thomas was a handsome, wealthy artist. He loved to read and study spiritual books. Bryan was a regular at the restaurant, yet we had never met. I was excited when he invited me to join him. Before the night was over, Bryan asked if he could take me out to dinner. I explained I just fought with my boyfriend, but I gave him my number and told him I'd think about it. Drake hadn't called by the next day, but Bryan did. He again extended the invitation to dinner; without thinking, I accepted. I called Drake right away and broke up with him; just like that, it was over.

Bryan fascinated me, we would drink wine, and he read Carlos Castaneda books to me. We exchanged ideas about magic, life, art, and music. He was different than most men I knew. Something about him intrigued me but also scared me. We talked for hours; he was the first romantic partner since Robbie that seemed to care about how I saw the world, my gifts, and my feelings. It was intoxicating.

I began seeing Bryan casually. After several failed attempts at relationships, I liked the casual, laid-back nature of our relationship. We had amazing chemistry together, but it never felt real. Then, one day, he sent me into his closet to fetch a tie. I looked around, finding a black duffle bag half-open. I was shocked to see tens of thousands of dollars in cash. Later he told me how he left Mexico City right after the crash of the Peso. He had owned a thriving, upscale hair salon. Overnight, he lost his business and all his money in the bank. When he returned to the United States, he didn't keep large sums of money in the bank because he didn't trust the financial system. The fact that he even had so much cash surprised me, mainly because he expected me to pick up and buy the wine and cheese before going to his house. I was a single Mom; it started getting on my nerves.

Bryan was partnered in business with a woman in La Jolla, flipping houses. He remodeled them, and they split the profit. He had his eye on an old wooden sailboat he wanted to restore next. He shared his dreams of the future with me. I listened and offered encouragement. Most nights we spent together included a couple of bottles of wine; he drank a lot. Months passed, and I was still singing Karaoke in La Jolla at the little restaurant we met. He never took me out to eat after our first dinner. Instead, he would show up at the end of the night to make sure I went home with him.

One holiday weekend, Brindi joined me at his house. She liked playing in such an ample space. He made glass bowl sculptures and oil paintings when he wasn't remodeling. Brindi enjoyed watching him paint. We seemed to be getting closer, but something kept me from opening up to him or taking him seriously. One night, out of the blue, he started talking about our future while in the kitchen making dinner. He told me he wanted me to marry him. That he wanted me to stay barefoot in the kitchen and have a dozen kids like they do in Mexico. I laughed until I realized he was serious. He went on to tell me Brindi would go to boarding school somewhere posh like France. I started listening intently. I asked why she would need to do that. He explained he wanted her to have a good education. As I pressed further about the hypothetical dozen kids, it became clear; they weren't destined for boarding school. I was to stay home and raise them all while my first-born daughter was sent away.

I woke up early the next day, gathered our things, and headed for my apartment. Bryan was still asleep, so I snuck out as quietly as I could. As far as I was concerned, things were over. I had set Bryan up to do voiceovers for phone systems that the company I worked for sold. He was happy to do it, as he had done some in the past. His voice was super deep and sounded authoritative but sexy. Avoiding his calls at home, I was forced to see him for the voice-over work. He begged me to go to lunch with him, but I made excuses. Feeling guilty, I finally called him. I explained I didn't want to get married, nor did I like the idea of sending Brindi to boarding school. After trying unsuccessfully to get me back, he finally gave up and moved on.

I was back to spending my nights and weekends studying metaphysics and spirituality. My mind was expanding, and so was my understanding. The more I learned, the more I could sense, feel into things and sort myself out. Unfortunately, I wasn't getting messages from the Angels anymore, yet I still thought they guided me. So, books on channeling and the Seth material became an obsession. Astrology, tarot, runes, I-Ching, and numerology books piled up on my bed, mysteries of the Universe became my obsession. The more I studied, the hungrier I became, wanting to fill myself with knowledge. Before long, I composed stacks of spiral notebooks filled with notes and journal entries.

One day a thought stream began to develop in my mind. These thoughts were not my own. Pictures, words, and metaphors filled my mind, creating a massive internal shift in how I perceived life. I began furiously taking notes as the information poured into me. I wasn't sure what was happening, but I knew something within me was changing, remembering, waking up.

12

A CRY FOR HELP

Finally, in Elementary school, Brindi was making new friends, feeling more secure, discovering herself. I was working as a Marketing Coordinator and Executive Assistant for an electronics firm. The intranet was growing, and the internet was born. Digital marketing was emerging as a new way for companies to find customers. Work was challenging as I took on two separate roles. Taking work home became routine. Late at night, I worked on graphic design and copy as the company began to embrace the worldwide web. Spiritual studies took a back seat, as did personal growth and healing. Brindi was enrolled in a Magnet school focused on music and the arts. She was bussed to her school from home, then dropped off at my office in the afternoon. She spent hours working on drawings as I worked. I had no child support from her father as he disappeared after our divorce. It was solely up to me to feed, house, and care for us.

Brindi was becoming very independent, stubborn, and her behavior was changing since she'd entered grade school. Her new attitude was reflected in how she talked to me; she started getting a little bossy, if not unruly. Granted, I held massive guilt over what her Dad had done to her. I indulged her with toys, special treats, anything I could to make her happy and make myself feel better. Unfortunately, temper tantrums were often happening, escalating into throwing things and screaming at me.

Mornings were spent struggling to get her ready for school and onto the bus. Each morning at the bus stop, she waited at the back of the line to get on. Then, just as her turn approached, she would turn and run down the street with me chasing her in heels. Finally, the bus driver and I devised a plan to avoid the dangers of her running near the road. I held her back until he was ready to close the door, then quickly put her inside, and he promptly shut the door. Once on, she found her seat and was a model bus rider. In fact, around others, she was an angel. However, at home, especially after a long week at school, she became demanding. We started arguing constantly. When things got too overwhelming, I'd lock myself in the bathroom to calm down. She was on the other side, putting something under the door, talking, screaming, and kicking it. She did anything she could to try and get me to come out and pay attention to her.

Work was demanding, and sleep escaped me most nights. I didn't notice the depression and anxiety building within me. Disconnected, scattered, and burned out, I began to snap. I had very little help from my Mom, who only lived 90 minutes away. If I took time to recharge, I had to pay a babysitter. Babysitters were often hard to come by. I did have a friend, Candy, a stay-at-home caregiver to a son with Multiple Sclerosis, who helped on occasion.

Hometown Buffet was Brindi's favorite restaurant. After a week of fighting with her, I figured we could use a treat on Friday night. Wearing stained, dirty clothes, I told her to change into a dress so we could go to dinner. Immediately she snapped back at me, saying, "You're not the boss of me." That didn't hit me right. I completely lost it. I began screaming at her to change clothes, or we would stay home. She rose to the challenge and roared back. I sent her straight to her room for a time-out. I was pacing in my tiny kitchen when I heard through our open windows, "Somebody save me; my Mommy doesn't love me."

"What? What in the hell is she doing?" I thought. I continued listening as she yelled through a fake cry, "Save me, please save me." I marched into her room, flung open the door to see her standing with her face pushed against the screen. Her room was barren as I had removed most of her toys earlier in the week as punishment for arguing. I told her again to stop and get dressed so we could go. Exhausted, hungry, and angry, I turned to leave. Just as I was ready to close her bedroom door, she grabbed her small lamp and threw it at me. It hit the hallway wall inches from my head. I marched into her room, closed the window, stripped her bed, and left. It became a war as I locked her in her room by tying a string from her door to the bathroom door to keep her in since the door had no lock.

She continued to kick the door, yell and do other crazy things. When emotions are out of control and reactions are entirely unconscious, you tend to lose track of reality. I was not in control of myself and most definitely not in control of her. I can only imagine what our neighbors thought. Finally, my neighbor Candy called to check on us. She could hear us going at each other. I explained what was happening and expressed my frustration. She laughed but told me if I needed anything to call. Well past midnight, Brindi fell asleep, with me lying on the floor in the hall. I felt like crap. Neither one of us had eaten, and neither of us had won the fight.

Bright and early Saturday morning, the yelling began as if we hadn't stopped from the night before. I called my Mom, asking if she would take Brindi for the weekend, telling her things had escalated between us. Not surprising, her answer was no because she had plans to go shopping at the mall. She didn't want to have to take her granddaughter with her. I hung up the phone, pissed but not surprised. The battle intensified:

"I'm not changing. If you don't take me to eat now, I'm calling CPS," *Brindi yelled.*

"CPS? Where did you hear that?" I retorted.

"The school told us that if someone is hurting you to call CPS. I'm calling CPS and telling them you are a bad Mommy."

"Oh no you don't! I'm calling CPS on you," I responded.

I was reaching a dangerous point in my frustration. I talked to Candy on the phone, telling her I understood how some people beat their kids or hurt them. She must have heard the desperation in my voice. She told me Brindi's behavior was not normal, and I needed help. With compassion, she gave me the number to the crisis line and instructed me to hang up and make a call quickly.

Without a clue as to what I would say to the nice woman who picked up the phone, I broke into loud sobs. She asked my name and had me take some deep breaths. In the background, Brindi was yelling. I calmed myself enough to retell the events of the night before. I asked her if it was normal behavior. She said, "No, honey, something is going on here, and you need help." I told her I didn't have insurance, couldn't afford counseling, and the school wasn't helping. I wanted help for her and myself. Her behavior in school was changing. She was getting in trouble for disrupting class. The crisis line woman listened intently before saying, "You two need to be separated for a while."

"Separated? What do you mean?" She explained she had a child with mental illness and behavioral problems. She went on to explain that she and her son were briefly separated to get help. Assuring me that it all worked out for her, she asked if I had family nearby. I explained the situation and Brindi's molestation, how we moved to start over. She seemed to understand what was happening. She instructed me to call 911 and ask for a police officer to come to get Brindi. Following her advice, I called and told them I was suicidal and had a five-year-old child. When the Police arrived, they were friendly but scary. They called the crisis line and spoke to the woman, then handed me the phone. She confirmed that Brindi would go with Child Protective Services, and we would get help. The officers told me I had to go with them to County Mental Health. A second police car arrived, taking Brindi into protective custody. I was placed into the back of a Sheriff's car and walked into County Mental Health.

Plain dull green walls, worn out from years of use, lined the County Mental Health hall. I suddenly felt like I was in trouble. While I hadn't done anything wrong, I felt like a criminal. The on-call Psychiatrist prescribed Zoloft and Xanax before sending me home. I had no way to get home, so I reluctantly called Drake for a ride. He asked what happened; I tried to tell him as briefly as I could. He wasn't surprised because he knew I was having a hard time with Brindi. On the drive home, he said I had scared him when we were together, mentioning that I felt I "had a dark cloud of shit that followed me everywhere." Then, without emotion or empathy, he pulled in front of my apartment, telling me to get out and took off.

Once inside, I found the card with the phone number to call and talk to Brindi. I wanted to call the crisis line woman first. She wasn't in, but I left a message for her to call me back when she returned. Then I called Brindi, reaching Brindi quickly at the temporary holding center. Surprised, she excitedly told me how it was a fun summer camp. Knowing she didn't understand what was happening, I explained she would have to be away from me for a while. She didn't mind, saying she liked where she was. It felt like I was out-of-body, not comprehending the seriousness of what was happening. I told her I'd call tomorrow and for her to have fun.

Hanging up the phone, I broke into a million pieces. Sobbing uncontrollably, I felt like a complete failure. How had this happened? Was I so damaged and broken I couldn't raise a child? Alone in an all too quiet apartment, I fell into an exhausted sleep. Startled, I was jolted awake by the sound of the phone ringing on Sunday. Answering it, the voice of the crisis counselor said, "Hi Bernadette, I'm the crisis counselor you spoke to yesterday." Glad to hear from her; she gave me several numbers to call to begin the process of getting help. I called in sick that Monday, telling my boss there were things I had to take care of. Social Services called to schedule a visit from my assigned caseworker for that same day. She was friendly and helpful in explaining how my case was unique. She said the agency wished more parents used the services like I did instead of beating their kids. Together we completed paperwork for Brindi to receive Medical Assistance. We also made written plans for reunification, made Psychology appointments and screening for both of us. She informed me that they located and secured a temporary Foster home for Brindi, not far from home. The worker estimated a year apart so we could both heal.

As part of our treatment plan, a screening was scheduled for Brindi to test for ADD and learning disabilities. Finally, someone was listening. The twenty-minute screening turned into weeks of repeated attempts since she couldn't focus long enough to get through it. After waiting a month, the psychologist diagnosed ADHD (Attention Deficit Hyperactivity Disorder) with impulsivity disorder. We were referred to an ADHD Specialist. Brindi and I met with her separately with the goal of joint counseling when she was back in my care. Dr. K recommended I study books specifically about the brain, ADHD, and Sexual Trauma.

Studying the early work of Dr. Daniel Amen, I began to understand the cause of Brindi's behavior and how it developed. Forced to hold attention and behave all day, she had no choice but to be unregulated when she arrived home. The Psychiatrists prescribed four different medications: Adderall for attention, Zoloft for Depression, Risperdal for Impulsivity, and another to keep her blood pressure from spiking, which is a side effect of Risperdal. Her school performance and her behavior began improving. Once a week, I picked Brindi up from her Foster home to take her to her appointments with Dr. K. Usually, the effects of the medicine had worn off, which made it challenging to hold Brindi's attention. Dr. K, a mother of 2 ADHD kids, was patient and persistent. I learned a great deal from Dr. K's sessions. She taught simple things like "Don't sweat the small stuff; everything is small stuff." She made me feel like I wasn't so terrible a person or mother. In the olden days, entire villages raised the children, not just one parent. Solo parenting wasn't helping, nor was the expectation that a child sits still, focusing, for 6 to 8 hours a day.

Time marched on as Brindi and I worked our way through the maze of living separately. I had gotten a new job as Director of Business Development in downtown San Diego. The location allowed easy access to Brindi's foster home and Dr. K. During one of our visits, Brindi told me her grandmother had taken her to McDonald's. My mother and I were not on speaking terms. I was informed by the social worker that my mother was very critical of me, no surprise. Mom had told the worker that I was a lost cause, and she intended to fight for custody of Brindi.

Custody? Are you kidding me? Hanging up the phone, I was furious, thinking, "The woman who had to shop the weekend this whole mess started, now wants to 'save' my child from me, 'FUCKING GENIUS" I screamed. The things Mom told Social Services about me resulted in supervised visits. Grandma's visits continued for a few weeks as we approached our first court hearing. The Foster Mom, concerned, told the worker and me that my Mom told Brindi I wasn't coming back for her. Until that restriction, I visited twice a week and took Brindi to her appointments with Dr. K. Now, limited to only supervised lunch visits, the foster Mom had to take Brindi to her psychology appointments.

Dr. K spoke up for me to Social Services; she divulged my childhood abuse from my Mom with my consent. Social Services interviewed Brindi and the foster Mom, confirming my mother had told Brindi I wasn't coming back for her. Concerned that she would be emotionally damaged, they remanded my mother to supervised visits and removed supervision limits from me. I was astonished at the lies my Mom was telling during the first court hearing. My brother sided with her. No one had been around her or me much since moving to California. Yet, my Mom was determined to take custody of my daughter. I was grateful the court was able to see through the bullshit.

The judge in the hearing went over the half-inch thick file and said, "Most cases that come before me are full of reports several inches thick. Your case is the smallest I've ever seen. I commend you for knowing your limit and loving your child enough to get help. Continue following the recommended counseling; I'm sure you and your daughter will be reunited quickly".

For the first time in months, I felt human again. Maybe I wasn't the worst person on the planet after all. Perhaps I wasn't all the things my mother had said either. I did do the right thing. I missed my daughter tremendously, but I knew we were getting the counseling and help we needed. Dr. K was teaching me patience and tolerance. I knew with continued work, Brindi and I would heal.

(Throughout the last 21 years of coaching people, I learned an interesting coincidence. Many of the clients that came to work through past sexual trauma were diagnosed with ADD or ADHD. So, I began to note the link and asked Spirit about it. From my limited understanding, the brain has to shut down certain areas to suppress the traumatic memories. It does so to allow the person to move on with life until they can process or heal. Sometimes, the brain shuts down the parts that control impulses, focus, and attention. Since the time of these events, PTSD has been discovered and added to the DSMV manual.)

13

CREATING A MAGICAL LIFE

Four months had passed since Brindi entered the foster care system. Wrestling with sadness, guilt, and grief, I began growing on many levels, and my new job afforded me many new opportunities. Getting hired as Director of Business Development for an all-female equipment leasing company was exciting. Susan, the company president, had hired me as head of the sales and marketing team. I worked tirelessly to prove my worth since I had no college degree, although I had a portfolio of successful marketing materials. One side of the business was for recruiting investors: the other side leased equipment to companies. The work was fun, and the pay was great, yet I struggled with 'imposter syndrome' daily.

One day, accidentally, I discovered Susan was a believer in the Spirit realm. Walking into her office, overcome by the smell of a pipe with cherry tobacco, yet not seeing smoke, I froze in confusion. I stood in the middle of her large office, turning in a circle, sniffing the air. She looked up from her desk and asked what I was doing. I asked her if she smoked a pipe. She broke into laughter that quickly turned to tears as she confessed that her late grandfather smoked. Then, she asked if I was a medium. "Shit, my secret is out," I thought to myself. I shrugged my shoulders, dropped the signed documents I held onto her desk, and quickly exited her office.

Feeling uneasy, I returned to my office, grabbed my purse, phone, and headed out for lunch. I felt like running home and hiding as if I had done something wrong, triggering an old fear. I made my way out of the building, almost dumping my purse as I frantically searched for a cigarette and lighter. I lit up and started walking briskly without any specific direction in mind. My thoughts were racing. What was I afraid of? Images from childhood began to flood my mind. I had flashes of angels, transparent spirits, and invisible friends that were my allies. Then, the images and sounds of my mother's voice scaring me into secrecy.

Making my way to a park bench, I grabbed a journal out of my purse and began writing everything down—the pipe smell, the images, the fear that I had done something wrong. I was terrified I was losing my mind. Yet, writing it all down somehow gave me peace. I decided to find a metaphysical store on my way home. I needed to find a book or maybe ask questions about it. When I returned to the office, I searched the yellow pages and found a metaphysical shop located just five miles away. All I had to do was make it through that strange day and get to the shop.

Following the store clerk's directions over the phone, I stood in front of a glass storefront window dressed in crystal balls, stones, books, and tarot cards. I was excited to go in., My energy calmed as soon as I entered. Incense was burning, relaxing music was playing, and the woman behind the counter smiled as she greeted me. She asked if I was looking for something specific. Feeling comfortable, I told her the events that brought me to the store. Her face lit up as she raised one finger, signaling for me to wait. She grabbed a cordless phone and walked to a back room.

When the clerk emerged five minutes later, she told me someone wanted to speak to me. "Speak to me? About what?" I said in confusion. The front door to the shop opened, and a friendly, brown-skinned man dressed in white walked in. He immediately approached me, grabbed my hand, and introduced himself as John. He asked me to follow him, taking me to a reading room in the back of the store. There he lit a candle and pulled something wrapped in cloth from his bag. He reached for my hand and said, "I had a dream about you." He relayed a story about telling the store clerk if a dark-haired girl comes to the store and is looking for help with her gifts to notify him immediately.

My head was spinning as I sat in that candle-lit space. I didn't understand why this stranger had dreamt about me. He asked if he could do a psychic reading for me. I had no money, but it didn't detour him. I gave my permission. He unwrapped his cloth to reveal something that looked like round seashells. He said a prayer, releasing the shells onto the table and cloth. A smile burst onto his face as he began to tell me things about myself nobody knew. What he said next both fascinated and scared me.

"Child, you are gifted with sight. So many spirits walk with you. You can see the dead, the angels, and evil. You should not be afraid of it." I didn't believe what I was hearing. He continued, "You have much to learn, but first, you must allow yourself to see again." I had no idea what he was talking about. "See again? What do you mean see again?" I asked.

John laughed as he waved a bundle of sage over my head. "Open your other vision, open your ears. Let Spirit guide you. You have a purpose; your gifts have a purpose." He sat down, wrote some notes, put his shells away, and looked me square in the eyes. "I know you are frightened and confused. You have seen much in your life. You will see much more if you are willing. Allow your eyes to open again. It will make things easier". He left the room to gather supplies, returning with a black candle, a typewritten prayer, and a sage bundle. He taught me how to smudge and told me to light the candle and say the prayer when I got home.

Once home, I poured myself a glass of wine, staring out the window at Mission Bay, unable to grasp what was happening. Hours passed before I finally read the prayer, lit the candle, and asked my vision to return. Nothing happened—no sudden flash of insights, nothing magical. I finished my wine, called Brindi to tell her goodnight, and went to bed.

That night, I had a lucid dream where I was sitting in a classroom. Rows of old wooden desks filled the space. I was sitting atop a desk with the teacher sitting on his desk in front of me. No other students were in the classroom. When I woke up, I felt refreshed, grabbed my journal, and jotted down the images in the dream. I couldn't remember the subject taught, just that I was in the class. I knew the dream meant something. Unfortunately, I didn't have time to look in the dream symbol book to find out. It would have to wait until after work.

Working Food & Beverage trade shows kept me busy, traveling every other weekend, with little time to think. However, my boss

Susan had a never-ending supply of new ideas and flashes of insight constantly. Unfortunately, she had a habit of sharing her thoughts through phone calls in the middle of the night. I was worn out, but I knew better than to say "no" to Susan.

As the company grew, Susan was occupied with investors and her new home. That gave me time after work to focus on myself. The first order of business was to catch up on bills. Paying bills was irritating. There always seemed to be more bills than paycheck. I sat down to write out checks when I had a sudden flash of insight. Almost audibly, something told me to light a candle, pour a glass of wine, and make bill paying a ritual. The voice in my head also told me to write the checks out in a state of gratitude.

"Instead of remaining in resistance, turn it into a fun event. Wine? Candle?" Why not? I grabbed my checkbook, sat down with some classical music, lit a candle, and began writing the checks. Each time I inserted a check into its envelope and put a stamp on it, I thanked the Universe that I got to pay the bill with a tenfold return. I imagined all the families that worked for the utility company receiving their paycheck because people like me paid bills. It made me smile. Instead of freaking out that I only had a little money left until next payday, I thanked the Universe for its providence.

While nothing magical appeared to be happening since my visit to the metaphysical shop, I felt better. My dream life was more lucid and active. I made a habit of writing them down in my journal as soon as I woke up. It seemed there were messages, teachings being strung together each night. I began to notice synchronicities, intuitions, yet I refused to give them any weight. Just as I thought about a vendor, the phone would ring with the very person I was getting ready to call. It repeatedly happened, so I knew it wasn't just a fluke.

Nightly, between dreams and what I can only refer to now as channeling, I furiously noted all the things I was taught by "the voice." A step-by-step process emerged that would allow me to create the life of my dreams if followed. I played with the techniques, began controlling my thoughts, and continued to study metaphysics, theosophy, quantum physics. Back in the 90s, there was no "internet" or google, yet somehow the correct information found its way to me, in sometimes strange, mysterious ways. Books were found on tables at a restaurant, with no explanation of who put it there. An angel book with round talismans arrived in my mailbox with no copyright inside, no return address, and no author.

One day on the way home from work, I stopped to grab some smokes. As the cashier got them for me, my eyes were drawn to a $1 lottery scratcher. I asked the cashier to add the scratcher to my purchase. I rarely played scratchers. I got into my car, lit a cigarette, and decided to scratch the ticket. I scratched the ticket with a quarter before looking at the symbols. As I peered at the ticket, I saw $500 twice in a row. Scanning the entire ticket, I saw a 3rd $500. Skeptical I had won; I turned the ticket over to read the rules of the game. Three matching amounts on any row wins that amount. Shocked, I took the ticket back into the store. Handing it to the cashier, I asked if it was a winner. He looked at me, at the ticket, and smiled. He said, "You won $500, congratulations, you're lucky." He then processed the ticket, handing me $500. You can imagine my excitement. I was so happy. There was a doll Brindi had wanted that I didn't have the money to buy. I drove straight to Toys R Us and got her the doll. When I called her that night, I told her I had a surprise for her. It felt good to have the money to get her something special.

As I practiced the steps I had learned, I found that consciously drawing in and creating things into my life was getting easier. The lottery win made me think about creating something more significant. All the material I was studying on quantum physics made me feel the things I received from "the voice" and wrote in my journal, gave me the ability to create my reality. "The Voice," which I began calling Spirit, told me I would teach others someday—reminding me of the vision I had before everything in my life fell apart. I brushed it off, but I wanted to put the "manifesting" thing to the test. I told Spirit if it works, I will teach others, but only if it works consistently.

Rent in San Diego was super high; I felt like I was throwing my money away. My dream was to buy a condo on the beach in Mission Bay. I couldn't afford one, but that was my dream. I wrote my desire in my journal and went to bed. Before I woke up, I heard a voice asking, "What about a boat? You can afford a boat". Before my eyes were even open, I responded, "I don't know anything about boats." Later that day, a friend invited me to the San Diego boat show. "Boat show? That's odd; I just had a dream having something to do with boats," I told him I'd go.

I was in shock as I walked through the boat show. These weren't boats; they were yachts. Many were nicer than my apartment. I asked my friend, a sailboat person, how much they cost. He ran through the various choices available in power versus sailboats. As we were leaving the show, he grabbed a Boat Trader magazine for me. I shoved it in my purse and forgot about it. At dinner, I asked about the possibility of living on a boat in San Diego. He told me some marinas allowed it. Availability was small, but it was worth checking. There were too many synchronicities with this crazy boat thing.

Searching through the Boat Trader when I got home, I found most boats were in my price range, just under $100,000. I excitedly wrote a list of everything I wanted in a boat. First, it had to have 2 bedrooms and 2 baths. I hated the dark, dank smell of sailboats, so I opted for a powerboat. Next, I wanted something light with lots of windows. Last, I wanted a bathtub. I wasn't sure bathtubs were available on boats, but if they were, I wanted one. Based on what I was reading, it didn't matter if I knew how it would happen; it was just up to me to ask for what I wanted. According to everything I knew, the "how" was up to the Universe. Manifesting a boat was the perfect test. I put my list away and went to bed.

Monday came, and I had done a ton of research on used boats. I walked into my boss' office and announced, "I'm going to buy a boat. I want to live on the water, and you can't get any closer than in a boat". Susan didn't have limitations. She lit up like a Christmas tree and repeated back to me, "You're going to buy a boat." I skipped back to my office, working on paperwork. When I got home, I wrote in my journal a prayer addressed to Archangel Michael, Guides, and Jesus:

I know you can hear me, and I hope you will answer. I feel like the boat idea came from you. It's perfect, although a little scary since I can't drive a boat. If this works, I promise I will do whatever you want. I finally understand the dreams about school. You are teaching me many things. Please watch over Brindi. Please direct me to the perfect circumstances and helpers to make this dream a reality. Thank you for guiding me, B

Attempts to make appointments to see a few boats in San Diego Harbor was a dead end. None had what I wanted, were too old, or just weren't suitable. Finally, my ex-boyfriend Drake who owned a new charter business, offered to fly me to Oxnard to see a boat I liked that was for sale. While he didn't believe I would go through with it, he played along. We flew up north for the day, sadly disappointed by the boats available. Once home, I started making calls to the local marinas. My friend gave me the address of a boat broker in San Diego Harbor. I walked into the sales office and asked to see available powerboats. The three salesmen barely paid any attention, telling me they didn't have anything I would like, quickly dismissing me. I was pissed! As I left their office, I whispered under my breath, "you condescending assholes."

I stopped at a marina down the hill from my apartment before heading home. I had been there before when Bryan Thomas took me to show me the wooden boat he wanted to restore. I had forgotten about it until just then. Seaforth Marina was small, but the broker, John, was a sweetie. I walked into his office and asked if he remembered me; he did, knowing Bryan well. I told him what happened at the San Diego marina and asked for help finding a boat. He immediately opened a binder of local boats for sale. I wrote down a list of what I wanted, how much I thought I could afford, and left. John said he'd check around and see what matched my list. The next day, he called with great news. He located a boat moored in San Diego that fit my list for $89,000. We made an appointment to see it at lunch.

Walking onto the 38' Sportfishing boat called "Advantage" was surprisingly comfortable. It had a large sun deck, bridge with plenty of seating upstairs. It was 2 bedrooms, 2 baths, light with a sliding glass door, skylights, and a bathtub. The galley was cute, including a three-quarter size refrigerator/freezer. It was perfect. I confessed to John that I didn't know much about boats or how to drive one. I'd driven ski boats, but this was much different. But he reassured me, if I bought it, he would help me find someone to teach me how to drive it. He also wanted me to know about a live-aboard slip available in the Seaforth Marina. I wanted to hug him. But, instead, I smiled, thanked him, and told him I would get back to him the following day.

I should have been concerned with no savings account, no credit, and no idea how I would get the money to buy the boat. Yet, I trusted in this process Spirit taught me, sure it was happening. Returning from lunch, I bumped into Susan and her new business partner. She had partnered with an independent bank to offer investments and ATMs. I had just finished our company's brochure package and media kit. Susan wanted me to show the partner my work. Once done, I started making calls to Boat Financing lenders. John had told me CIT was the lender most boat owners used. Since boats are "rolling inventory," they are harder to finance than homes. However, that didn't discourage me. According to my calculations, to cover the downpayment, expenses for the survey, licensing, and taxes, I needed $25,000 to purchase "Advantage." The broker at CIT ran my credit, the numbers and let me know I could qualify if I had a big enough down payment. My calculations were correct; it was close to $25,000. Magically, my dream was manifesting.

Refreshed, I woke up the next day and headed into the office. I hadn't even put my purse down before Susan came storming into my office. She announced, "Our partner company likes the marketing package you did for us and wants one like it. It needs to be done quickly and not during normal business hours. They are willing to use you since the quotes from the agencies are so high. It pays $25,000. If you want it, the job is yours, but you've only got a week to have the final product done. They have a trade show and need the materials." "Yes, I want it," I told her, barely believing what I was hearing. I met with the partner at 5 pm to get all the digital files, orders, and instructions. As soon as Susan left my office, I called John and told him I wanted the boat, promising to bring a deposit the next day.

Adrenaline must have carried me through the following week. Aside from working 7-5 pm for the leasing company, I worked 5 pm to 2 am every night to finish the job. The project was due to be delivered the same day I was to take possession of "Advantage."

Wednesday at 2 am, I headed to San Diego for a final press check on the brochures. There was one small paper problem that was thankfully was caught before it went for the final print. I made it home at 3:30 am. Then, I drifted off to sleep. At 5 am my alarm clock shook me out of what felt like a deep fifteen-minute nap. I brewed some coffee, jumped in the shower, and thanked God for helping me finish the project on time. When I arrived at work, Susan waited at the door to see if the project was printing. I told her it was and went to my office. I was exhausted. I jumped out of bed at 5 am Friday, grabbed a bag with a change of clothes, and headed for the office. The print shop delivered five boxes of materials by 8 am. Susan and her partner were happy the job was complete. She hugged me and whispered, "Your cashier's check is in accounting; take the day off and get your boat." I ran to accounting, grabbed the envelope, and headed for the marina.

John was waiting when I arrived. The CIT broker waited as I signed all the papers, took the check, and offered to drive us to San

Diego harbor. It was a done deal. I owned a 38' Sportfishing boat. I sat in silent gratitude on the way to get the boat. John showed me how to fire up the boat and had me untie it from the dock. Once beyond the surf, he stepped to the side of the bridge and let me drive. It was a beautiful, sunny day in San Diego. The waves were mild, as was the wind. I was the Captain of this boat. It felt amazing. John took command and drove the boat to the slip as we approached the jetty. Parking it meant reading the current, using both engines, and carefully sliding it in without hitting another boat. He made it look easy. I knew it wasn't. We tied off the boat, turned off the engines, and plugged into the shore power. He showed me a few things I needed to know and assured me he would be available if I had any questions. His office was within sight of my slip. On the way back to his office, he introduced me to an old boat owner named Al, a friendly man in his late sixties who lived four boats down from my slip. At the time, I didn't know Al would play a part in my boat education. I left John, walked to my car to grab my overnight bag, a bottle of wine, and went to celebrate on my new boat.

I felt great appreciation while watching the sunset and absorbing all that had happened in just two weeks. The test had worked with everything lining up without force. The down payment lined up, the boat that matched my list was located, and the financing fell into place quickly. While the work to earn money took sheer determination, it was well worth it. I was overcome with tears of joy as I wrote in my journal.

Dear Angels, God, Universe, Guides:

Thank you for everything. I finally feel like everything is going to be ok. From this point forward, I will not doubt you. However, you want to use me, demonstrate through me, I'm all yours. Please continue to teach me the mysteries of your ways. Open my eyes to see, my ears to hear, and my heart to understand all you wish me to know. Teach me how to co-create with you in every moment of my life. I miss hearing from the Archangels. Please return to me.

Just as I finished the last word, a stream of thought began pouring in. My body was suddenly energized but also filled with deep peace. Rather than try to figure out where it was coming from, I started writing.

Child, we are here for you always. You've studied well, following your intuition and our guidance. You created the boat because you wanted a home of your own. It was your desire, imagination, and faith that lined up all the people, opportunities, and events. You've done it before but never realized that was what was happening. When Ody gave you the ten thousand dollars to record your demo, you co-created that. You were writing songs with a strong desire to record them. The joy you held from singing made it easy to manifest the circumstances to bring into physical reality. We've never left you; we never will. You, in your ignorance, were taken off track by the events of your daughter's abuse.

You fell into despair, fear, and depression. We are on a much higher frequency vibration than you are in your reality. Fear and negative emotions drop you even lower. It is love, joy, hope, and gratitude that allows you to connect to the subtle realms. When you were a child, it was easy to connect. As you got older, the veil of illusion dropped firmly in place. The veil doesn't allow you to see or connect to the subtle realms without raising your vibration. Don't misunderstand; we are still here for you, you just can't sense us. For now, use this form of communication. Try to remember that you must be in a state of peace, gratitude, appreciation, or hope to connect to the stream of consciousness we are.

Continue to study, pray and be of good cheer. We know you are worried about Brindi. You may use the same method to bring this circumstance to conclusion as you did to co-create the boat. Write down what you desire, have faith it will come, and the rest will be taken care of. Rest now child.

The words flowed as if I was transcribing from dictation. It didn't feel like my own thoughts or sound like my words. "This had a different feeling to it. That's it! It had "FEELING" to it. When I analyze things, I'm not feeling; I'm thinking." Somehow it was different; these were words birthed from feelings. "Channeling," I heard and felt. My books were still at my apartment, but I know I had one that mentioned channeling. I sighed as I remembered I still had to move out of my apartment. Most of my furniture was already sold or spoken for. Brindi's toys were divided between a storage unit and the boat. Her new room had a queen-size bed with storage cubbies. I was so excited to show her our new home. I hadn't seen her much in the last two weeks. I had plans to take her to the park for a few hours on Sunday, though.

I fell asleep from the back and forth rocking of the boat, with the sound of waves hitting beside my bed. Waking up to the sound of barking sea lions, it took me a minute to figure out where I was. The clock said it was 6 am. I grabbed my shorts, a hoodie and put on my Ugg boots; I headed out to grab some coffee. Just down the marina from my boat slip, a cafe run by the deep-sea fishing charter was open and busy. I sat at the counter, ordered coffee, and took in all the sounds of my new life. Everyone at the cafe was warm and friendly. Something about the ocean relaxed people: I was excited to be part of this atmosphere and this marina community. I finished my coffee, went back to the boat, grabbed my purse, and headed for the apartment. This would be the easiest and best move I've ever made.

I breathed a sigh of relief after loading the last of my belongings on the boat. So much of my possessions and my furniture were gone. Letting go of old things was overwhelming at first. However, once everything was sorted, it felt liberating. I kept a few files, books, toys, and bikes in a small storage locker; aside from that, I started my new life with minimal belongings. Living on a boat meant everything had to be secured and tied down when not docked. The less I had to do when I was ready to leave the dock, the better.

A few days after arriving at the marina, Al stopped by to see if I needed anything. We talked casually, and he asked to see the boat. While letting him look around, he wondered how good I was at driving it. I began laughing, "I don't know how to dock it or anchor it properly." His face lit up as he exclaimed, "You can learn. I can teach you." I had prayed that someone would show up to teach me about owning a boat. Old Al was the perfect teacher.

One afternoon, Al pulled my boat into the bay, away from the docks. He shut down the engines as the boat rocked back and forth. He taught me about the engine room, the control panel inside the boat, and the radio. He taught me how to start the engines and cut one or both in an emergency. Next, he had me spin the boat around, steering it with only the throttle. Using forward and reverse, I turned the boat in place several times.

Once Al was satisfied with my ability, we drove over to the fuel dock. Since no other boats were around, he felt safe having me glide the boat to the dock, using only the engines. Gauging the tide, the current, and distance, I approached the fuel dock slowly.

While a little scary, I accomplished the task on the first try. Al wanted to challenge me, so instead of pulling away from the dock, he told me to back it out straight, perpendicular to the dock. While a little more challenging, I backed it out, turning the boat away from the dock without incident. It may sound simple, but it's not. Driving a large boat using only forward and reverse throttles, pushing against the current, took serious concentration. I had a new respect for boat captains. We drove back to our marina where I now had the task of parking my boat between 2 others. It took a few tries to pull in, back out, and start over, but I finally did it. Unfortunately, the current in the bay was a more significant factor than I realized. The boat drifted dangerously close to hitting my neighbor's boat. Thankfully Al was able to correct my error in judgment and avoid a collision.

Grateful for his instruction, I went to the market to grab a 6-pack of his favorite beer. Sitting on the back deck of my boat, drinking and talking, felt amazing. Before long, other boats were coming in from fishing. I met a few boat owners that had slips across from mine. Al knew everybody; he was the marina staple. But I heard weeks later, they all assumed my Dad or rich boyfriend bought the boat for me. Who was I to correct them?

I was feeling more at home than ever before. I ached to share it with Brindi. She knew I had moved onto the boat, but she had no reference of what living on a boat meant. She loved the water. It wasn't hard for her to be excited. Barking sea lions, seagulls, pelicans, and weekend fireworks from Sea World, were enough to make her happy. Six months had passed since going into Foster care. I had met all of the counseling requirements; now, it was up to Social Services.

Initially, the goal for reunification was one year. However, things were not going well at the foster home. The social worker called me on a few occasions reporting problems between Brindi and some of the other girls. Elva, the foster Mom, had been a foster parent for over nine years. She had many girls that lived with her for over two years. Brindi was one of the youngest girls. She and Elva's biological daughter were fighting.

14
____

LIVING IN A POSTCARD

As I left a sales meeting, I received an urgent message to call the social worker. She asked if I had time to talk about Brindi and the plan for her return. She explained the circumstances and recent problems at the foster home. Brindi had accused both foster parents of hitting her, which meant social services opened an investigation. As a result, Elva no longer wanted Brindi to reside with them. The social worker congratulated me on making so many changes before asking if I would allow Brindi to come home early.

"What do you mean 'allow' her to come home?" I asked. She explained that it was in everyone's best interest if she came home. They didn't want to place her in a new home or return to the temporary holding center. It was music to my ears. "Of course!" I exclaimed, barely believing what was happening. Spirit was right; I could control circumstances when I asked for what I truly wanted, believing with faith, it would happen.

When I arrived at the foster home on Friday afternoon, Brindi ran out of the house screaming with joy. We quickly gathered her belongings and jumped into the car. Everything on the boat was ready for her arrival. One of her favorite treats, bread, and brie with grapes, was waiting for a celebration dinner. I saw her excitement building as we boarded the boat. She was so happy to see her new room and some of her old stuffed animal friends on the bed waiting. All the months of separation and stress were now behind us. Our new life and new adventures were laid out before us. I was beginning to believe anything was possible.

Seaforth Marina was located just west of Sea World. Every weekend, at 10 pm, Sea World had a large fireworks display. We sat on the flybridge together, waiting for the show. I was excited about Brindi being home, and I can only imagine what her six-year-old brain had to process. So much had happened with so many new things to accept. "Kids are very good at being in the moment," I thought as I watched her face light up with joy. I had no idea where life would lead us next, but I was thrilled the past was behind us. Our relationship was better now that I understood how her brain processed things. I still had work within myself. I still hadn't forgiven myself for placing her in foster care or being weak, depressed, and still feeling like a failure. We were still going to counseling appointments. Luckily Dr. K was close by, making it much easier to get to our counseling appointments. I was learning not to "future trip" so much and create overwhelming emotions of worry. I would go to sleep that night, grateful for answered prayers and miracles.

Life in the marina was peaceful. Each night, the sound of waves slapping the boat along with the gentle rocking motion made for the best sleep. We perfected our morning routine, dropping Brindi off at school and driving ten minutes to work. Weekends were spent out on the ocean, deep-sea fishing, or cruising to Catalina Island. Brindi often fished off the dock, catching plenty of fish and kissing them before releasing them. Grant came down a lot in the beginning. My depression was lifting, and my anxiety was gone. As our lives forged ahead, Grant came down less and less.

After losing our cat to feline leukemia, there was a void in our home. I wanted an animal companion for Brindi and me. I boarded a friend's Jack Russell Terriers for a month before Brindi got home. It was nice having dogs around again. On a whim, I searched through the classifieds. I came across an ad to rehome two Siberian Huskies. Something inside me jumped at the idea of having another Husky. I had owned one before, named Siba. They were great dogs with unique personalities. I called the number in the ad and made an appointment to see the dogs. They were both very active, young dogs. Neither had much training or manners. Shasta, a red-colored husky, seemed to be very curious about me. The other one didn't care I was there. The owner ended up rescuing them but couldn't keep them anymore. If they couldn't be rehomed, they were headed to the animal shelter. That was all I had to hear to decide to give Shasta a home. Putting her on a leash and walking her to my car was nearly impossible. She had no idea how to walk on a leash. As soon as I opened the back door to my Maxima, she jumped in and laid down.

The first stop was to get a proper collar, leash, bowls, and food. Supplies in hand, we made our way to her new home on the boat. Shasta was a little unsure of walking the docks at first. However, once she saw another dog heading toward her, she forgot about her apprehension. At the boat, she jumped right onto the swim step and boarded quickly. I took off her leash and let her explore once the transom door was closed. She calmly walked through every inch of the boat, exploring inside and out. She made her way around before sitting at my feet. Brindi loved her instantly. The first night she slept in the cubby at the end of Brindi's bed. We were creating our own little family, and it felt complete when Shasta arrived.

Sunday morning, we decided to take Shasta to Ocean Beach, the local dog beach, to let her run. I needed to get her energy spent so I could start training her on basic commands. She loved to run but didn't care much for balls or fetch. She chased the dogs that chased balls, but that was the extent of her play. Other dogs would sniff and check her out, but she was a bit snobbish, ignoring them. It didn't take long to figure out Shasta was unique and didn't think much of other dogs. As the weeks passed, she became more regal, stoic, and proud. She was no longer challenging to walk; she learned fast and seemed to know she had found her people, place, and forever home.

An emotional bond formed between us quickly. She reminded me of Quincy as well as a dog Robbie and I owned named Max. Shasta had an easy time telepathically communicating with me. I always knew what she wanted just by asking her. Pictures, words, and feelings formed if I slowed down long enough to listen. She picked up on my thoughts and feelings too. Shasta knew what I needed when I was feeling down or out of sorts without saying a word. It's as if she was "mothering" me. If I were journaling or praying and feeling sad, Shasta would sit with her head on top of me. If I cried, she snuggled up next to me. If I was agitated, she demanded a walk. After a while, I understood that her demands were as much for me as they were for her. Even though she was a dog, she behaved like the kind of loving mother I had longed for but never had. She taught me so much about love, affection, and patience. She was my fierce protector, guide, and comforter. I have no doubt that had she been two-legged instead of four-legged, she would be the epitome of a parent. To me, she was the mother I prayed for so many years ago.

Sleeping on the boat was the best I've ever experienced. Feeling relief from the constant onslaught of other people's energy allowed me to grow in my understanding. I began connecting to the other side through mediumship. One morning while sipping my coffee, I heard a very familiar voice speaking almost audibly yet in my head. *"Hi Berni, can you hear me?"* Looking around to be sure no one saw me talking to myself, I replied, "Grandpa? Is that you?" Suddenly, a warmth wrapped around my body while the hair on the back of my neck stood up. There was Grandpa, who had just died a few days prior. While alive, he didn't communicate much with me, now here he was. Intrigued, I began questioning him.

Me: Why are you talking to me now?

Grandpa: Because you can hear me.

Me: But why now?

Grandpa: I'm here to help. You've been struggling with going to my funeral or not going.

Me: I wish to pay my respects and all, but I don't want to be in the middle of the family drama.

Grandpa: Then don't go, there will be a lot of drama.

Me: Yeah, I didn't plan to.

Grandpa: If you want, we can visit each other during the funeral.

Me: That might be more fun.

Unsure if I was making it all up, the day of his funeral arrived. Grandpa kept popping in and then disappearing as if he was running between 2 different rooms. I found it fascinating how he described some of the events and characters. It was hilarious how he pretended to be a sports announcer and referee. Grandpa announced the events playing out with a tone of sarcasm and humor. I found out much later that the events, conversations, and drama occurred just like he described. I learned that my Grandpa had a great sense of humor. While alive, I never experienced that side of him. He explained that he was very lost while alive. He was angry, limited, and very convinced that life was hard. From that perspective, he could only behave like an angry, unhappy man. It was refreshing to get to know another side of the man I feared. He shared things with me that I treasured and helped me understand my mother and her shortcomings.

While not the first spirit I communicated with, Grandpa was persistent in getting me to listen to those who had crossed over. Along with a group of souls who wanted to be heard, he convinced me it was not wrong or evil to communicate with them. As I engaged more and made time to commune with the spirit realm, my gifts began to grow. I began to question the validity less and accept the guidance more. Doing so allowed me to communicate with those who crossed over, guides and angels daily. Life was changing again as I learned how to walk between worlds without losing my sanity.

15

SPIRITUAL PUBERTY

Two years on the boat afforded me an experience I will never forget. I grew closer to my daughter, Shasta, and the spirit world in tight, small quarters. I was also in a new relationship that was blossoming. Newly engaged and partnered in business, my fiancé' Mike and I moved in together. It was time to move to a larger home. I put the boat up for sale as I transitioned to living on land, creating a new life as a family.

Mike was a student of spirituality and didn't mind playing with new understandings. He had loved ones on the other side and wanted to connect with them. Unsure of my gifts, we used a Ouija board to contact them. I don't recommend using one unless you know how to open and close it properly. Stories told about increased paranormal activity in homes where ouija boards have been used are true. It can create an open gateway or portal for spirits to come in and out. It's imperative to properly close the doorway to the subtle realms to avoid lower dimensional beings or entities from using it.

One day, Brindi went to the park to meet her friend and walk the dog. Somehow, Shasta got away from her. Brindi was freaking out; after she was stung by an insect and couldn't catch Shasta. At that very moment, Mike and I got a message on the Ouija board saying, "Brindi's in trouble; she needs help." We looked at each other, quickly closed the board, running to find Brindi. Driving down the hill to the park, we saw Brindi crying. Shasta was off in the distance. Immediately Shasta ran to the truck and jumped in.

During this same period, I was playing with astral travel a lot. For me, it was an exploration into the subtle realms but also an escape. I was having a hard time wanting to be in my body. Some days I stayed in bed for 18 hours, escaping into the astral realms. I was learning a lot, meeting a lot of ancestors, guides, and teachers. Archangels communed with me daily as I sought understanding of the hierarchy in subtle realms. My understanding of the dualistic nature of reality grew. Light/dark, good/evil, physical/nonphysical began to make more sense.

Astral traveling gave me an excellent education, but it also brought spiritual attacks. Lower dimensional entities chased me, looking to steal energy. Anytime I was in the astral, negative spirits plagued me while incubus/succubus visited my dreams. So, I went searching for books on psychic protection as I encountered beings I didn't know existed.

Physically I began to struggle as events were playing out with people who were psychic vampires. A psychic vampire is someone who steals the energy of those around them. It can be a physical being, or it can be a discarnate being. I didn't understand how to rid myself of these vampires. I prayed for help. At one point, months after experiencing spiritual attacks, the angels delivered a message. I was no longer allowed to play in the astral. It was time to focus on living my life in third-dimensional reality.

I went back to the metaphysical store I had found when the accidental mediumship incident happened, hoping to get help from a psychic. There I met with John, the Santerian Priest I had met before. After reading with shells, he invited me to do a cleansing ritual to clear me of these attacks. As we worked together, he asked if I would join them. All I knew about Santeria was that they walked in between worlds. In some ways, I was honored to receive the invitation to join them. But, on the other hand, it didn't feel right for me. Mike insisted that I was only allowed to participate if he could as well. John immediately dismissed the idea, saying Mike wasn't invited.

The cleansing ritual did wonders for me. Before the ceremony, I was losing handfuls of hair. After John's spiritual work, my hair grew back, and my physical energy began to return. Following John's instructions, we destroyed the Ouija board and stopped using it. He told me I didn't need it and using it would only draw lower vibrational entities. He voiced his concern about Mike, warning me that dark days were coming. I had no idea what he was talking about. All he would say was, "secrets and lies will be revealed." He told me to be careful and be faithful to my spiritual calling no matter what I had to lose in the physical world. I wrote about the messages in my secret journal, not even sharing them with Mike.

Mike didn't drink, but he never told me why. Out with friends, he gave into peer pressure and did some shots of tequila; but he didn't stop there. I could always stop drinking when I wanted, but Mike couldn't once he started. Finally, he confided that he was a recovered alcoholic, and this was his first relapse; many more would follow. "What? Why didn't you tell me?" I screamed. It was the beginning of the end for us. For several months he would battle alcoholism and relapses. John was right, "Dark days were coming."

Meanwhile, Shasta wasn't acting like herself since we had moved into the house. She wasn't happy that Mike's dogs had become part of the family. While visiting a friend, Shasta, and Chloe, Mike's female dog, got out of her backyard. It was pouring rain, and Chloe didn't know her way around my friend's neighborhood. Shasta, however, did, and she had no issue taking Chloe on a run. Once we realized they were gone, we found Shasta walking up to the house alone. Chloe was nowhere to be found.

We drove the neighborhood for hours, searching for her. Unaffected, Shasta took a nap in the back seat of the truck while we called for the missing dog. She was determined to be the only dog in our house. Knowing her the way I did, I could TOTALLY see Shasta purposely leading Chloe away and ditching her. Shasta had a keen sense of smell and direction; Chloe didn't. We checked all the shelters for two weeks; she was never found.

16

———

HORSING AROUND

As I settled into living in a bigger space, I longed for land and horses, wanting to pursue my dreams of rehabilitating horses again. Two years of manifesting whatever I desired had shown me that these Universal principles were real. I bought a couple of rescue horses and was already training them. Dawson, a big black warmblood, and a cute Morgan/Arab mix named Lad for Brindi, leading me back to a childhood dream, as well as my spirit animal.

Dawson needed a lot of attention and rehabilitation. He would never be a great riding horse, so I continued to look for one. I was offered a great deal on a Grand Prix Dressage horse with attitude problems named Bo. As I worked with Bo to get his attitude straightened out, I realized he wasn't trying to be a jerk to his riders; he just had no tolerance for bad treatment. The longer I worked with him, the more I liked him. Finally, I bought him and started training him to jump.

While training Bo to jump, I began to wonder why I shouldn't pursue horse training full-time. With a purchase offer on the boat, I wrote a list of things I wanted and began hunting for the perfect property. I found a 10-acre Horse Boarding and Training facility just 20 minutes south of downtown San Diego within just a few days. The property was vacant and available for lease. It didn't take much convincing for Mike to see the possibility of us working and living there. I used the proceeds from the boat sale to lease the property and set it up with new equipment and stalls.

The Bella Farms venture took a couple of weeks to set up to my liking. It only took a month to reach capacity. The barn was full with eight of my horses, and all available boarding stalls outside were taken. I manifested a successful business quickly. Every time I set out to create something, it was easy when my heart, mind, and emotions aligned. I was engrossed in running the ranch, training, and getting through the physical demands daily. I had two helpers that alternated feeding and stall cleaning. Juan worked during the week, and when he was off, his brother Javier worked the weekends. We had it all down to a well-organized system of caring for over 30 horses. I was giving riding lessons, training problem horses, and managing the business. It required a commitment of 7 days a week, most days from 5 am until 10 pm. If there was an issue with one of the horses, I stayed up to keep watch.

One of the great things about working with the horses was learning about their personalities. For example, one of my clients was looking to buy a horse. We found Will, a thoroughbred that had a lot of training and was pretty good at dressage. Will was a beautiful chestnut-colored, 16.1 hand thoroughbred with an impressive stride; he was flashy and gorgeous. However, he needed some training to lengthen his choppy stride. So, my client bought him and put him in full training with me.

During our first training session, I set up trotting poles to see if Will would lengthen his stride. He was super responsive as we rode around the arena until we headed for the poles. Horses are meant to step OVER the poles; Will stepped ON them. Immediately he stopped trotting, stood still, and his entire body began to shake. I jumped off him, thinking he injured himself. Instead, I heard his voice clearly in the tone of a gay man, "Oh my Gawd, Oh my Gawd! It hurts, it hurts, it's broken!" I turned to see if someone was in the arena with me. No one was there but me and Will. It took me a few minutes to realize I was hearing him telepathically.

Stunned by his dramatic voice and overly dramatic body shakes, I started laughing. Will was holding his left front leg up off the ground. I saw no blood or visible issue with his leg. "It hurts, it hurts, it hurts," he continued to cry. He was offended by my laughter but too scared to stop crying. I grabbed his leg, telling him repeatedly, "It's NOT broken." Finally, I explained that he stepped on the ground pole with one foot, making it feel like something was wrong. I demonstrated by stepping on the pole with one foot, showing him how uneven my legs were. It took twenty minutes of hand walking and reassurance to convince him that he didn't break his leg.

Will and I worked on his fears and his bad habits of shortening his stride for weeks. His owner was amazed to see his progress when she returned from a business trip. I took a chance and disclosed our trotting pole debacle, even letting her in on the telepathic communication. Not only was she open to it, but she wished she could hear him too. Knowing that we understood his personality, fears, and needs, he could finally trust us. He fell in love with his new owner and became the spoiled "Diva" he yearned to be.

Shasta had become the guard dog of the barn. One night, a pack of coyotes was roaming the property. We had adopted a tiny kitten named Jasmine that Shasta was fond of. While she didn't care for other dogs, she seemed to enjoy the kitten. Sitting at my desk in the kitchen, Shasta became very agitated. Jasmine wasn't in the house for the night. I was afraid Shasta wasn't going to rest until she came in. I stepped out the back door to call the kitten, but she didn't come running in. The coyotes began howling in a circle near the arena. Shasta bolted out of the house straight for the coyotes. I caught a glimpse of her with something in her mouth minutes after I heard the coyotes run off in the distance.

Shasta calmly walked toward me, unphased by her battle with the coyotes. Even though four coyotes were against her, she somehow chased them all away without even a hair out of place. I could finally make out what she had in her mouth when she walked to the porch. Held gently by Shasta's teeth, bleeding yet calm, Jasmine dangled from her scruff. Shasta walked right past me and gently laid Jasmine on the kitchen floor. She stood over her, licking her fur, then turned to look at me as if to say, "She's hurt, help her."

Running for a first aid kit, I examined Jasmine and found a puncture wound on her shoulder. It wasn't anything that required stitches, so I cleaned her up and treated the wound. The whole time I worked on her, Shasta sat beside me like a worried Mom. After feeding Jasmine, I sat her down next to Shasta, who quickly picked her back up and walked her over to the dog bed. The two snuggled up for the night. Shasta was unwilling to leave Jasmine's side.

The ranch taught me so much about animals, telepathy, and I felt like my family was expanding again. Shasta was a mother not only to me but Brindi, Jasmine, and the other kids that hung out. Unfortunately, life on the ranch was busy, so I had little time to do much inner healing. Nevertheless, progress was being made, just not from a clinical perspective. I felt more relaxed with who I was, and on the surface, our lives looked normal. But, of course, unhealed wounds remained, waiting for my attention.

17

FALLING INTO MY PURPOSE

There were days I wondered if I had made a colossal mistake taking on this venture. Mike wasn't helping at all. He was traveling for work, and his on/off drinking created more problems than I could keep up with. We were making great money, but I started noticing significant bank withdrawals when he was out of town; money never accounted for either. I later found out he was on a drinking binge while out of town for business. I was beginning to burn out from dealing with his drinking and the increased chaos. I loved the horses and the kids, but life was becoming unbearable.

On a long weekend, Mike went missing somewhere in San Diego for almost four days. I had to stay focused on the ranch and Brindi. All hell broke loose on the farm Monday morning. I woke up from a dream in a panic to a message from Archangel Michael saying, "It's time to go, you're moving to Colorado; you've had five years warning." Covered in sweat, my heart was racing as I stumbled to the bathroom. I washed my face, put on my barn clothes, and headed out to check the horses.

By 9 am, still feeling a sense of dread and panic, one of the boarding clients came running into my office in the barn announcing the water wasn't working. I ran to check the stalls, the house, the bathroom, and there was no water. So, I called the water company and was informed that I had called to shut the water off late Friday afternoon. "What? I didn't call to shut the water off. The horses need water," I pleaded. The water company employee insisted that someone did call, pretending to be me. To restore the water, I had to give a new deposit and pay a reconnect fee. When I provided my bank account information, the customer service agent told me, "I'm sorry, but the charge was denied." Shocked, I called the bank to find out the $30,000 we had in the joint account was gone. I was grateful I had a check from a border; I went to the bank, opened a new account, and called to restore the water.

Mike called from rehab that night, explaining that his sister had talked him into getting help. He apologized for disappearing. He was furious when I told him what happened at the ranch. His sister blamed me for his drinking and decided to ruin my life and business. She had called the water company pretending to be me. She didn't care about the threat posed to the animals; all she wanted to do was inflict pain on me. She mistakenly thought I was spending his money. Little did she know that the money from my boat opened the ranch and was in our joint bank account. She convinced Mike to clear the bank account before being admitted to rehab. Not only did I lose the remainder of my savings during his binge, but now, I was unable to keep the bills paid.

Almost audibly, a voice spoke to me again, "It's time to move to Colorado, close the ranch." Feeling desperate and with little sleep, I sat down to meditate. By now, my relationship with Spirit and the Angels was secure. Announcing himself, Archangel Michael began to speak words of encouragement. I resisted moving to a state I had no ties to. I begged, pleaded, and bargained to stay in San Diego on the ranch. Each request was denied; I was urged to have faith that moving was in the grand plan for my life. I had promised to be a vessel for God's will; it was time to do my job and fulfill that promise. I was afraid I wouldn't have an income if I left the ranch and my business. I told Spirit, "If you want me to move fine, I need a home that is super affordable." Archangel Michael instructed me to write down what I needed to move, and the Spirit world would come to my aid.

As soon as I stopped resisting the abrupt turn of events, things began falling in place. I received guidance to sell the new stalls, equipment, and six of my horses. I notified the boarders that I had to close the business, explaining what had happened. Mike's sister made further threats that prompted me to hire an emergency moving company, placing my personal belongings in storage. It all happened so fast it was a blur, but somehow, I made enough money from the sale of things to pay the bills through the next month. I asked my guides and Angels for a bit of a break before moving to Colorado. Synchronistic events led to a Spiritual retreat in Sedona, Arizona.

Brindi was in Washington visiting my Dad as I left for Sedona, leaving Shasta with my friend Mary in San Diego. Javier, my stable hand, took care of the horses and ranch. My friend Ross was going through a considerable crossroads in his life and decided to join me at the retreat. I spent four days hiking, meditating, and clearing my head. Spirit directed me each day, encouraging me to have faith in the help from unseen realms. Messages poured in; I continued to record them in my journal. I had no choice; by blind faith, I did as Spirit asked, believing the words I was hearing. "That which you forgive in others will be forgiven in you. That which you hold against others will be held against you."

Matthew 7.1 "Judge not lest you be judged."

Judgment, anger, and a touch of victimhood were keeping me stuck. Spirit kept imparting teachings that would allow me to forgive, heal, release and move forward. I was angry at Mike and his family, mad at my Mom for a laundry list of things. But worst, I was ashamed of myself for every mistake I ever made. "Whatever you judge against others causes judgment to fall on yourself. When you forgive others for their MIS-takes, you allow them to be imperfect. The imperfections you allow in others, allow you to be imperfect as well," kept repeating in my mind. Spirit continued to teach me that forgiveness and acceptance are the keys to freedom and love. When you accept others as they are without expecting something in return, you are operating at the highest level of love. Holding a grudge based on something you feel was taken from you allows anger and resentment to build. Forgiving ourselves for mistakes and imperfections is also very important. The biggest MIS-conception we have is that we have to behave perfectly and always make perfect choices. We seem to forget that no matter what choice we make, it is the "perfect" choice for that moment based on the information we have available.

On a hike in Sedona, I had a crucial lesson shown to me. I was a bit unsure of what path to take up Cathedral Rock. The path I chose was a bit steep and rocky, it was getting hot, and I wasn't making progress. So, I prayed for some spiritual guidance, asking to be shown the best path to reach the top of the peak. The most beautiful message was received when I quieted my mind enough to listen. Suddenly, a small garden snake got my attention. Stopping dead in my tracks, I heard, "Take a step to the right," then Spirit guided me to climb through some brush and over a rock just beyond the snake. Although I wasn't sure it was the correct path, I followed the guidance. Within minutes I realized the new route was much smoother, cleared by many people who traveled it before me. The most surprising part of the change in the path was that within 10 minutes, I reached the peak. I didn't even realize I was ascending, my breathing was steady, and my legs didn't strain to climb. Once at the peak, Spirit gently spoke, "Every path leads to the same place. You have the freedom to choose which one you want to take. Do you want to take the hard, rocky path, or do you prefer the easy path that has been cleared before you?"

The message I received that day gave me great insight. I realized how often I had chosen to take the hard, rocky path in life, somehow thinking it was necessary. I always seemed to choose the hard way, resented others and myself. However, as soon as I released the need to be perfect and have everyone else be perfect, my path became easy and effortless. Of course, I am not saying that every moment will be easy, but the more we allow unconditional acceptance and love to enter our hearts, we open up to the easy path of life. Ultimately, every path leads to the same place, and we will reach our final destination, regardless of which path we choose.

Forgiveness allows us to freely choose our path and the freedom to walk without fear or resentment. When we hold resentments and grudges against ourselves and others, we become burdened with a hefty load. Forgiveness allows us to release that load and travel through life lightly, unencumbered by anger. By forgiving others and especially ourselves, we allow joy to flow freely in our lives.

Ross and I drove from Sedona up into Colorado, looping back around through Nevada and home. I told Spirit I would move if they found me a place for the horses, my dog, Brindi, and I to rent for under $500 a month. My logic was that it couldn't be done, but I would move if it did. Three phone calls later, I found a 2-acre property already fenced for horses for $450 a month. I made a deal with Spirit; now, I had to keep my end of the agreement and move. Everything about it lined up to what was on my list. Sight unseen, I rented it over the phone. Within three days, Brindi and I were on our way to our new life in Colorado, the great unknown.

18

THE MIDDLE OF NOWHERE

Late August, just before Labor Day weekend 2000, we were packed and ready to go. Driving away from our lives in San Diego felt exciting but scary. I had no idea how I would earn an income, but I was optimistic with a strong sense of faith. I wanted to show Brindi Sedona's red rocks, so we detoured off the main freeway and drove the moving truck, car in tow, to Oak Creek Canyon. Brindi loved the red rocks she could see in the distance.

We could only afford to take two of the eight horses with us, so I chose which two we would bring. I rehomed Brindi's horse, 23-year-old Lad, to another trainer, knowing he would live his life out in the pasture. Because of his age, I was unwilling to put him through the altitude change from 0 to 6000 feet. The Colorado snow would be a huge adjustment for him. Lad was going blind, developing arthritis, and while he seemed healthy, it didn't seem reasonable to expect him to survive such a drastic climate change. Dawson and Bo were the two I kept. Bo was a perfect lesson horse for advanced riders, and Dawson was the first horse I acquired after years of not having any. While Dawson had terrible hips and was primarily lame, I didn't want to chance him going to slaughter. The other six horses were sold or rehomed quickly. It gave us the money to pay for the moving truck and horse transport. Bo and Dawson were at a farm awaiting transport, scheduled to meet us at our new home within a few days of our arrival.

My head was still swimming. Everything had come unwound so quickly. I prayed that Spirit would ease our minds and hearts, making this transition less painful. Brindi was great during the drive, catching me up on all she had done while visiting her Grandpa and cousins. She seemed almost excited to move somewhere new, even though our whole lives were changing.

After a couple of years on prescriptions for ADHD, I had searched for alternatives to get Brindi on something more natural. Unfortunately, once a child was diagnosed and medicated in California Schools, you had to continue the regimen. Before signing the lease for our new home, I called the school Brindi would be attending and found out they didn't require that medication. After reading several stories of parents losing custody of their children to C.P.S. for medical negligence, it was a total relief. Weaning Brindi off her meds allowed her personality to brighten and reemerge. She hated taking them, so that might have had something to do with her NOT being resistant to the move. She didn't seem bothered too much about leaving her friends in school, maybe because she had been on summer break.

Timing and the ease at which everything fell into place hadn't escaped my notice. Although I hadn't had time to process the breakup with Mike, synchronicities were happening daily. It was as if I was in an ongoing conversation with Spirit and the Angels. Not a normal conversation like humans have, but certainly, one that guided me and confirmed things I was hearing. Guidance was always available whenever I took the time to ask questions and wait for answers., I had plenty of time to talk to Spirit on that 15-hour drive to Colorado. While Brindi napped, I let my tears flow as I spoke to Spirit about the heartache, my fears, and confusion over the events that had just transpired. As I began to process everything, Shasta was right beside me, head in my lap, occasionally licking my hand as if to comfort me.

Long-distance driving always seemed to put me in a meditative state. I began looking back at the amount of hurt, healing, and blessings over the previous five years. The number 5 was becoming very significant for me. Five in numerology is the number of transformations and sudden change. It's even shaped like a rocking chair, threatening to roll forward at any moment. I didn't know if I should embrace the number 5 and all of its energy or be afraid of it. Spirit reminded me of the five-year warning about a move to Colorado. As the conversation with Spirit continued, I began seeing fives everywhere. Looking at the clock just as it turned 5:55 became a daily occurrence. Change at the grocery store or gas station of $.55 or a bill for $5.55 caught my attention. I should have known something huge was going to happen had I been paying attention.

By the time we arrived in Colorado, the sun was setting. I was worried we'd get lost. I wanted desperately to get to our new home and out of the moving truck. Still thinking like a "city girl," I figured we would unload the car and run out for dinner after we got there. As we turned down the dirt road leading to our new house, a deer and her baby walked right in front of the truck to greet us. I felt calm and peaceful energy surround me as they looked right at us before continuing on their way. Within five minutes, we parked in front of our new 2 bedrooms, 2 bath, mobile home. It was cute with lots of windows. We were pleasantly surprised at how fresh it looked; as we checked out the inside, Brindi's hunger grew. I went back outside to unhook the car from the tow dolly in the dark. We grabbed Shasta and headed out, thinking we would find food close by. I had no idea where we were or even the direction of town, so I turned right.

Within a few minutes, we came upon a Mexican Restaurant that had just closed. I explained we had been driving since early morning, and my daughter was starving. They offered her a peanut butter and jelly sandwich, but she refused it. I felt so bad that everything had closed for the night. I was used to restaurants being open late. The ladies at the restaurant explained everything closed by 8 or 9 pm, even in the summer. Brindi was crying. "Let's go home to California, Mommy; I hate it here."

How do you explain to a 9-year-old that it wasn't possible to go back? I handed her an open bag of Doritos and a bottle of water we had from the trip. That night, we slept on the floor with beach towels for blankets, tired and hungry. I cried as I drifted off to sleep, praying tomorrow would be better.

Bright and early, the sun streaming in the windows woke us up. The first order of business was to unload some of our clothes so we could shower and find food. Driving into the little town of Ignacio, about 15 minutes from home, we found a restaurant that was bustling with customers. Brindi ordered a full breakfast and a side order of pancakes with hot chocolate. I was determined to make up for missing dinner last night. In the light of day, things seemed a little less overwhelming. I asked our waitress for directions to the best grocery store and received directions to Walmart, about 30 minutes away. Brindi and I jumped in the car and headed to Durango for food, water, and supplies. It was a beautiful drive with rolling pastures and farms. Durango was a charming little Western town in the middle of the mountains. The beauty of our new environment was enough to give me hope that Spirit had a plan for us, and we would be alright.

As I was unpacking the moving truck, a neighbor girl greeted Brindi. The girls were about the same age and hit it off instantly. Grateful for the distraction, I let her play as I worked. Unloading the truck alone was difficult. I called my Realtor Kaeon to see if he knew of anyone who could help me. After a couple of phone calls, I had a couple of guys agree to move the big furniture into the house for $20 each. We got the truck unloaded, and I was able to return it the day after we arrived. It seemed like everything I needed and asked for was easily manifested. Moving to a new state with no friends or family was a scary proposition, but Spirit assured me I would not be alone for long. Brindi and I explored Durango's downtown, looking in stores and seeing what was around. It was a tiny town, but we felt safe and welcomed.

Here I was, with no clue what to do for work; I sat down to meditate and channel. I pre-arranged to have the phone line and the internet turned on before we arrived. I'd already seen the local paper, which wasn't much help, aside from service jobs. Things were looking bleak. Spirit had promised I would still be giving riding lessons, but it wouldn't support us financially. Marketing positions were slim. The only one I found paid $10 an hour with a 45-minute commute daily. I began to panic, thinking I had made a grave error in judgment moving here. My ego fears were loud and making it nearly impossible to sit still. Meditation wasn't happening, so I checked my email and surfed Yahoo. I noticed an ad for free psychic readings and heard loudly, "click on it."

"Oh, you want me to get a reading so I can find out where to find a job, Spirit?" Immediately I heard, "No, you are going to give readings. Time to use your gifts to help others". I panicked. I immediately began arguing with my guides. Instead of looking into becoming a "reader," I signed up to receive a free five-minute reading. I asked the reader about employment opportunities. What followed surprised me. Matter-of-factly, she said, "You are a gifted psychic and medium; you will be doing readings, using your gifts to help others." I couldn't believe what I was hearing. I almost fell off my chair with laughter. Laughter from the subtle realm erupted simultaneously from what seemed like an entire committee as she explained how easy it was to sign up on the site to become an advisor.

Within an hour, I set up my profile and was ready to hit the button, allowing people to call me. Spirit poured an overwhelming blanket of peace over me. For a moment, all fear drained from my body as I heard a whisper, "Just try it. You have nothing to lose." With no other options for making money, I hit the button to make myself available for callers. Minutes later, the phone rang, and I delivered my first professional reading. The caller was genuinely grateful for the messages delivered. It felt good to be able to help someone with my connection to Spirit. To my surprise, that day, I earned $45.00. I had no idea how to price myself, so I started at the minimum 79-cents per minute, of which I made about 35-cents per minute. Being a new psychic on a brand-new site, I needed feedback and a rating from callers to get traction. By the end of that first day, I had good feedback and a 5-

star rating. The next day Spirit told me to raise my price to 89-cents per minute, finishing the day with $90. I had no idea you could make money doing psychic readings, let alone on the phone. After that, things felt a little less hopeless, knowing at the very least I could make enough money to pay our $ 450-month rent, our utilities, and food until I found a "real" job.

Within two weeks, Spirit had guided me to incrementally raise my rates until I reached $1.99 a minute. The lower rate meant I had calls stacked up back-to-back with little time for anything. The number of calls I was taking was taxing to my energy, emotions, and body. I noticed the type of client was changing as I raised my rates. The higher the rate, the more the caller seemed to honor the guidance I was giving. When my rate was low, people pushed me for information quickly. I began nicknaming the types of callers. "Rapid-fire querent," "Nosey Nellies," and the ones who started emailing me for free readings became "Leg Humpers." Every day I received a few emails with people giving me sob stories, wanting a free reading. At first, I agreed to do it; being an empath, I could feel their desperation. I was regularly gifting free minutes until Spirit put a stop to it. Spirit explained that people who expected me to work for free had no understanding of energy exchange. I received a download of information about protecting my energy, exchanging it, and knowing when to say "no."

Boundaries were a constant weakness throughout my life. Feeling other people's emotions as my own has been the most challenging part of being an empath. I didn't just empathize with people; I absorbed their emotions and pain. If someone was hurting, I felt it amplified within my body. The only way I knew how to make it go away was to help the other person shift their own feelings or thoughts. It was so bad I would give someone my last dollar and go without just to relieve myself of their pain. Working as a professional psychic, I was learning that I needed to gain control of my empathic gifts.

Empaths are highly sensitive people that experience a wide variety of challenges in life. Living in the city, I knew I was sensitive; it was hard to drive in traffic, shop during holidays, or attend concerts. However, I didn't realize how much other people's energy affected me until we moved to the country. Living on the boat, I learned how much my energy changed versus being in the middle of the city. When I moved onto the boat, my energy was calmer and more centered. I slept more soundly and peacefully than at any time in life. There weren't a lot of people living on their boats, so at night it was peaceful. As I began to research more, I began to understand what being an empath was all about.

In an article *Adapted from The Empath's Survival Guide by Judith Orloff, M.D., she writes:*

As a psychiatrist and an empath, I often get asked, "What is the difference between empaths and highly sensitive people?" Following are the similarities and areas of overlap.

Empaths share all the traits of what Dr. Elaine Aron has called "Highly Sensitive People," or HSPs. These include a low threshold for stimulation; the need for alone time; sensitivity to light, sound, and smell; and an aversion to large groups. It also takes highly sensitive people longer to wind down after a busy day since their ability to transition from high stimulation to being quiet is slower. Highly sensitive people are typically introverts, while empaths can be introverts or extroverts (although most are introverts). Empaths share a highly sensitive person's love of nature and quiet environments, their desire to help others, and their rich inner life.

However, empaths take the experience of the highly sensitive person much further. We can sense subtle energy (called shakti or prana in Eastern healing traditions) and actually absorb it from other people and different environments into our own bodies. Highly sensitive people don't typically do that. This capacity allows us to experience the energy around us, including emotions and physical sensations, in extremely deep ways. And so, we energetically internalize the feelings and pain of others — and often have trouble distinguishing someone else's discomfort from our own. Also, some empaths have profound spiritual and intuitive experiences — with animals, nature, or their inner guides — which aren't usually associated with highly sensitive people.

Being a highly sensitive person and an empath are not mutually exclusive. One can be both, and many highly sensitive people are also empaths. If you think about this distinction in terms of an empathic spectrum, empaths are on the far end; highly sensitive people are a little further in; people with strong empathy who are not HSPs or empaths are in the middle; and narcissists, sociopaths, and psychopaths who have "empath-deficient disorders" are at the far opposite end.

The gifts of sensitivity and empathy are precious. We want to keep opening our hearts and break through to new heights in the empathic spectrum. We need these gifts now more than ever.

Being empathic had always felt like a curse, but I understood that it was a blessing. There are so many insensitive people in the world. It seems the gift of empathy is waning with the rise of technology. Tuning in to the emotions and energies of others is helpful as long as I don't take those energies on as my own. I tried to process everyone else's stuff in my own body, mind, and emotions for many years. It's no wonder I felt so depressed and heavy growing up. There weren't any books about it, and no one talked about it. Thanks to the internet today, empaths and sensitives have infinite sources of information on the topic.

Continuing my search for a real job resulted in more frustration than opportunity. The most I could find was waitressing jobs. Resistance from my limited understanding and old beliefs convinced me that the psychic advisor position wasn't an actual career path. I began having dreams of being in a classroom. Each morning I would wake up and write the dreams down in my journal. I diligently looked up the symbols and began learning from the information. My guides were schooling me at night; every dream ended the same, with the teacher telling me I had a lot to learn before I could graduate. Piecing the dreams together, I understood that intuitive work was my "calling" and soul purpose.

I began having flashes of the vision I received when Brindi was a baby, recalling it as if I had just seen it yesterday. Finding the journal of notes from 1992 helped me understand that I was helping others by shining light and wisdom into their lives. I gave up on finding a job and accepted my new career while working from home. Word spread quickly; the more grateful I became, the more my business grew. Each day, I had a waiting list of clients eager to speak to me, allowing money to flow abundantly.

Studying, meditating, writing, and taking calls daily, were having a massive effect on every area of my life. Brindi was making friends at school, the horses were in the backyard, and I had picked up a few riding students. The loss and devastation I had encountered in San Diego were becoming a faded memory. The massive leap of faith I took to follow Spirit's guidance had paid off. Living in the country, nature in the backyard with fewer distractions, was helping me grow rapidly. I began teaching a psychic development class in a Yahoo chat room weekly. I was making all kinds of friends online even though I didn't have many friends locally.

During my studies, I got instructions about staggering my sleep. Spirit told me to stagger my sleep and waking time purposely. Adjusting your sleep cycle helps bring awareness to creativity; it allows you to walk between worlds, accessing far greater creativity and intuition. Your body can adapt to the sleep/wake cycles better too. It's important to understand that it isn't about productivity; it's about rhythm and playfulness. It's about freedom.

Free play at night when no one is awake allows you to do whatever you want without the same time constraints or rules. It creates a space of free choice. In that state, you can create whatever you want. The unconscious mind holds more power to affect your reality than your conscious mind. Just as your dreams contain more information and hidden wisdom than does your limited, forced thinking. If you want to expand and grow, you must destroy the divisions in your own life, self, and practice. You divide yourself even in how you explain the life you lead. Work, home, relationships, spirituality, hobbies have all been neatly categorized, creating division within you. You have a public and private life, a family life, and social life. The list goes on and on. Changing your habits with sleep begins to shift your entire life. Spending that time in meditation, creating art, writing, yoga, dance, or study rather than sleeping feeds you on high levels. It creates conditions for optimal integration of your soul and physical body.

The human brain has biological pathways that allow one to achieve the state that helps conscious participation and interpretation of the unconscious and dream activity. The more you merge the conscious and unconscious, the more activated the biological pathways become. There is crucial therapeutic information given in dreams that are meant to be recalled. This information becomes accessible when you minimize the division between wake and sleep. Unfortunately, the division between waking and sleeping states during 8 hours of sleep creates a more significant gap in the conscious and unconscious mind.

When you stagger your sleep by only sleeping 4 to 5 hours at a time, or 2 hours awake, 2 hours asleep, you set up optimal conditions for the free flow of communication between the conscious and unconscious mind. Within this flow, old programs or beliefs and built-up emotions can be addressed more quickly. As a result, your mind is more open, creativity heightened, and intuitive information is allowed to flow.

After 5 hours of sleep, the body wants to move; the muscles crave movement. When you sleep longer, you slow down the body processes and dull the senses. Longer sleep sessions disconnect you from memory recall and dream recall. When you sleep too long, you create inertia in the physical body that takes longer to shake, making a more significant division between conscious/unconscious and wake/sleep states.

19

______

HIDDEN DARKNESS

As I began to experiment sleeping for 2 hours, wake and study for 2 hours, my gifts began to strengthen. I was learning and retaining information so much better. My dreams were lucid, and I could consciously react to things within my dreams, knowing I was dreaming. Even more important, I was healing a lot of my old wounds from childhood. Past issues were resolving quicker, and my beliefs were expanding. It's a practice that takes discipline, but the reward is worth it.

Late-night studies and readings put me in touch with some interesting people. Word spread through testimonials, and I excelled at connecting to those who crossed over. Mediumship was a regular part of the services I offered. For example, just after Christmas, I received a call from a very distraught woman from the inner city of Detroit. She asked me to connect with her 12-year-old son. He was found dead in their apartment laundry room on Christmas Eve by his 5-year-old sister. Without any other information but his name,

I connected with him quickly. As he began showing me how he died, I relayed the information as accurately as I could. She was sobbing, saying, "I knew it, I just knew it." It was clear that two people were responsible for his death, a man and woman. He innocently stumbled upon them in the laundry room while they were doing drugs. Unfortunately, since it was Christmas Eve, the police quickly dismissed the case as a suicide. My client overheard one of the officers say, "Let's wrap this up so I can get home for Christmas dinner."

Confirming her son didn't die by suicide, my client was relieved but overwhelmed and angry. She asked for direction on how to get his case re-opened so she could get justice for her son. This boy was smart, got straight A's in school, and was looking forward to Christmas. He had gone to retrieve their laundry when he ran into the strung-out pair, embroiled in a violent argument. Amid a physical altercation, the boy was "accidentally" killed. Before hiding in their apartment, the couple hung him from some loose cable wires to make it appear a suicide. It took a couple of years, but I received a call from her thanking me for the reading. She shared the good news that the police found the couple, a drug dealer and prostitute. They had lived in the building at the time but had since moved out. Police arrested them, allowing the boy's family to move on. Unfortunately, the daughter that found the boy in the laundry room was experiencing PTSD; she hadn't spoken much since that day. After we ended the call, I wrote down the little girl's name, said a prayer, lit a candle, and asked the angels to heal her.

Missing persons and murder investigation work began to occupy my nights. Doing mediumship work for the families of those missing pulled at my heart. One of my clients was a private investigator that requested help on a few of the cases she was working on. I agreed to help and partnered with her to try and bring closure for the families. Offering to work pro bono was my way of giving back. It felt good to be of service, and while heavy, I was unaware of the darker side to the work. Pam, the P.I., asked for my help on a missing person's case in the Midwest. A 7-year-old girl went missing with no leads. Using her name and description, I connected with Spirit and asked for help locating her. With some coaxing, she came forward so that I could speak with her. I knew she was dead, but there was something strange about where her spirit was located. She hadn't fully crossed over, and she wasn't alone. Besides being extremely frightened, there was something else I had never experienced before: A darkness with a strong sense of evil was present.

I quickly took notes as images, a location, and information flooded my mind. This beautiful, frightened child revealed everything she could recall: her killer's nickname, the mobile home where he lived, the street, the house number. Before she disappeared, at least a dozen other girls were revealed, standing in the shadows behind her. As she faded, my guides started filling in the missing pieces. The killer was part of a Satanic cult, and these murders were ritual killings. All the bodies were buried in a way that allowed him some sort of control in the astral realm. They couldn't cross over; they were stuck in a strange in-between place. I typed up my notes, ready to send them off. Thinking of the killer, I whispered, "I got you." I was in tears, sick to my stomach, and desperate to help in whatever way I could. I called Pam, relaying all the information. She promised she'd let me know if there were any developments.

Around 1 am I had let Shasta out for her nightly run. Being an escape artist, the only way to keep her from escaping was to let her out in the middle of the night. She usually ran for an hour and came home, scratching the door to be let in. Around 1:30 am I heard the scratch. As I got up to let her in, I felt a little spooked but shook it off. Opening the door, Shasta paused briefly. The thud of something she dropped at my feet shocked me. She never picked anything up in her mouth. Shasta ran past me, immediately climbing under my bed to hide. She was terrified. I flipped on the hall light. The sight I encountered was of a freshly severed deer head with its tongue sticking out. At that exact moment, I heard a whispered sound in a creepy male voice, the words, "I got you too!"

Shaken, I turned every light in the house on. Quickly locating a trash bag, I put the deer head in it and ran it to the trash bin. I came inside, locked the door, and checked all the windows. This guy wasn't anywhere near us, but his presence was palpable. I jumped on my computer and began messaging my psychic friends who were good at spiritual warfare. I explained the situation and begged for help. I had never considered a scenario like this. Not only did I locate him, but he knew who I was, energetically back tracing my connection to him. He was powerful. My friends and I jumped on a conference call and went into prayer. We cleared his energy and created a strong cube of protection with blackened walls so he couldn't read or connect to me. After an hour of additional prayer and cleansing, pure exhaustion set in as I laid on the couch. I woke up from a dream just as the sun was coming up. In the dream, angels surrounded me, reassuring me I would be safe from harm. There was nothing left to do but focus on work and help Shasta feel safe again.

Two nights later, Pam called to say she was going to the address I had given her. It was a couple of states away, but she had to check it out. She was a retired police officer, fearless with great hunches. Pam drove to the address and discovered it was exactly as I described, right down to a sticker on the window next to the front door. After poking around, some not-so-friendly police officers showed up. She described the town as a rural, redneck kind of place. Things unraveled quickly as the police escorted her over the bridge and the state line, warning her not to return. She felt threatened, believing that something sinister was going on. Pam did more digging and found that the chief of police and the killer were related. Unfortunately, the "good ole boy" style of protecting relatives didn't allow for further investigation on her part. We didn't have a location of the bodies, so there was nothing we could do. I had to let it go somehow, yet it left me feeling heavy, depressed, and helpless.

Weeks passed, but the heaviness I felt wasn't lifting. I made the decision I wouldn't do any more missing person investigations. I removed all references to being a Medium from my website. I didn't want to make it easy for the killer to locate me. He scared the shit out of me. As soon as I decided to stop using my gifts that way, things started to shift. Letting go of the possibility of helping the kids was one of the hardest things for me to do. My guides explained that it was part of my education. I learned more about evil things done in the astral than I ever wanted to know. While I'm grateful I had a team of people to back me up when I got into trouble, I wasn't willing to take chances like that again. I learned new ways of protection, clearing, and setting up energetic grids. I learned how to consciously travel into the 4th dimension, tapping into those who crossed, doing my best to avoid the darker spirits that resided there. My knowledge of the dimensions helped me hone my gifts, making regular life much easier.

Being a medium without control or a way to shut it off was interfering with my life. One time while driving through a small neighboring town, one such event nearly caused a car accident. Slowly driving down the main street, a boy on a skateboard jumped in front of my car. I went right through him. There was no sound when he hit my car. As I slammed on the brakes, all my passengers were flung forward, and the cars behind me began honking. It took me a minute to realize he wasn't real, and he was a ghost. Things like that happened quite frequently, and it was always alarming.

Spirit began to teach me that I could set rules the spirit world obeyed, and life became much more manageable. While I still offered mediumship to a select few, I let those who crossed over appear only when reading for someone or if I was in meditation and wanted to connect. When a spirit wants my attention, flickers of light blink, my ears ring, or a sudden flash occurs that makes me stop and listen. It's made life much easier and allowed me to feel more in control of walking between worlds.

20

I'M NOT YOUR MOM

For a long time, Joshua, a little boy I began dreaming about almost nightly, started appearing in visions when I was awake. In 1995, when I first started receiving messages about moving to Colorado, I had dreams of him. He kept referring to me as "Momma." When the dreams started, I laughed it off. Now five years later, I was bombarded in dreams and visions by his presence. His eyes were steel grey, his smile sweet and innocent. I wasn't interested in having another child, aside from the fact that I was single.

Nevertheless, this little boy kept appearing and calling me "Momma." Finally, I told him, "I'm not your Mom. Can I maybe help you find her?" Joshua wasn't convinced; he continued to follow me around the house quietly, or he'd pop up unexpectedly as if waiting for me to acknowledge him. Usually, I just brushed it off, determined it would eventually make sense.

Dream interpretation and symbology were a lot of fun for me. I began teaching a class in a Yahoo group. One of the students, greeneyes_24_f, and I became close and would chat throughout the day. She was a gifted intuitive and empath who regularly attended the weekly group classes. During class, she began to divulge information from a dream she had. The dream was about Jesus flying her to a beautiful meadow by a river. Jesus landed an old broken-down shed with her when a swarm of bees flew around them. She said it didn't scare her since Jesus was there and the bees didn't sting her.

As she continued to describe the place, I began to have major concerns. The place she was describing was my sacred space, a place I created in meditation to meet with my guides, angels, and teachers. What was she doing there? It felt like a massive invasion of privacy. The class wrapped up quickly, and I decided to click on her name to ask her more about the dream. Just as I clicked to start a private message, I saw the name "greeneyez_24_m." It wasn't her; in fact, it was a man.

I demanded to know who this person was. He was just as confused as I was. While looking for help interpreting his dream, an invitation to my private class popped up. Strangely, I didn't invite him, and no one I knew did either. As we began to talk, he divulged that he was from Canada and his name was Stan. He got into more of the details of the dream, which started to get even stranger. It was MY sacred space, and the whole thing was making me angry. I told him I needed to meditate and ask my guides what the hell was going on.

Upset and shaken, I went into meditation, asking for guidance. Jesus appeared, calmed me, and confirmed the dream. He said that it was important that we keep an open mind until more was revealed. With that, I felt more peaceful, knowing that whoever this was, I was meant to speak to him. My screen name at the time was "b_the_psychic_vampire_slayer," recently changed from "beez_is_a_girl." The reference to the old shack and swarm of bees suddenly made sense. Spirit was directing him to me, and all the synchronicities that lined up were confirmation to both of us.

After hours of chatting, we began to develop a relationship. Weeks later, we arranged for him to fly out for a visit. It all fell into place quickly, which was a sign that it was happening for a reason. During our visit, we hit it off immediately. We had ease with each other even though he was nine years younger than me. We were soulmates of some kind which added intensity to the mix. Within a month of returning to Canada, he made plans to return to Colorado permanently.

Stan began driving from Canada to Colorado, but there was a problem with getting his car across the border. We had to figure out how to get him and his cat to the Southwest in a pinch. In need of cash, I prayed for a solution. My friend, greeneyes_24_f messaged me that her boyfriend proposed marriage. She wanted to share her good news even though they didn't have a ring yet. An image of the engagement ring worth $5,000 Mike had given me flashed in my mind. I asked her if they would be interested in buying it for $800, which was just enough to pay for airline travel. She was overjoyed. She made arrangements to wire the money, and just like that, a solution was in hand.

Locating an airport within driving distance from me became a challenge. A cold winter front had moved in, and planes were only taking pets as far as Las Vegas. Everything was working out. I made the ticket purchase and planned my drive. Within a few days, Stan was on a plane with his cat, arriving in Vegas. Brindi and I, along with Shasta, drove 10 hours to meet him. While confident we were meant to be together, things were moving at the speed of light. Little did I know they were going to move even faster.

Stan and I had already discussed getting married since it was the only way for him to stay in the States with me. With all the maneuvering to get him here and the unexpected trip to Vegas, we decided to tie the knot while we were there. Three days later, we pulled up to our house with two new members of the family. Life had become a whirlwind of unexpected events, synchronicities, and circumstances. It took a few weeks for things to calm down and reality to set in. I was married again. We had to hire an immigration lawyer, and we had to make a plan for our lives.

Brindi was nine years old at the time, and I wasn't planning on having more children. However, marriage to a younger man created a need for me to consider the possibility. Stan was only 25 years old, but I was 34 and considered a "high risk" for problems with pregnancy. As soon as I agreed to have another child, only days passed before I conceived. Both and Stan and I knew the moment of conception. I shared the visions and dreams of Joshua with him; he didn't seem shocked or surprised. Convinced I was having a boy, a doctor confirmed my pregnancy the following week.

Living a life led by Spirit was exciting, but I'd lie if I didn't tell you I had reservations, fears, or doubts. Throughout my pregnancy, I was sure I was meant to bring the little Spirit of Joshua into the world. However, I wasn't confident that Stan and I were going to make it. Months into my pregnancy and our marriage, we began to disagree on every issue. Right before the end of my first trimester,

Stan wanted to call it quits. He didn't want to be married, and he didn't want to have a child together. Somehow, we patched things up and held our marriage together, albeit by a thread. While not a blissful relationship, as soulmates, we were undoubtedly causing growth for each other.

Just before my due date, I received shocking news from the midwife I'd hired and paid in full. She had lost a breech baby during delivery due to complications, and she was quitting. With only two weeks to go, I needed a miracle. Calling on my guides and angels, I demanded a solution to calm my nerves. Jen, the midwife's assistant, contacted me within hours. While she wasn't certified yet, she was willing to be at my delivery unofficially. I felt confident she would know what to do if there were any complications. Faith paid off again, and my peace of mind was restored.

On January 22nd, I began having stomach pains and feeling irritable around 8:00 pm. I wasn't sure what labor felt like since I had so many drugs with Brindi's birth. We called Jen, telling her it was possible I was in labor. Answering questions and timing the cramps, she confirmed labor had begun, and she was on her way. Trying to relax, I decided to take a warm bath. By the time Jen arrived, it was well after 10:00 pm, and the contractions were regular but not unbearable. I sat in a candle-lit room, rocking gently, staring at the moon. By 2 am I couldn't get comfortable no matter what I did. I wanted to be fully present for this birth and thought I had planned well for this miracle. As I began to hit transition, all I could do was lie in bed as the pain increased. At one point, Jen checked my progress, encouraging me to rest as much as possible. I had closed my eyes tightly, afraid to open them and terrified of making the pain more intense. I remember grabbing her hand and begging her to tell me how many more contractions before the baby would come out. She laughed, "I'm not the psychic honey, you are." For what seemed like an eternity, she coached me to ride the pain like ocean waves that crested before calming.

Finally, on January 23rd at 4:00 am, I delivered a healthy baby girl in my own bed at home. While not the boy I was expecting, her steel grey eyes were unmistakably the same as Joshua's. Ironically, we had only chosen a boy name but decided days before to pick a girl name just in case. Isabela, meaning "God's promise," perfectly described the spirit that spent five years convincing me to be a mother a second time. Some cultures believe children born with steel grey eyes are gifted seers and healers. I had a strong sense she was both.

Bela's eyes were striking and intense. One day while shopping at Walmart, with her feet sticking out of the car seat in a shopping cart, she got the attention of an older man. The man walked right up to her, smiled, and asked if he could touch her feet. Bela stared right into his eyes intently. He was mesmerized by her, mentioning he had been sad until he saw her. Touching her feet, he smiled, straightened his posture, and walked away smiling.

Powerfully gifted with telepathy, Bela taught me quickly how to recognize someone else's thoughts and intentions. At age 1, I started to notice her quiet, piercing stares as if she was searching your soul. By age 2, I realized she was not just staring; she was reading people's energy. Whenever meeting someone for the first time, Bela would stare at them, sometimes getting them to do things for her without saying a word. When my Dad moved in with us, she sized him up quickly, and I swear she dropped ideas right into his head without detection. Her preschool teacher said a few things that made me think she was a victim of Bela's telepathy too. She reminded me a lot of myself as a child. I knew she was sensitive and would need to learn how to protect herself.

Before Bela's birth, we had been making plans to build a bigger house. Four people in a 2 bedroom were cramped, primarily because I worked from home. Stan wasn't working, so he took care of Bela while I worked. We learned about homes that the local building trades class at the community college built once a year and auctioned. One of my friends bought one at an incredible price. After viewing the southwest-style house, it seemed perfect for our growing family. Stan thought we should have a larger space than the 3-bedroom, 2-bath house. We decided we would bid on the college house after discovering that the slope to our land would allow us to build a floor underneath and connect it to the house from the college. While different, we would end up with a much bigger home at a fraction of the cost of building the whole thing from scratch.

It was time to manifest the winning bid on the college-built house and a construction loan to build a bottom floor. Auction day came quickly. We kept our spirits high, sure that we would win the bid. The bids were opened at 5 pm. We had the winning bid. I had to get a loan from the bank to build the bottom floor, move the college house to our property 45 miles away and have it placed on the constructed bottom floor. It seemed like a crazy project. I didn't want a simple basement under the top floor; I had a vision of lots of windows. But, crazy or not, I was determined to make it all happen. Stan wasn't employed even though he was a permanent resident, which meant it all fell on my shoulders to make it happen. Within a week, I secured a construction loan, lined up contractors, and kicked off the project as the General Contractor.

My dream of building a home manifested through a series of mishaps, long days, and help from both the seen and unseen realms. There were days I was so tired I wanted to give up. The project went way over budget, leaving my income to cover any extra expenses. Then, the stucco contractor quit without finishing the job, stealing money I had given him for supplies. Thankfully, his crew of eighteen-year-old helpers was willing to finish the job. One day, working in my office after the stucco contractor had stopped showing up, one of my guides decided to help motivate the remaining stucco crew. They knew I was a psychic, but none of them asked questions or gave it much thought. Then, as I was hanging up a call, one of the boys came barreling into my office confused and concerned. An old Native American man dressed in cowboy boots and a hat had appeared to all three boys on the crew. He was supervising the work and keeping watch. As he told me what happened, I instantly knew it was one of my guides, one with a sense of humor. I explained that they had seen one of my guides, a protector, ensuring the house got built on time. I did my best to impress upon them the need for efficient, quality work, especially with my guide forcibly making his presence known. The boys accepted it, and while slightly shaken, they took it seriously. Their pace and quality of work improved immediately. We finished the project on time, with all-hands-on-deck, receiving the Certificate of Occupancy on the construction loan deadline. If we hadn't received it, we would have to pay high interest until it could be converted to a standard home loan. You can imagine my relief when we finished.

There is nothing that we can't accomplish, manifest, or create. It is only the fears and doubts in our minds that hold us back. Manifesting and construction of our new home tested my faith and patience daily. Anytime I became overwhelmed by my exhaustion and sheer effort, I was surprised by Divine providence. Money, resources, supplies, and help all arrived at the perfect moment. The house was huge, 3,248 square feet, 5 bedrooms, 4 baths, sitting on just over 2 acres. I couldn't believe how much life had changed or how much I had created since leaving San Diego, broke and uncertain.

21

SPIRITUAL BATTLES

Within weeks of finishing the house, a new client was referred to me for healing work. He had been to every major specialty hospital, yet no one could help him. He was unable to eat, unable to drink, and his life was on a downward spiral. I wanted so badly to help him.

Clearing his energy on my massage table, I noticed strange reactions in his body as I moved around him. I ran healing energy, calling in the Angels to assist. He was lying on his back as I approached his heart center. Sensing a strong block, I was shocked at what happened when I increased the energy. This man's shoulder blades, head, and heels remained touching the table, but his back, chest, and abdomen arched off of it. Freaked, I quickly prayed and asked for immediate help. I heard the angels whisper, "Pray a binding of the dark spirits, breathe and stay calm." He didn't even seem phased. His eyes remained closed while I went to work on binding the entity attached to his heart.

I did as much clearing work as I could, binding entities as I went. Once finished, I struggled to explain to the client what had happened. He didn't seem surprised by anything I told him. Before the session, he hadn't been able to drink. Now he was suddenly thirsty. I was relieved he drank without vomiting the water. It was obvious he needed help; I was willing but unsure of what to do. Finally, Spirit told me to invite him to stay for a few days or a week until we could clear all the entities attached to him. It seemed like a crazy idea, but I knew I wouldn't be able to help him if he left. He seemed relieved by the idea and agreed to stay in our guest room.

Putting a stranger in the guest room, upstairs from the family, with protection in place, was a crazy idea to me. I always listened to my angels and guides, so I had to see this through. I put a circle of salt under his bed to protect him and a line of salt at the bedroom door to contain anything still attached. It seemed to work. The following day he was able to eat a meal and drink water without any issues. I began formulating a plan to free him of these negative attachments.

Days of clearing work included surrounding him in a circle from a hose with running water outside, working while Brindi was at school. I had a helper who was fluent in Latin help me as we worked to clear the demons. During one particular attempt, the most miraculous event occurred. My assistant and I were reciting prayers calling the demons out to release him. The air was still and warm without a hint of a breeze. Then, out of the corner of my eye, I saw a large streak of silver, and both my assistant and I heard the sound of large wings flapping. Just as the energy was intensifying and the demons were losing power, a brisk whirlwind surrounded us. The whirlwind was located to the right where we were sitting. Taller than the roof of my house, I saw a glimpse of Archangel Michael with his sword drawn. We continued to pray as the wind continued to swirl around us. It was like being transported to some other place. Finally, two of the three entities left, the wind instantly disappearing with them. It was over, at least for the moment.

That night, exhausted, I fell into a deep sleep almost instantly, then at approximately 1 a.m. I realized I was in the middle of a lucid dream. After being pulled into hell by two giant thug-like demons, standing between them, in front of a beautiful desk, sat a very handsome man. He was gorgeous with blonde hair and blue eyes, wearing a navy, double-breasted blue suit. I instantly knew who it was. Without introduction, Satan began to speak about my client. I felt paralyzed and mesmerized all at the same time. He was gorgeous, dressed just as I would like my perfect match. I tried to stay focused as he arrogantly told me that I needed to stop helping my client. Announcing that he owned his soul, and now he owned mine as well. I laughed right in his face saying, "He isn't yours; he belongs to God." As for me, you don't own me; I'm free; all I have to do is wake up." I felt panic for a moment, wondering how I was going to wake up. Just then, the fire alarms in the house began loudly chirping for no reason. My assistant, husband, daughter, and client woke up, followed by me, still half out of it.

Just as fast as the fire alarms started, they stopped on their own. I immediately checked that everyone was ok before announcing, "I was just in hell with Satan, and the Angels needed to wake me up." I'm sure they thought I was crazy, yet no one seemed shocked or surprised by anything that happened. Finally, we all went back to sleep, agreeing that we were indeed protected. The following day, as evening approached, my assistant and I put the client in a salt circle in the dining room. The angels instructed me to put two bowls of water in the circle with the client. As we spoke and prayed, it was made clear that this entity was not leaving. Checking the water bowls, I had my assistant look at what I was seeing. In the water, a reflection of the little bugger was looking right at me. His face resembled Dobby from Harry Potter. I would have doubted it if it wasn't for my assistant seeing it too. Telepathically he told me that he didn't have to leave since the client was holding onto him.

Relaying the information to the client, he confirmed that he had been with him for so long, he was afraid to let him go. He didn't want to send the bugger to the Abyss, requesting I somehow save it. I tried to reason with him, but he wasn't willing to release it. Finally, after a week of working daily to clear him, I decided to send him home. Freewill is a Universal law. No matter how much we want to help someone, they have free will to choose in the end. He understood there was nothing more for me to offer and left the next day. I ran into him outside a restaurant a few years back before leaving Colorado. He looked at me and quickly walked past when he realized who I was. He looked fine physically but felt slightly tortured—nothing like he had when I first met him, though.

We settled into the new house, creating new routines and filling the space. My private client schedule was packed, all from referrals. Psychics, healers, and tarot readers became clients as well. Referred by her brother, an older tarot reader asked for help with a wealthy client. She was having issues with accurately predicting events about a romantic relationship the client had. At one point, she had me do readings for her to deliver the information to the client. Eventually, I got tired of it, demanding the client call directly if she wanted a reading from me. Madge, the wealthy client, became a regular for a few months. She still paid the tarot reader for in-person sessions but called me to validate the readings. Soon, Madge stopped using the tarot reader. Instead, she relied solely on me, which angered the tarot reader, resulting in a demand that I tell Madge to stop calling. The entire thing was ridiculous! I refused to be manipulated, telling the tarot reader to "grow up" and ending all communication with her.

Things were calm, and I enjoyed not having to do construction. Fall in the Rocky Mountains was beautiful. As I did some housework, I suddenly felt a wall of negative energy hit. Looking outside, I noticed four giant vultures circling the back pasture. Tuning into Spirit, I asked what the message was. Images and words tumbled through my mind. Someone was sending some bad juju my way. Pissed, I immediately grabbed supplies to cast a protection circle. I laid an unbroken circle of salt on the floor around me, marking the four directions with candles. Next, I started a protection prayer, performing a reversal without first checking my anger, returning the negative energy and intentions to whoever sent it multiplied 7 x 70 times. Sensing the energy had dissipated, I closed out the prayer, ended the ritual, and cleaned the circle. Once it was over, I thought, "Who the hell is trying to zap me? Whoever it is should know the rules of magic. Whatever you send out can be returned." Still a little pissed, I journaled to release the remaining energy.

At 7 am the following day, I answered the phone to an angry man demanding, "What did you do to my sister?" "Aha, that's who sent the juju," I thought. "I didn't do anything to your sister. What did she do to me?" I asked. Louder, he replied, "You gave her a heart attack." Calmly, I explained to the man that I had only done a "reversal" when I sensed the hostile attack. Ignoring what I said, he yelled, "She's in the hospital; you gave her a heart attack," before hanging up on me. Stunned, I grabbed my journal to read what I recorded after the reversal, and then I saw it. "7 x 70 times." SHIT! Whenever I performed a reversal, I "returned to sender," 7x the power sent to me. I felt terrible for a minute, but then I remembered the power and intention of energy she sent my way. Unfortunately, the zinger she sent was full of bad luck, illness, and arguments. So, when I returned it to her multiplied, she had a heart attack. I never heard from either her or her brother again.

Lesson: Don't cast spells or send energy balls full of negativity toward someone. If you do, remember the rule of magic, what you send out comes back to you multiplied.

My Lesson: Don't perform reversals or send out energy intentionally when you're angry. Calm down and pay attention to your words. If you can't calm down, do a protection ritual and perform a reversal later.

22

IN COMES DAD, OUT GOES HUBBY

My father overcame and recovered from throat cancer, retired, and moved into our second master bedroom from Washington. Within weeks of Dad moving into the house, my marriage abruptly. Coincidently, Stan's Permanent Residency Card was approved just a week earlier. One of my biggest fears was manifested; I was now a single Mom of two girls with two different Dads. Thankfully, I wasn't alone. New Mexico made it easy to file a non-contested divorce. I prepared all the paperwork and filed it jointly with Stan. Within 24 hours of filing, the divorce was final. With my Dad in the house, things weren't complicated; it was easy. He was great at helping around the house and with projects. We each had our own space; the girls and I had our own family room downstairs, where the master suite and girls' bedrooms were located. Dad's master bedroom, my office, and guest bedroom, kitchen, and living room were upstairs, allowing a significant bit of space for us to cohabitate.

It took a long time for us all to find our groove. Dad had to deal with my style of parenting and keeping house. He also had to learn to trust and have faith in Divine providence. Born in the 40s, he never felt secure enough to be self-employed. He believed a steady income could only come from working for a company. My income was never guaranteed. From day to day, I didn't know how much money I would earn. It drove him crazy at first. After several months of watching how I manifested intentionally, he began to relax and trust me. We spent many hours in my office talking about beliefs, life, and God. For the first time in my life, I got to be myself with my Dad. Seventeen years living on that property bore many projects, lessons, and blessings. It was the longest I had lived anywhere, let alone on one property.

My office became the gathering place in the mornings when the family woke up. As I sat at my desk drinking coffee, Dad would sip his from the recliner. He shared many stories of his childhood during our morning talks. It turns out that Mary, Dad's mother, was a healer and clairvoyant. I learned how she healed people of twisted guts and other ailments using her hands, plants, and herbs. It took thirty some odd years to find out that my grandmother was a healer and psychic. She died within months of visiting us in California right after I was born. I felt so relieved to know that my spiritual gifts weren't just random; they were inherited. Knowledge of her gifts gave me peace and a feeling of connection. So, it was no surprise when she started materializing in visions and various places in the house.

One night, Bela, just four years old, came running into my office to say a woman walked right through the wall and the wood-burning stove downstairs. While she was a little scared, she didn't feel threatened. Bela said she was wearing a flowing dress and just walked in; I instantly knew that it was my grandmother. Bela's spiritual gifts were confirmed, and communication with my Grandmother began. She shared many things with me during her visits. I learned a lot from her about our family. She showed up a lot when my Dad and I were in disagreements. When we were fighting, she was adamant about being good to him and trying to understand him. She also appeared when something was going on in my extended family.

In 2009, while I was fighting a second bout of Leukemia naturally, Grandma kept coming around. Initially, I thought she was hanging out because of Dad. But I kept hearing her voice and sensing her energy around me. I mentioned to Dad that I was searching for natural remedies, and his Mom kept appearing. I kept seeing in my vision a handwritten recipe book that Grandma kept, full of her natural remedies. I asked Dad about it, and he didn't know who might have it. He remembers her making remedies for people but wasn't who might have it. Grandma assured me that there is a collection of her recipes and notes for healing. Many of Dad's 11 siblings have died. Theresa, one of his sister's might have had it, but it appeared to be long gone.

Dad and I were talking in my office a few days later when suddenly Grandma showed me a White Rosary and a prayer cloth. She said, "I want you to have these, pray with them, and you will heal." I told Dad what I heard. He remembered a Rosary, and the prayer cloth was something she wore on her head. We started making calls to Hawaii. After talking to my Uncle Alan and explaining what happened, he said he remembers a purple rosary but not a white one. His house had flooded, so the boxes containing the items were in storage. He assured me he would look. Within a couple of weeks, I received a package from Hawaii.

Inside was a picture of Grandma, two rosaries, and the prayer cloth. One of the rosaries was purple, Dad took that one, and I kept the white one with the prayer cloth. The white rosary looks just like it did in the vision, a perfect gift from the Spirit realm. I keep it next to my bed, and when I doubt my abilities, I look at both items and pray a prayer of thankfulness that here and on the other side, I have great Angels and Spirits watching out for me!

It took six months to put the Leukemia in remission. I do not doubt that God, my ancestors, Angels, and guides were by my side every step of the way. With so many stories to share, the Leukemia battles don't hold as much significance to me as the others. Let me share this; it seems that with every spiritual battle I fought, a severe illness seemed to run parallel.

After a series of intense spiritual battles involving a close friend, I woke up one morning in May of 2010 to extreme neck pain. I could barely turn my head, and the pain was overwhelming. I went to see the chiropractor but left disappointed that the pain had lessened. Monday, I was back in the chiropractor's office desperately wanting relief. After adjusting my neck, he referred me to the hospital to get an MRI. I drove 45 minutes to the hospital, worried about the cost. I didn't have health insurance and knew this wasn't going to be a cheap test. Angels comforted me on the drive, assuring me it would be affordable. I had no choice but to have faith that the money would be there to pay for it.

MRI machines are noisy, scary machines and not fun for a claustrophobe. As I laid there in the tube, I prayed an affirmative prayer stating, "I know I'm being taken care of." As the radiologist technician came to get me off the table, he had a look of grave concern. He spoke firmly, saying, "I'm not supposed to say anything about the results of your test, but you need to go immediately and get a neck collar. You can get them from Walmart. Put it on and be very careful with your neck. Don't get any chiropractic adjustments. Go home, lay flat and wait. I can't say anything more than that. Your doctor will call you with the results after the radiologist reviews them and writes his report".

Shocked and a little scared at the seriousness of his tone and words, I went straight to Walmart to get the neck collar. I called my chiropractor in the parking lot and told him what the technician said, asking if he would please follow up. "What the hell is going on," I thought, "All I did was go to sleep and wake up," I would have to wait until the following day.

Results of the MRI, a CD of the x rays, and radiologist report were waiting for me at the hospital. My chiropractor briefed me on the seriousness of my condition, referring me to a surgeon ASAP. I had severe disc degeneration, three herniated discs, and an osteophyte or bone spur in the shape of an arrow pushing into my spinal cord. It looked like someone had shot an arrow right into my spinal cord. The spiritual battles I fought for others over the years usually left me drained for weeks but never physically incapacitated.

It would take surgery to remove the osteophytes and address the herniated discs. There were no local spine surgeons with experience to address it. Frantic, I went into meditation and prayer, gaining peace of mind enough to look for a solution. Tons of research turned up everything from quacks to neck fusion and approximately $300,000 worth of surgery in the United States. Without insurance, most hospitals couldn't even quote the price for neck surgery. When asked, doctors and hospitals were at a loss on how to calculate self-pay. One doctor in San Francisco suggested I take a 2nd loan on my house to have him remove the herniated discs, allowing the bones to fuse naturally. CRAZINESS!

As usual, Spirit led me to a solution I hadn't even considered. I found a blog by a lawyer in the United States; he ventured to India to have disc replacement surgery. His neurosurgeon used to teach at Harvard but was now teaching in a hospital in Bangalore, India. I contacted the man and began exchanging emails. He gave me the contact number for a company that did medical tourism. Brazil, Germany, and India were doing the disc replacement surgery for ten years with excellent results, although it wasn't available in the United States. Disc Replacement was superior to fusion, as you maintain mobility and flexibility of the neck. Through a series of contacts with medical tourism advocates, I had a phone consult with the neurosurgeon my new friend used.

With the MRI uploaded to the web, the neurosurgeon, Dr. Rajakumar, read the radiologist's report and made his recommendation. Disc C6-7 was herniated and needing to be replaced, with suspicions of damage to disc C5-6. The osteophyte would need to be removed carefully to take the pressure off my spinal cord. It would cost $18,000 for the surgery, a month's stay in a private hospital room, and a week of physical therapy. Dr. Rajakumar instructed me not to lift anything heavy, quit smoking immediately, and get there as soon as possible. He explained the risks, the possibility of permanent loss of voice, even paralysis from the neck down. If I did nothing, I was sure to be paralyzed as the osteophyte posed an immediate danger to severing my spinal cord. The surgeon would enter through an incision on the front of my neck, clamping the blood vessels and vocal cords to the side during surgery. It sounded gruesome, painful, and frightening, but paralysis sounded worse, especially since I financially supported the family.

I prayed for Divine Providence, needing the money for the surgery, a passport, and a plane ticket. Blessed to have been able to pay all the household bills without Dad's help for six years, I needed his financial assistance now. Without hesitation, he dipped into his retirement savings to help. I felt so much guilt, but there was no choice. If I didn't have the surgery, I would become a burden, we would lose the house, and everyone, including my Dad, would be homeless. I worked, paid the bills, and took care of myself and everyone else throughout all prior illnesses. This time, I would have to learn how to receive help from others, a more significant issue for me than I ever realized. So, I took the loan from Dad, and we started a fundraiser to help. I'd be lying if I didn't admit I was scared, SHITLESS!

Reviewing the risks of the 3-Level Disc replacement was intense. I would be the first 3-level replacement. It was common to do 1- or 2-disc replacements, but they hadn't done three yet. With intense pain, headaches, and the inability to walk without falling, the risks were well worth it.

In a great deal of pain every day, I found a way to be grateful for the surgery, though. I was depressed for a few days thinking I could end up paralyzed. Working with the medical tourism company based in the U.S., the arrangements were made to travel to India. The process was so overwhelming and a bit discouraging at times. To make matters more stressful, an Air India flight crashed in Mangalore, killing over 150 passengers. I was sad for the passengers and their families, sent prayers out before addressing my fears. I prayed, asking God to let me dream, to give me clarity about the trip. I wondered if maybe I should worry. I woke up with a feeling that everything would be ok. I watched several video testimonials of patients from the US that went to India for the same surgery, using the same Doctor. It helped to put my mind at ease as I committed to making the trip.

While waiting to leave for India, I saw Onye, a healer friend from California. Onye did a drumming circle in Durango, and it was a Divine night. Although I couldn't dance with the drumming, I did get to stand with the group and pray for others. Onye pulled me into the circle for prayer. Suddenly the pain from the pinched nerves eased up considerably. My tailbone pain which had been flared up since the whole ordeal started, was relieved as well.

I made it thru the night on Advil instead of painkillers. The painkillers were killing my memory, not to mention my stomach and liver. I was trying to save them for the long flight to India and only use them when I absolutely couldn't stand it without them. (I would make a horrible drug addict, lol) Prayers were relentless to keep my neck stable enough in the collar, so I didn't need painkillers. I had just gotten my liver working on its own six months before. I didn't want to give it a reason to shut down again. An IUD with hormones caused that liver issue. Once the IUD was removed, my liver was restored.

My poor Dad was just as stressed as me; although stoic as he is, he tried to hide it. Brindi was pretty stressed too. I've never been away from my girls that long. Three weeks out of the country seemed like an eternity. Bela had her 2nd-grade graduation field day amid all of this. I felt so bad that I was out of it and unable to give her attention before departing. Arrangements were made for her to split time with her best friend camping and her Dad while I was gone.

Brindi was due to receive an award at her high school graduation ceremony. I wanted to be focused on her, but even that was challenging. The day after her graduation, I was scheduled to leave. Unfortunately, the company I used for my emergency visa and passport screwed something up, missing the delivery date. On the phone with the passport company, I missed her speech. Thankfully I got to see the recorded replay.

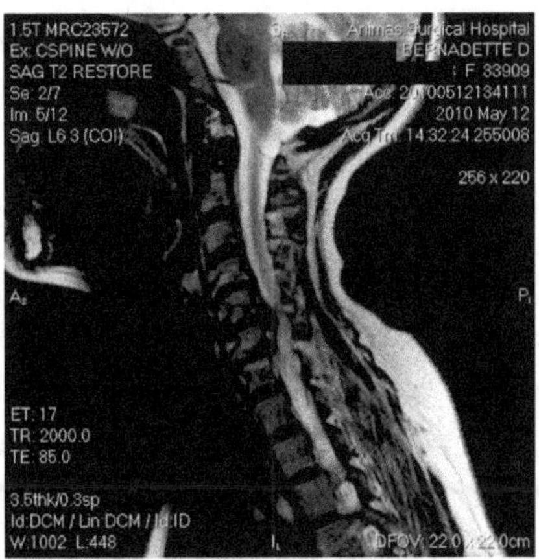

My pain primarily centered in my neck, shoulders, and arms increased, radiating down my legs. I tripped more than a few times, walking slowly, caused by sudden weakness. The headaches became debilitating, and I was getting worried. The Doctors told me any new symptoms were a cause for concern; there was nothing I could do but pray.

Thursday, June 10, 2010, I arrived in India at 3 am after 30 long hours of travel. Thinking I would be taken to the hotel for five days waiting for surgery, you can imagine my surprise when I was informed that I was going directly to the hospital for surgery. Dr. Rajakumar's schedule changed while I was traveling, and I arrived just in time for surgery. Before 8 am, Pre-Op X-rays, MRI, CT Scan, and blood work were completed. Then I briefly met Dr. Rajakumar in person before being wheeled to the operating room. I had surgery at 8:30 am and was in ICU around 4:30 pm. Dr. Rajakumar said I might be a little taller because my bones are so small, and the discs are larger than my normal-sized discs. All three discs went in, and I did not get fusion, so I was happy.

I woke up sometime late afternoon June 11th, in the ICU in massive pain. As soon as the staff knew I was awake, I complained of a burning in my throat and pain radiating across my neck and shoulders. I heard a man telling me the surgery went well, and I had three new discs. Disoriented and barely conscious, I asked for water. Once I became oriented, I could NOT believe the amount of pain I was in. Taking in my environment, I was a little scared. The ICU reminded me of the operating rooms in the TV show Mash. Unfortunately, it wasn't anything like ICU in the United States. They gave me sips of water and ordered some hot tea to ease my throat. As the day continued, the pain persisted, and I could barely move. I went to sleep in the operating room with a single IV and woke up with at least four more. I begged for pain meds but was told that I already received the limit. Sleep would evade me for the next 12 hours. Finally, I asked for something to help me sleep around 2 am. I'm not sure what time I finally got to sleep, but it only lasted a few hours.

By 11 am the following morning, they took out my catheter and escorted me to the bathroom. Once able to walk and take care of "business," I was transferred back to my room. That afternoon, Dr. Rajakumar visited before departing for his conference, reviewing the surgery and explaining that my bones were unusually small. Therefore, they had to use an extra drill bit to make extra space for the discs to fit, stretching the length of the surgery. That night Dr. Ankit, one of the residents, checked in on me and explained the pain med difference from the US to India. He said that I was on 650 mg Dola, which is equivalent to Tylenol. Holy Hell! No wonder the pain was so bad. In the US, you get morphine after major surgery. I was instructed to walk to speed up the healing and recovery time. Again, not something hospitals in the states recommend.

Thankfully I didn't lose my voice, but my throat felt like it had something big stuck in it, and I couldn't clear it. When I woke up from surgery, my mouth and throat were dry and burning. The mouth sore caused by the breathing tube wasn't fun either. My throat had a lovely 3-inch incision running top to bottom. Both sides of the front of my neck were hard and swollen. Most of my pain was located in the back of my neck, where the new discs were implanted, and in my shoulders. The strange leg and foot pain was gone.

I started having a cough a few days after the surgery. I thought it was just an innocent little cough from the throat healing. Or maybe from my trachea being pushed to the side during surgery. In any case, the cough made me feel like I had a Lego lodged in my throat. Swallowing was an ordeal since the surgery, informed later that it was caused by the clamp that held everything as they replaced the discs. Well, that little cough created quite a problem because the neck muscles and tissues had not yet healed. The tightness, soreness, and swollen parts of my neck were highly reactive.

To make matters worse, it felt like my head was exploding with each cough. Do you remember the movie "Scanners," the part where the guy's head explodes? Well, that's what I imagine it would feel like to him. It was bad! Determined to heal quickly, I walked every day. The staff all said I was doing great and healing ahead of schedule. I would be discharged as soon as Dr. Rajakumar returned from his medical conference. Dad was due to arrive right before the new discharge date. Unfortunately, our flight to return home wasn't for a couple of weeks.

When the coughing started, I told the nurse and doctor. They both felt my head (not a good indicator) and said, "no fever, you feel fine." I was on antibiotics to prevent infection, but they don't use therMometers to take your temperature. "They don't take your temp here, weird?" I thought. They also have no idea what a heating pad is. So, I made a homemade one from a towel I brought from home, boiled water and slipped the towel into a Ziplock freezer bag, put another towel over it to protect my skin, and VOILA - heating pad. It helped a little.

I had only been eating porridge while in the hospital; I didn't like the food at all. I don't even know what porridge is. I couldn't wait for my Dad to arrive. He slipped some summer sausage and Laughing Cow cheese in his suitcase for me. I don't know if that was allowed since cows are sacred, but I was looking forward to eating it. You can't imagine how much I wanted a home-cooked meal, a cup of home-brewed Chai Tea, my shower, tub, my bed, my pillow, the list goes on... Seriously, just trusting the water was a big deal. I even missed being woken up five times a night by Tank (my active bladder Labrador) and his cohort Moto (Tank's best friend, our rescued cat). At least I was in my room, and the door was only five feet away. I even missed Prince Furby (Alpha Dog of the house - Cockapoo with a Napoleon Complex) fighting me for bed space. Most of all, I missed my girls, Bela and Brindi. I missed Bela telling me she's hungry every 30 minutes. I missed sitting down to eat something Bela says she doesn't want, only to have her decide I had to cook her something else while my meal got cold. I missed Brindi's phone calls telling me she wouldn't be home.

The whole adventure brought a greater appreciation of my life. Even though my move to the "Sticks of Colorado" had been an enormous adjustment, I was still in the process of accepting it ten years later; I was grateful for it. I still missed living in San Diego, missed the beach, the weather, and my friends. Colorado is rugged living all the way around unless you ski, like drinking and doing recreational drugs (i.e., meth), or a cowboy raising cows. But being in India, I realized just how much I have. The air is so clean back home! The skies are blue. I had land to grow my own food.

I was hoping for early discharge, dreaming of good food, and anticipating Dad's arrival. I wish he had escorted me through the entire trip; I would not recommend going out of the country for surgery alone. However, I opted to go alone to save money and spare other people the inconvenience of watching our animals and kids. I woke up in the ICU wishing I knew someone. It would have been much easier if my Dad was with me, especially in the middle of the night when I couldn't sleep because my pain was that bad.

Once discharged, we changed hotels and moved from Bangalore to the rural countryside in Mysore. Upon our arrival, I was very sore, had muscle aches, and overall felt horrible. That night I came down with a fever. We were staying at a beautiful palace called Brindavin Gardens. We went for a walk in the garden, following the advice of the Doctors to walk daily. Before even reaching the front of the hotel, I was in terrible shape. My stomach began cramping, and I suddenly had the urge to use the restroom. Unfortunately, I didn't make it to the bathroom on time, not the prettiest picture. Within an hour, I couldn't sit up. The muscles in my shoulders felt better, but my stomach was a MESS!

Struggling on the floor in the bathroom with a temperature of 103 to 104 for four days, concerned, Dad called the hotel front desk for a doctor. The local Shanti doctor confirmed a diagnosis of Dysentery. He prescribed five medications: One for the stomach cramps, an anti-diarrhea pill, an anti-parasite drug, medicine for good bacteria, and finally, one for Electrolytes. Finally, the doctor offered me an injection for stomach cramps and pain. I opted to wait for pills.

The Shanti Doctor came back in the morning to make sure the meds were working and give me a final fit to fly. I hadn't eaten in three days. It seemed to run straight through me, no matter what I would drink, double what I took in. At that point, I was pretty worn out and had broken down more than once. My poor Dad had to witness all of this. He felt helpless. He wanted to get me home, and we both felt trapped. I've heard it said that you either love India or you hate it. I do not love it!

Recalling all the strange events that led to surgery and even the time spent on the bathroom floor in Mysore, I felt like there was more to clean up in the spiritual realms. The bathroom walls at the hotel were open to the outside air at the top. The entire time I lay on the bathroom floor of the hotel room, unable to walk to the bed, crows stood above me in the bathroom window. Crows are messengers, but sometimes the message predicts death. Dad kept chasing them away but as soon as he left the bathroom, they returned. He was visibly scared of the ominous sign as the message felt like a warning. Strangely, as soon as the Shanti doctor arrived to treat me, the crows left and didn't return.

Before leaving for surgery, I shared some private information regarding my condition and trip to India with a fellow psychic. She was very supportive before and after surgery. She offered to do a custom essential oil formula for me. We had discussed the unique blends she was mixing for clients and how powerful they were. I was excited to see what Spirit wanted for me. Late in September, I received the email reading detailing the formula, mixing it, buying the oils from a reputable company, and the reason each oil was selected. I immediately went online to purchase my oils.

"Guardians of The Gate" was the name she gave my oil formula. She wrote, "Your formulation refers not only to those who guard you but to you as the guardian, all working towards the same purpose." This custom oil formula was for protection and healing. Both of which I needed, although at the time I received it, I wasn't aware of just how much.

Two days before the oils arrived, I found out that the friend I tried to "save" from involvement with dark arts was moving in across the street. It was during the attempts to reason with her that my neck was injured. The newly placed mobile home took up the view from my office window. Having to see her come and go rocked me. I felt she posed a threat on many levels, both spiritually and physically. With that shocking news, I called the psychic and told her how accurate her reading was and how much I needed that oil blend. (It's always nice as a Psychic to get validation.) I was determined to enlist the aid of Spirit, the oils, and prayer to get my new neighbor to relocate.

When my essential oils arrived, I happily mixed the formula and applied some to my hands. I closed my eyes and inhaled the sweet aroma, instantly feeling a tingling from head to toe. I felt what I could only describe as light, around me and through me. My mind was clear, and my body felt invigorated. Next, I placed crosses in oil on every window and over every door of my home, praying for protection. Then, I went online and bought four pounds of black tourmaline, spreading it around my house and property for further protection. After applying the essential oils to my windows, doors, and various parts of my home, I felt peaceful, calming energy.

Moving day for my old friend came on October 1st. I didn't have the usual sinking feeling when I watched from my office window as she unpacked her belongings. Instead, I felt at peace and kept applying my oils to my hands, slowly inhaling their beautiful, sweet aroma. To my utter amazement, my old friend moved within five days of moving in. By day six, she was gone and out of my life for good! Within a few months, the mobile home was removed from my neighbor's lot as if it had never been there.

Five, the magical number of change and transformation seemed to always warn me before ushering in significant changes. Five months of physical and spiritual battles had finally concluded, my faith tested to the max. Miracles, solutions, and guidance always seemed to arrive at the perfect time. For many years I questioned the extreme events and experiences of my life. Finally, I accepted that for each thing I have overcome, there is someone out there I can encourage, knowing I have triumphed over similar issues. So many people are fascinated with psychic gifts without understanding the importance and sometimes the burden of our experience. I've dedicated my life to being of service to God. Many times, amid trials, I wondered if God was punishing me. Once the tests were over, I accepted the growth of faith, courage, in awe of the mysteries surrounding us. We have to be open to receiving guidance and answers in ways we aren't even aware of. We're called to surrender, knowing the infinite intelligence called God is REAL and available when we believe.

23

I CHOOSE TO LIVE

Superbowl Sunday (damn if that day wasn't significant in my life), February 2, 2014, after finishing chores around the house and taking care of our goats, I ventured to town to get groceries. I was going to take my granddaughter Addie for a ride to Durango, 45 minutes away. At the last minute, Brindi told me to leave her home. After a sleepless night, I figured I could run to get groceries in a mostly empty store since everyone would be home watching the football game. Happily, I journeyed to town to fulfill my shopping list and to talk to Spirit.

When I drive alone, I tend to use that time to talk to Spirit. It's a great time to listen and channel information for myself or enjoy communication with my guides. Just a few minutes into my trip, a download of information about "vulnerability" came through. I was enjoying the information flooding my mind about that topic. Information was being exchanged rapidly; answers to questions I asked were received simultaneously when suddenly a strange vision took over the windshield of my car.

While I could see the road, I was mesmerized watching this holographic vision play out. I was driving in my car, wearing the exact same sweater. My car was on the same highway but farther ahead from where I was currently traveling. Suddenly I watched in horror as my hands went up in front of my face, and all I could see were shards of flying glass. Next, the scene changed, and I watched as my lifeless body lay in a hospital bed with a bunch of tubes and machines hooked up. I see and hear the doctor explaining to my Dad that they needed to "pull the plug" on the life support machines. The doctor explained further that I was brain dead, and even if I somehow gained consciousness, there was so much brain damage, there was no point.

As the vision continued, I watched the life of my oldest daughter Brindi play out in quick succession. Her life went to shit, and she committed suicide. I didn't know what happened to my granddaughter. My Dad in the hospital room came back into view as he listened to the doctor, crumbling into a thousand pieces. Bela was there, but she was quiet, stoic. As I watched the vision play out, thoughts began running through my mind. "What a crazy thought. Do I need to buy life insurance or something?" Seeing the effect on my family, I thought, "money isn't going to take care of this." Quickly calculating the payoff on my mortgage, I knew that money wouldn't solve the problem, even with a life insurance payout, especially with large hospital bills and funeral expenses.

Just as the vision was fading, I said out loud, "I can't go yet; my kids need me, my Dad needs me. I get it. I have to stay. What a stupid, random, suicidal thought," thinking this was just a random thought. I was slightly annoyed by the intrusion of the vision since it interrupted my conversation with Spirit about vulnerability. Wrapped up in the strangeness of the hologram, I slowed down from 65mph to about 60mph on the two-lane rural highway. The vision was so real that it put me in a split consciousness. It was as if time stopped while it was happening.

Within mere seconds, heading west, I noticed a white Toyota 4Runner pointed eastbound, stopped in the emergency lane. The tires of the car were slightly over the line, with the wheels cranked left into traffic. I glanced over at the parked car. As I passed, I watched in horror from my drivers' side mirror a big blue Dodge truck traveling 65-70 mph hit the parked 4Runner, bounce into my lane, inches from my rear bumper. The airbags of the Dodge deployed as he continued into oncoming traffic.

Thankfully there were no cars behind me or in front of me for miles. Then, realizing he drifted into the other lane, the driver of the Dodge cranked his steering wheel hard to the right, into a ditch. His truck hit the ditch and rolled three times before coming to a stop in the pasture beside the road. I immediately pulled over and called 911. Shaken, I knew that if I hadn't had the vision that caused me to slow down, he would have bounced off the white 4Runner and hit me head-on. I told the 911 operator that a white 4Runner was in the middle of the road, but the passengers were okay, running to aid the Dodge. Still on the line with the 911 operator, "It could have been me." Fifty feet ahead of the impact zone, I backed up to check on the victims and report their status. The Dodge was lying on its roof, smoke billowing out from the engine. Unable to walk, I stayed on the side of the road in my car, 20 feet ahead of the 4Runner.

Waiting on the phone with the 911 operator for the police to arrive, I worked on calming down. As soon as the police showed up, I called my Dad. He offered to come to get me, realizing how upset I was. I refused. In shock, a part of me thought I was dead, that the vision was real. It was so confusing because the Dodge didn't even slow down when it impacted the 4Runner. There were no skid marks until he had hit the front of the 4Runner. One of the drivers just ahead of the Dodge slowed down because he saw the 4Runner, saying he could tell it was about a foot into the lane, positioned to make a U-turn on the blind hill. Just as I passed the 4Runner, it pulled farther into traffic when the Dodge hit its front end.

When the police arrived, still shaken, I started babbling about the vision. I'm sure the officer thought I was crazy, failing to mention I'm a psychic. I was telling him how I saw it in a vision and slowed down, avoiding the accident. He was pleasant and asked if I needed to sit down as I gave him my report. I just wanted to leave, get my groceries, and go home. The officer told me how lucky I was that I was driving seconds slower. He said that the Dodge would have impacted my vehicle head-on, and I would be dead at that rate of speed. After being released by the officer, I slowly drove to town.

Walking through the grocery store, it felt like people were giving me strange looks. Maybe it was because I had the look of shock or my tear-stained eyes. I was crying on the way to town because of the enormity of what had just happened. But, realizing that the words I spoke and my choice to stay as I watched the vision play out saved my life. The weight of what I witnessed hit me like a ton of bricks. The Universe gave me a choice, and once I chose to live, I avoided the collision.

My mind was reeling, with the knowledge that I could have been in that hospital bed, Dad having to let me go and unplug life support. Aware of my Do Not Resuscitate instructions, he would have to agree with the doctors. It took a lot of time to process how many lives would have been ruined by my death, something I didn't want to consider.

Passing the tow truck that held the Dodge on my way home from the store was equally shocking. The truck was mangled; I could only imagine what my car would have looked like had I not slowed down and missed the accident. I was grateful my Dad and kids didn't have to know or experience that. Knowing alternate realities exist in other dimensions, I also thought about the possibility that I was hit in a different reality or plane of existence. It was hard to consider that some version of me was in a hospital bed, the family dealing with the loss. Playing that possibility out in my head, I imagined the other versions of my family as stronger and able to handle it.

Clearly, I had a choice to live or die that day, and I chose to live. There are moments where we experience intersection points in life. I've read Richard Bach's books that talked about those points. This incident, I have no doubt, was an intersection point. I recognized that a part of me didn't want to be alive, but something deep within me shifted due to the accident. I had just gone through a breakup the week before, so I was filled with varied emotions while I processed the event. When the vision first ended, I questioned myself thinking, "What are you suicidal? That's crazy." Quickly those thoughts were put to rest as the accident unfolded, and I realized it was a premonition. Seeing the wreckage to my family, I knew I hadn't fulfilled my purpose.

Looking back to the neck surgery in India, I could see it was one of those intersection points. We had to choose to spend the money and get the surgery in a 3rd world country or face paralysis. If that had occurred, I would have had no quality of life and would be a burden to my family. Even in India, I prayed to live, lying on the bathroom floor with dysentery for five days, not wanting to go out on a bathroom floor in India.

I walked around in a daze throughout that day, receiving understanding and insights about my life. My life hasn't been, and probably never would be, normal. Accepting a higher purpose for my life, knowing it wasn't about pure personal pleasure. It was about holding sacred space and creating an intentional, vibrational reality for whoever walked into my life, lover, client, friend, or family. No matter the role I play with others, my life as a healer, a psychic, or a Mom is about taking care of and loving other people. It isn't about pleasure; in reality, my life hasn't been a very pleasurable ride. Don't get me wrong, I've had the honor of sacred communication in Spirit, but my human life was challenging. I wasn't born into a life of love, joy, and satisfaction on a base level. Instead, it's been a rollercoaster ride. But, like all rides, there have been highs and lows.

Sitting with all of this, I finally hit a place of peace, accepting that it doesn't matter whether I get to be "in love," have enormous wealth, fame, or not; I CHOSE to stay, and what matters most is that the people that I have soul agreements with, will be okay. I am not ready for my family to crumble, so I stay. I don't mean from an egoic place but from a "knowing" that there are things I energetically hold together at this time for family, clients, and friends. After this event, I felt great joy. Telling my family about the event was impactful for them too. Brindi couldn't handle listening to it, and Dad just kept saying, "You can't go anywhere; we need you here." I shared the whole event on Hidden Wisdom Radio, my old BlogTalkRadio show, four days later. That episode felt surreal, knowing I could have been gone. This incident would help me through the enormous challenge of facing colon cancer just a year later.

24

MIRACLE IN THE DESERT

In 2015, after eight years of ignoring a growing mass in my intestines, I was faced with the biggest cancer challenge of my life. A tumor the size of a softball that started as Endometriosis tissue breached my abdominal wall, turning to colon cancer. Surgery was not an option, and I wasn't unwilling to risk chemotherapy or radiation treatment, certain I wouldn't survive it.

My health was beginning to fail on many levels. My family practitioner was agreeable to holistic treatments, making it easier to cope with the challenges of avoiding doctors. However, when my weight dropped, she became concerned with the mass in my lower intestines, mainly because it was now protruding. Surgery to remove the mass wasn't an option; the only treatment offered was chemo or radiation. If I were going to get rid of this tumor, I would have to do it quickly and naturally.

Eating became both difficult and painful, leaving my energy levels deficient. However, I was stubbornly acting as if everything was fine. It wasn't until I was unable to eliminate my bowels without the assistance of an enema that I finally sought treatment. Treating Leukemia wasn't as hard; I knew the supplements, herbs, the diet, and the protocol to treat myself. Unfortunately, treating this tumor was different, more painful, and way scarier, but I was out of options.

First, I would need to tell my kids about the secret I'd been keeping. I booked a week in San Diego at a beach house at the beginning of March. Then, I arranged to have Grant, his girlfriend, his sister, and my best friend meet us for an epic party weekend. Brindi, her husband, and my granddaughter met us there. While I didn't disclose the reason for our vacation that weekend, I wanted to create great memories for everyone; just in case things didn't pan out the way I planned with my treatment.

San Diego was both fun and stressful. My energy was low already; needless drama caused by drinking and individual agendas made the trip rough. It was great to laugh and hang with my crew after so many years away, but my emotions were boiling. My boyfriend Ned tagged along, being the only one that knew what I was hiding. I wasn't aware that Ned had his own agenda, only coming along to visit his friend who lived there and surf. He spent most of the trip uninterested in anything but himself. I paid for the house rental and expected he would be thoughtful of my intention for the trip, wanting to spend time with me.

Before leaving for vacation, unhappy with the room he was renting, Ned manipulated a move into my house, and things began to change after that. I found out later that Ned secretly talked to my son-in-law, pushing my daughter's family out of the house. Ned began to assert control over everything; it started on our way home from San Diego. From the passenger seat, Ned started a fight. Exhausted from cancer and driving the 10 hours home, crying, I struggled to keep the car on the road as he ranted about his displeasure that I needed to be left alone in the morning. Bela tried explaining that everyone knew that I took my time in the morning to remember my dreams and record any messages I received. Unphased, Ned wasn't happy about that, nor did he care what I needed. My desire to wake up slowly, in a sacred, intentional way, interfered with his demands of sex in the morning. We weren't even halfway home, but I wished the drive was over as he continued criticizing me and his all-expenses-paid vacation.

Once home, I began Colon Hydrotherapy treatments with Ozone, restricting my diet to almost nothing. I took countless supplements and layering Medical Marijuana patches and edibles with high doses of CBD and CBN. Several weeks passed, but the tumor wasn't shrinkings; Ned was concerned. He called a friend in Arizona that is a Native American Medicine Man. Ned asked for his help. Miraculously, his friend agreed to meet me to see if he could do anything.

I completely respect the Native American traditions, beliefs, and ways, being similar to that of my ancestors. Being open to herbs, ceremonies, and even attending Native American Church meetings was not a stretch for me. My biggest concern was that somehow, they wouldn't accept me into their ways. I was wrong! They not only accepted me but also welcomed me into their family and their tipi. They did so much to help me.

We drove all over Arizona and even Northern California to attend Native American Church (NAC) meetings for months. Taking the medicine weekly and praying all night for others was such a blessing. I was also taking some Native herbs I received from the family in Arizona. The combination of everything I was doing was making a difference, but I needed to host my own NAC healing meeting. Arrangements were made to hold a NAC ceremony in Arizona in August 2015. There were many preparations to make it happen; unfortunately, even as I was preparing for the ceremony, things with Ned deteriorated even more. In June, I wrote Ned this email after constant arguments that had him moving in and out of my house:

I have written a short list of the complaints and things you have regarding my life, my home, and what you have attempted to change or want me to change.

1. *How I handle my business.*
2. *How I handle my family relationships.*
3. *How I handle my clients.*
4. *How the chickens are taken care of.*
5. *Having the chickens.*
6. *Having the dogs.*
7. *Having Moto.*
8. *How the yard is taken care of*
9. *How the kitchen is handled.*
10. *How we eat, what we eat.*
11. *How the garden is watered.*
12. *What is planted in the garden.*
13. *Having the garden.*
14. *How and what I think.*
15. *How and what I feel.*
16. *Not humble enough.*
17. *Don't exercise enough.*

18. *Don't have sex enough.*
19. *Work too hard.*
20. *Don't rest enough.*
21. *My resistance.*
22. *The way I listen.*
23. *The way I talk.*
24. *How I communicate.*
25. *How I take care of things.*
26. *My independence.*
27. *My codependence.*
28. *The electric fence is wrong.*
29. *Taking the lawn mower key out is wrong.*
30. *I'm not self-responsible.*
31. *Ego*
32. *I apologize like a child*
33. *Don't wake up the way you like*
34. *Grumble*
35. *My emotions and emotional energy is too intense for you*
36. *My abandonment issues, fears, past hurt that has caused me to be cautious or guarded.*
37. *Vulnerability*

I need to be free to be me, not to be constantly criticized, monitored, and controlled. I don't think you hear that. In order for me to heal the rest of this, I am getting messages clearly that says I need to re-empower myself and feel good about my life, my body, me, period. That you can't see how destructive these things have been to our relationship or me is worrisome. I, too, want to move forward, but we can't move forward until we resolve the past and change what is happening, and has happened, and continues to happen. The list is all over the place because you have literally found fault all over the place with me and my life. It has to stop. You talk about the power of words, and these are words you've spoken. What power do you think they have? Of course, it's all me again, my trust issues? OMG, you betrayed my trust, and of course, that's my fault too? Until you can see these as patterns in your life, it won't and can't change.

I want to be well; I want to get this cancer done, out, over. I will stand up for myself. I liked my life before you came. I like my property, my business, my income, my family, myself. I have never stopped working on myself since I was an adult. I am putting up boundaries, limits of how I am treated. I know you love me, but your issues have affected how that love is expressed, and until you see that, we can't move forward together. As long as you constantly say it's me, my issues that create your criticism or control, there is nothing that can be done. I will go to counseling with you; you have the insurance. You have to set that up. Emotional healing is what has to happen now for the physical to heal. I am clearing everything I can, including this. I want respect for myself and my family. That is non-negotiable. It shouldn't even be a conversation. I have not demanded it; it has not happened. There was never an apology to my father for the night you left here screaming at him. You hid from him until he was leaving. In the meanwhile, you have continually tried to make everything be done your way. If it isn't, you complain, criticize and cut down. I've lived here for 15 years and tried lots of ways of getting stuff done in that time period with a lot more animals and people in this house. I've kept it running smoothly for years; bills paid, jobs done, kids fed, emotions soothed. You walk in and act as if everything is wrong. I can't take that anymore.

I did not, I repeat, walk into your life and try to change you, distrust you, question you. You did that to me. It is a fact. I paid the price in tears, repressed feelings, pain. It doesn't just go away because you say, "I'm sorry." As you said, that's a child's apology. You have to earn that trust back once you betray it, not just sweep it under the rug. It's been three weeks, dropped discussion, no more. I'm just supposed to get over it all. Meanwhile, handle everything alone because you aren't present when you are home if you are home.

I love you. I want a healthy, equal partnership, not one in which I fully submit to you, and there is no equal exchange. We have to both feel good about decisions, not just one of us. You are used to making all the decisions, no kids, no animals, no commitments. I am used to making decisions based on what is best for the entire family, not just me. You should think about that. I may not have had a committed partner for the last 23 years, but I have been committed to caring for others for that long, if not longer and held that commitment. I have lived with others the entire time I've been on this property, too: husband, children, animals, friend, father, and boyfriend. I've juggled it all and kept it going, managing to create what I wanted in my life.

I'm not making blanket "always" statements, but these are things that can't keep happening. Actions have to be taken to repair past damage. You can't just pretend it didn't happen. I've suggested we schedule dialogues with Imago. That hasn't happened either. You agreed to it, saying we need to work thru the stuff but then complained to me yesterday you've spent so much time on this relationship. Well, so have I, and I don't complain to you about the energy it takes.

If you want to let it all go, that is fine. If you want to work on it and improve it, then we need a solid plan and commitment to get that work done. It does take time, energy, and consistent effort. You stated you needed a lot of alone time yesterday. My immediate feeling and reaction were fine; take it, be alone. I confess that was a reaction and defense, but at the same time, what else am I supposed to feel? You have lived most of your life outside of committed relationships, not in them. You need a lot of alone time, and perhaps you are happier alone.

I wish I could say the email improved things; it didn't. I received a scathing email in return, but Ned wouldn't leave. He just got better at manipulating me. By July, my Dad moved to California to live with my brother. He couldn't deal with Ned anymore. Ned had no respect for my Dad, doing anything and everything he could to drive a wedge between us. Weak and confused, I couldn't see what was happening clearly. Finally, I yelled at both of them to stop fighting.

In the end, Dad left, unable to stay, knowing Ned wasn't going to take care of things around the property, so I was so upset when he moved, knowing I was left with double the work. It felt like no one understood or cared that I was sick. It was the opportunity Ned needed to try to get me to sell the property. He tried to convince me we could find another property to buy together. In truth, he wanted me to sell the house and put his name on a new property. Thankfully, I was too weak and sick even to consider it. I eventually learned he had a way of doing things like that to benefit himself.

July was a difficult time for me. Dad was gone; I was driving myself to all my Ozone treatments while treating myself at home. I worked every day, taking calls and teaching my Charmed Life class weekly. I was exhausted from doing 3-4 enemas a day to detox my liver, lymph, and colon. I spent a lot of time hiding in my room, unable to climb the stairs to get to my office. Then, one day, the pain in my stomach was so bad I couldn't get off the bathroom floor. In tears, I prayed for help, questioning whether I was going to live through cancer.

I decided to write letters to my daughters just in case I didn't survive. I made a video for Brindi, including pictures of all the things we've done, accompanied by her song, "Sandcastle Dreams." I wasn't giving up, but I was no longer confident I would get through it. Between self-treatment and the emotional roller coaster I was on with Ned, I was drained on all levels.

August 8, 2015. After four days of cooking, we arrived in Arizona, ready for my NAC meeting, grateful my cousin Bernee and my daughter Bela attended. Even though I knew the meeting was focused on healing cancer, I had no idea how hard it would be. I can't divulge details of the ceremony, but I will share some of my experiences that night.

Sometime after midnight, one of the elders said something that completely shifted my consciousness. Whether a vision or dimensional shift, I suddenly found myself under the fire, the coals. I couldn't breathe. I believed I was dead. I remember telling Ned my heart wasn't beating and that I wasn't breathing. He didn't understand why I was saying that since my eyes were open and, to him, I looked fine. I was watching my funeral, watching as my casket lowered into the ground, thinking it was happening in real life, yet it was only a vision. I wanted to leave, asking him if we could go home. Then, he disappeared, the funeral disappeared, and I was in the center of the earth, connected to the roots of the medicine. The roots lit up, as did my body. As soon as my body began to glow, I knew I was going to live. Suddenly, my consciousness returned to the tipi as the meeting continued for several more hours.

Sitting there as the sun rose the following day, I was flooded with gratitude for every person in the tipi. I was grateful for every ancestor that aided in my healing. I thanked Creator and felt over-whelming peace, joy, appreciation. I thanked everyone for coming and for their prayers on a tough night as the meeting ended. I declared I was healed, knowing I was. When I felt my stomach, the lump was gone. Stumbling out of the tipi in the morning, I was grateful for a helping friend, Erik. He grabbed my arm and helped me walk around the tipi to complete the ceremony. Ned had gone ahead of me, unaware that I could barely walk. No one seemed to notice Ned's disregard except Erik, my cousin, and Bela, the blessing of healing outweighed everything else.

Thinking back on the beauty of the meeting, I understood the sacred rotation of everything reflecting the Sun, the moon, the earth. To me, the fire represents God's creative and destructive force, and the water represents the emotional, nurturing force. The sacred movement of the instruments symbolizes how we communicate with God, how our bodies move around on the planet, and how the earth revolves around the sun. The ceremony is done with conscious movement, thought, intention, and emotion, all in order, no chaos.

Within the tipi, all earthly problems are brought before the fire as an offering, a sacrifice, held by the community as you sit up all night, in prayer and communion with God. I witnessed the holi-ness of the feminine nurturing and life-giving energy represented by the woman bringing in the water that delivers sustenance and relief to the family around the fire or metaphorically around the world. The fire purifies, the water soothes and sustains. The smoke carries the prayers to the throne of the Creator. I viewed the orientation of the tipi as the womb; as the sun rises, it gives birth into the physical, heralding the divine entrance of life and creation into this reality and dimension.

During the midnight hours, anything blocking you from connecting to the Creator is purified. It's the most challenging part of the meeting, feeling tired, worked over by the heat of the fire, as you become aware of every fear, ego concern, or worry. You feel like quitting, just like life. The hardest part is when the fire is testing you, but when the 2 am window is reached, things begin to lighten, burdens begin to lift, and gratitude replaces suffering.

I will forever be grateful for the sacred fire and the beautiful Native American family that embraced me. There are no words to describe the wisdom of indigenous ways. It is pure experience, connection, and honor for all beings. The ego must be laid down, and the heart opened in a humble way to receive the blessing from our loving Creator.

Returning home, I had to continue Ozone therapy and treatment for a couple more months. The mass was gone, but liver functions hadn't fully returned. After the meeting, I began to experience severe depression. Depression wasn't something I had dealt with in many years, but suddenly I was crying, losing my mind, and feeling very confused. Ned was blaming me for anything and everything. Finally, Ned decided I needed help understanding the changes I had to make for him to be happy. So, I agreed to see a counselor with him, one who specialized in Cancer grief. Little did I know this counselor would change my life and, in many ways, save it.

Our first intake session with Dwayne was to provide context and history. I chose him because he had experience with narrative therapy, which Ned studied to get his degree in social work. Ned also interviewed Dwayne before confirming the appointment, explaining I was sick and how the sickness impacted our relationship. The session began with Ned telling Dwayne all the things about me causing the issues. First, he didn't want me spending so much time with my granddaughter and didn't like that I could not meet all his "needs." Before ending the session, Dwayne asked Ned how my sickness factored into our relationship and my inability to meet his demands. Ned brushed over the question as if I had a cold. I couldn't believe what I heard as silent tears fell down my cheeks.

Dwayne asked me how I felt about it. Speaking quietly, I said, "I have been battling colon cancer; I don't understand what more I can do." Dwayne looked shocked but remained quiet. Our session ended with the agreement to schedule another session. Thankfully, Ned and I took separate cars, so he could go straight to work after the appointment. As I drove home, the floodgates opened, and I couldn't stop crying. Praying, I heard Spirit whisper, "Call Dwayne and speak to him privately." I dialed Dwayne's number and asked if he could counsel me over the phone in private sessions. I explained Ned couldn't know about it but that I needed some help. He agreed to keep our sessions confidential and quickly scheduled a session.

Journal Entry 9/4/15

Feeling sad for two weeks. Counseling yesterday brought up a lot. I've been able to suppress my emotions for several months, but they want to come out. I think because I was so ill and full of pain, I didn't want to break.

Realizing when Dwayne asked how the "illness" played into this and having it glossed over really shook me up. Truly Ned has left several times, withdrawn his love, placing more and more demands on me throughout this ordeal. Now I know he'd instantly say I do not appre-

ciate what he has done or how much he has "taken on." The reality, though, is not much. Yeah, a family, but that is a given. If he didn't like it, he could have opted out. Dad is gone, and I've had to take on a ton because of it.

How do I feel?

Sad, grieving, alone. My Dad left in the midst of my battle with cancer, on my word that Ned would help. He has done only what he wants. Sadly, he had NO clue I was not expressing myself. He says I don't listen or care, but that is a projection, not true. He's been given a lot and appreciates or acknowledges very little.

Yes, all things that created the cancer are all things that want a voice. So, I write. My appointment with Dwayne is Wednesday. Ned did the tit for tat when I told him I'd be seeing him alone. I figured I better tell him because if he found out, he would be furious. Of course, he started saying he wanted to meet with Dwayne alone, too, since I couldn't handle his emotions.

So many weapons were used to hurt me. Why? It hurts that my sickness hurt me. It hurts that Brindi avoided me. It hurts that people are so selfish they can only see what they need and not what someone in need of support and love needs. I fought for God, for my family, and for him. Do they care? Does it matter to anyone?

My heart is aching, and it feels like it's being squeezed. Ned said he wants and needs "agreeable communication." What he means is that I listen, agree, and support him and that everything he says is right.

Dwayne said, "actions are an important part of relationships, not just language," in response to Ned praising his own use of language. I feel put down like a child. Ned said I couldn't communicate. It's wrong, hurtful, insulting, and attacking.

I've allowed his projections and attacks throughout my whole cancer battle, but they've grown. They have started gaining momentum. He is always right, must always be right even when he's wrong.

I'm tired. I'm sad. I release all this pain tied to the unfairness of it all and am tired of Ned adding to the weight of it rather than being loving and supportive. He thinks and says he "knows what's best" for everyone but especially me. He's full of shit!

That first private session with Dwayne was an eye-opener. He confided in me that he had no idea I had cancer. Ned had only mentioned I had an illness. As our session continued, he told me to research "Narcissistic Personality Disorder" and that we would talk about it in our next private session.

Researching "Narcissistic Personality Disorder" explained more than just my relationship with Ned. It identified and defined the relationship I had with my mother. Keeping my research secret, I began to understand I was in a cycle of Narcissistic abuse from Ned.

Narcissistic Personality Disorder (NPD) - The DSM Criteria

Narcissistic Personality Disorder (NPD) is listed in the American Psychiatric Association's Diagnostic & Statistical Manual (DSM) as an Axis II, Cluster B (dramatic, emotional, or erratic) Disorder:

A pervasive pattern of grandiosity (in fantasy or behavior), need for admiration, and lack of empathy, beginning by early adulthood and present in a variety of contexts, as indicated by five (or more) of the following:

1. has a grandiose sense of self-importance (e.g., exaggerates achievements and talents, expects to be

    recognized as superior without commensurate achievements)

2. is preoccupied with fantasies of unlimited success, power, brilliance, beauty, or ideal love
3. believes that he or she is "special" and unique and can only be understood by, or should associate with, other special or high-status people (or institutions)
4. requires excessive admiration
5. has a sense of entitlement, i.e., unreasonable expectations of especially favorable treatment or automatic compliance with his or her expectations
6. is interpersonally exploitative, i.e., takes advantage of others to achieve his or her own ends
7. lacks empathy, is unwilling to recognize or identify with the feelings and needs of others
8. is often envious of others or believes that others are envious of him or her
9. shows arrogant, haughty behaviors or attitudes

Dwayne advised me to consider leaving the relationship during my next phone session with him. With the continuing cycle of Narc abuse, he was very concerned that if I stayed with Ned, cancer wouldn't entirely go away. The stress of the relationship was taking its toll on every part of my life from finances, to work to my relationships. Bela and Brindi couldn't stand him, watching helplessly as my physical and mental health deteriorated. I took Dwayne's advice seriously and began to pay close attention to what was happening.

With his constant demands, criticisms, and growing resentment, I had the perfect opportunity to end things. Using what I had learned about

Narcs, I sent him an email telling him I couldn't change due to all I had on my plate. I knew he wouldn't be happy unless I changed, so I felt it better to end things so he could be happy. To my delight, he agreed. Ned's response was something to the effect that we were on the same page. He announced he'd be moving but wouldn't pay rent for the time he remained. I refused to let him stay any longer, especially rent-free. Within two weeks of the breakup, Dad moved back from California. By the end of the year, I was cancer-free and healed on many deep levels. In addition, I healed deep wounds from my "mother issues" that created so much pent-up anger. It wasn't easy, but I learned a lot!

Many miracles, helpers, and healers, including the very special Native American family, came to aid me in fighting for my life. I have closed out and healed from the many things that created cancer in my body, celebrating a new beginning in August of 2018, 3 years after the tumor disappeared. It was a monumental battle for me that includes things I have vowed not to write about to uphold the sacredness of the healing. I genuinely believe there are natural cures available to heal disease. If you have faith, determination, and commitment, Spirit will guide you to the miracles, people, and cures you need.

Journal Entry 9/18/15

I just watched the movie "The Fault In Our Stars." The film brought up a lot of thoughts and feelings for me due to my own cancer battle. Most people will never know the intensity of facing a life-threatening illness, but those who have, know the thoughts that accompany it.

If I die tomorrow, I am grateful for what I know to be true about my life and me. If my heart stops beating, my lungs stop breathing, I know I loved deeply and gave everything I had to give.

I know that no matter what has happened to me in this life, it has a purpose. Whether that purpose was to teach me forgiveness, patience, tolerance, or simply unconditional love, it all had a purpose.

Most people choose to battle their cancer using Western medicine's treatment of surgery, chemotherapy, and radiation. I have battled cancer alone using alternative therapies. I've fought it in bed, from the bathroom floor, and in my mind. Most people in my life have no idea the extent of the pain I've endured both physically and emotionally, not to mention the daily mental battles to overcome fear, doubt, sadness, and despair.

I've made it through each day drinking nasty herbs, driving to colon therapies, taking endless supplements, and searching for cures with my head held high. I've done it alone, without doctors, nurses, or a team of caretakers. I've continued working, helping others, and caring for my children as I would if I were well. I may not be doing everything as perfectly as I would if I was well or as quickly, but I push through each day as best I can, even when I want to scream out loud, throw a tantrum, or even quit fighting.

I'm not saying I didn't have support; I did. I've had the love, acceptance, and help of God's human angels appear in my life at just the right moment. My loved ones, while concerned, can only offer support for a battle that I have to fight alone. Until a couple of months ago, my Dad lived here. He checked on me incessantly, tried to cook for me even though I couldn't eat most days. I work every day, do what chores I can accomplish, and keep the bills paid on time, food on the table, meals prepared, business growing, gardens watered, and animals, as well as kids, are taken care of. When it's time for self-treatments, I hide in the bathroom and administer painful enemas while crying silently. At night, when the pain is the worst, I hide it and try to fall asleep as quickly as I can to attempt to outrun it.

During my NAC ceremony, my dear friend said to me, "No child should have to care for their parent..." What she didn't know or realize is that my children didn't have to take care of me through this. My youngest daughter, who is 13 years old, helps with chores at times and helps with my granddaughter when she is here. If I stay in bed for the day, she checks on me to be sure I have water, but she never has to take care of me. I haven't stopped living because of this disease. I try not to complain about my pain or even let anyone know how much pain I'm in. I've hidden it from everyone. Why? Because I love you, I love you enough to not burden you when it so obviously scares you. I hide it because sharing it will not decrease its effects on me but could potentially over-whelm you. Instead, I spend time with you, cook for you, I'm fighting for my life to spend another day with you.

As I sit writing, all I can think is that this battle is not over. So, I wonder, if this were my last day, did I feel loved? Did I love? Did I give? Did my life count? I did my best to help others, remain peaceful, be thoughtful, give, grow, and stay connected to God. Was I successful at it? Can one ever be sure?

What I am sure of is, I loved deeply, hurt deeply in silence, struggled greatly, and remained loyal to God and my calling. No one will ever really know the amount of shear effort it took to get through these last several months or even several years. But I know, and more importantly, God knows.

Was it worth it? Yes! Love is always worth it. Does it matter? It does to me. I know that I have done what I can to recognize beauty, love and to spread it, even when I feel like crap. I know that I got up every single day in gratitude and hopefulness for another loving day, the gift of life.

So, if tomorrow doesn't come for me, I did my best with what I had. It is enough for me. And when I leave this physical body, I will fly! I love my kids; I love my family, and I love all the people who've crossed my path. I've tried to be kind and sometimes failed, but I gave it my best as a human.

I've spent years working on myself, studying, growing, healing past trauma, hurt, and illness. Through all of it, I've grown, and I like myself. So, if today is my last, I am grateful for the experiences and opportunities I've had. For love, I gave and received. It has been a good life. I don't think I'm dying from this cancer; I believe it's just a bump in the road, a bump that is spiky, rough, and unpredictable.

If God grants me one more day, I will cherish it and make use of it to be a loving, gentle human upon this beautiful earth. The best gift in life is to have the choice in how we live and express our humanity. I'm proud of who I am and the person I've become. I'm not perfect, but I like myself.

That is all anyone can ask.

Studying and learning everything I could about Narcissistic Personality Disorder gave me much understanding of the struggles I faced with abuse. Spirit deepened that knowledge with visions and clarity of how the spirit of narcissistic people was injured. It might surprise you to know that many narcs are empaths that were wounded early in life. Instead of coping with their trauma, they turned all feelings for others off, only focusing on themselves. It is true that hurt people hurt other people.

Empaths and sensitives are the perfect food source for the ego of the Narcissist. Naturally wanting to heal others by loving them, we draw them to us. They seek the qualities they lack, searching for the emotional feed we provide. For many years I was hurt by the projections and callousness of Narcs without understanding the dynamic. After years of clearing my old programs, fears, and self-doubt, light flooded my entire being when I finally had a name for it.

I am forever grateful for that counselor who quickly identified the Narc in my life and encouraged me to leave. There were too many times in relationships I felt like there was something wrong with me to evoke such cruel treatment. It's crazy when someone takes credit for things you did right and projects their own bad behavior onto you. Reality becomes fuzzy, and you are afraid to speak or act. Unsure of what is truth, you question everything. The cycle of narcissistic abuse became clear once I understood it.

Love bombing, idealized treatment quickly turns to devalue and ends in dismissal or discarding. In the beginning, the Narc builds you up, telling you all the things you ever wanted to hear. You believe that you are finally being seen, heard, and understood. Without warning, the Narc begins to criticize and complain, exposing any fault or fear you have. If that weren't enough, the Narc then dismisses you, turning cold, giving you the silent treatment. You try hard to please their craving for the original love and attention. Empaths naturally want to please the people they love, giving everything possible. Before long, you're drained, exhausted, and unable to give to yourself or anybody else.

As an empath, I never understood or comprehended that people couldn't feel empathy for others. I knew I felt the emotions of others as my own, but I didn't know how it deeply affected my reactions or behaviors. Once I understood it, another Narc came along, plugged into my emotions, and was able to steal the energy

I freely offered. Faced with cancer, you realize you only have so much energy. I had to choose to save myself emotionally, mentally, spiritually, financially, and physically. But the Narc had no empathy for me.

At the same time I was going through the cycle with him, my mother began to use my struggle as a personal attention plea. With so little energy, I had limited conversations with her. Most of what she knew came from her reading my blog or Facebook posts. I received an email from her after seeing a post she wrote on Facebook. The email was accusatory, making her the victim. She used my struggle with cancer to get attention from others. I cut all contact after reading, "Go gentle in the night, my daughter. Peace and love are with you. God's grace be upon you." My instant reaction was, "I am not going to die!" Who the hell writes something like that to their own child fighting colon cancer? I chose to end all contact, accepting that she is who she is.

During my healing ceremony, I battled the hurt, anger, and resentments that I carried in my body from the relationship with my mother. I had to release it all and let it go. I had to accept that she was one of my greatest teachers in life. It was her choices and actions that led me always to put love first. From a very young age, I thought of her anytime I had a big decision that potentially benefitted me but could be hurtful to others. I would ask myself, "What would she do?" and then I'd do the opposite.

Before we are born, we choose the family, circumstances, and life that will cause the most significant opportunity for soul growth. There was no mistake in the life I've led or the family I was born into. Each person has offered me an opportunity to learn. Some lessons took much longer but rising above the actions of others and no longer personalizing it allowed me to discover the truth of who I am at a higher level.

We are individual expressions of God, Infinite Intelligence. Sometimes we wear distressing masks on our journey to remembering who we are, yet beneath the mask, God resides. As we muddle around this planet, trying to become a better version of ourselves, we all find our way eventually. Some find their way early in life, others at the last breath. I'm still learning, growing, and remembering who I truly am. I am grateful for the lessons, even the pain and discomfort of disease. If I hadn't been through so much in my life, I wouldn't have the knowledge, wisdom, or skills to help others. Life is a confusing journey. It's filled with ups and downs, just like an amusement park. We would be bored if it weren't for the rollercoasters.

25

FULFILLING MY PROMISE TO TEACH

As technology has evolved, reaching and helping others has become easier. In 2001, I channeled my book "30 Days to a Charmed Life." It's a workbook I provided to clients that wanted to learn about manifesting. Because I was busy with the house, divorce, and raising kids, I didn't pursue publishing it. Within a couple of years, many Law of Attraction books had become popular. I was angry at myself for not publishing it, yet I had a feeling there was something I wasn't aware of that would be revealed about the information in the book.

2014 the online coaching industry took off with a slew of new technology platforms that allowed online group classes. For a few years, clients who had read Charmed Life asked for a workshop, a course to help them do the exercises outlined in the book. With the new technology, Charmed Life Online began. I taught 17 hours' worth of material in a Live classroom that met twice a week. Students who participated were making massive breakthroughs in their belief systems. In Charmed Life, the work is very deep, blending brain reprogramming, healing, and spiritual practice in a practical format. Relationships, money, and health issues were improving for each of the students. As the class continued with the element of live weekly coaching, miracles kept unfolding.

Taming the ego and healing the past are the most potent results of the work in Charmed Life. It's the process Spirit took me through for years to heal my past. As issues are healed, many of the students' intuitive gifts became stronger as their self-worth improved. The exercises can be challenging when you do them alone, but within a group experience, the dynamic allows for support in that process. I love teaching Charmed Life, and it keeps me growing and evolving right along with the class. Depending on our age, we have layers upon layers of old beliefs, unconscious programs, and fear. Doing the focused work to become consciously aware of the layers allows you to heal and reveal more of your authentic self. The more authentic and genuine you become, the easier it is to live a magical, charmed life connected to God, The Universe, Source Energy.

One of the most important things I've learned throughout my journey as an Empath and sensitive is that to live a peaceful, connected life; you have to rise above the ego, fear, and material concerns.

I have carefully chosen the stories shared in this book. Rather than boring you with more of my personal experiences, I want to share some lessons I've learned on my path of awakening. On the following pages, I want to share some of the most common experiences my clients have had when going through Spiritual Awakening.

After going through various awakening experiences, I now understand that what I experienced was a "Dark Night of the soul." "Dark Night of the soul" refers to a temporary crisis that affects someone at a deep, existential level on a journey to discovering union and a relationship to God within you. Living s very ego-centered life, there comes the point in our spiritual journey that we must learn to shift our perceptions. So, instead of living from ego, we strive to live a heart-centered, soul-based life. Many people discover or begin spiritual studies after experiencing a "Dark Night of the soul." It brings about change and transformation at a deep experiential level.

Triggered by external events like the early death of a loved one, divorce, sudden job loss, medical crisis, a "Dark Night of the soul" leaves you feeling lonely, in an uncertain world. Your sense of reality and meaning is shattered, leaving you confused and feeling hopeless. It's a period that stirs deep reflection and questioning of everything you believe to be real and valuable. "Dark Night of the soul" signals the death of the first layer of the ego. From this place, your perception and understanding of the connectedness of all things begin to form.

Imagine you have a big, beautiful mother tree. Every year the mother tree drops her acorns, and the acorns are planted in fresh soil, becoming new trees. While the acorns are attached to the mother tree, you can easily see that it's a seed attached to the mother tree, including the branches and the leaves. If the leaves were to fall, wouldn't the tree still be the tree and the fallen leaves a part of that tree? Yes. When the acorn falls, is it still part of the tree? Yes! Is it still part of the mother tree when a freshly planted acorn blooms into a new tree? Yes! It may have its own structure, leaves, and branches now, but it's never separate from the mother tree. It came from that original tree, and while different in its uniqueness, it is still part of the mother. Just as you could take an acorn from a tree in the front yard, plant it in your backyard, and now you have two trees, yet it's always going to be a part of the original mother tree.

You and I will always be a part of God, the original energy from which we came. We were birthed from the seed of Source energy, the same energy that pumps our hearts and gives us breath. Life-force energy can't be seen with the human eye, yet science has proven it is real. When you're angry, you can't physically see the energy coming off your body or out of your mouth. However, if you were to take a device capable of measuring electrical changes in the particles of the room where you expelled your anger, you would see it. Just because you can't see it doesn't mean it doesn't exist. You may not be able to see Spirit; you may not be able to see Source Energy, God, Creator, but you are a part of it, and it is in you. You can't see what houses your consciousness, what creates your thoughts, your creativity, but you know there's something. That something is God, Creator, Source energy. You can call it whatever you want; it is the ONE energy from which everything emerges. The Tao calls it the "Mother of ten thousand things, the nameless."

When you experience an awakening and realize that you're so much more than human, so much more than your physical body, a cascade of light releases, and your understanding is expanded. Once your knowledge expands, everything you gave meaning to in the past is gone, and your present reality shatters. So, whatever triggers an awakening for you will impart an existential understanding that you Spirit, made from Source Energy.

Awakening can happen when you realize that you're not your material things, job title, or role in the family. This awakening is your true self saying, "I'm not my ego, my body, and I'm not my looks, or what's in my bank account, I'm not any of the things I've used to identify myself." One of the biggest hurdles to overcome in our thinking is, you aren't your story, experiences you've had, and certainly not the judgments from others. You're not even the labels that mental health professionals have given you. You are so much more than your past and your cumulative experiences, no matter your age. If you haven't had an awakening and you're just now starting to dip your toes in the water, don't stop there; there's so much more for you to become.

When things no longer hold the same meaning as before, your ego is put in check because of its attachment to all those "things." People often mistake the "Dark Night of the soul" for depression for a good reason. You are suddenly in unfamiliar territory, stripped of identity, of all the things that you thought you knew. It brings a new awareness, and while it's super exciting, it's uncomfortable because you haven't been living that way. Once everything you gave meaning to no longer has any purpose, the ego begins fighting you tooth and nail, attempting to return to what is known. Experiencing a "Dark Night of the soul" can present all the mental and physical symptoms of depression and anxiety.

During a "Dark Night of the soul," I found myself asking, "Now what?" as I entered a "void." Spirit explained the "void" as a phase we can get stuck in, unaware it's a space to create anew; it can be highly uncomfortable energy. Some people will get stuck there for months or even years. It is challenging because you don't know where to put meaning, and while it's only the beginning stages of awakening, you have no past reference to navigate it. You're in what feels like unfamiliar territory of an unknown emotional, mental and spiritual plane. It will affect you physically if you don't continue moving forward on your journey.

Sensitives and empaths can get stuck in the "Dark Night of the soul" when they realize much of their reactions were not their own but were caused by other people's emotions, environmental energy, and ego. First, they get stuck thinking that being an empath and being so sensitive is a curse; then, the ego grabs onto the label of "empath" and crafts a story or an understanding that leads to acceptance of the curse. Without the education, wisdom, and tools to unplug from outside energies, being empathic can feel like a curse.

When you experience the void, everything you thought you knew is removed. Everything your ego is attached to, including your story, identity, values, and the things you've been chasing after for years, lose all meaning and validity. There's a blank space, and for a lot of people, it's a scary space. Yet, it represents the potential death of the ego. Our egos are very attached to stories, labels, roles, medical diagnoses, and everything in the physical, third-dimensional world. As you work on releasing the many ego attachments, the ego will grasp even tighter to maintain control and keep you safe. Because of those attachments, you may experience resistance, fear, and confusion as you force behavioral changes.

It is a mistake to judge the "Dark Night of the soul" as bad or negative; on the contrary, it's a beautiful thing. There is no shame or condemnation, no matter how long you get stuck in it. Instead, view the void as a place of birthing something new. Letting go of something old and creating something new is accompanied by a pause. Like the breath, when you inhale deeply, just before exhaling, there is a space. That space in between the breath is a powerful place of creation, "the void."

Many have asked how long a "Dark Night of the soul" can last. The simple answer is until you move forward, embracing the unknown. People get stuck when they are attached to things having meaning, rather than simply experiencing things as they are, without meaning. So how do you get unstuck? By releasing all of your attachments to things, labels, old stories, and forgiving anyone you're holding responsible for past hurts. As humans, it's normal to be attached to stories about our childhoods. But when you realize that your parents didn't know much and did the best they could with what they knew, you will be free from the tendency to blame. Forgive them and LIBERATE YOURSELF.

We live in a time where technology allows us to grow faster, learn and experience more, to expand our understanding far beyond any time in recorded history. It IS possible that your parents didn't know much. It is equally likely, if not probable that they were just products of their environment. If you're going to hold things against them for their lack of knowledge and wisdom, who are you holding captive, them or YOU?

We are often attached to our past accomplishments, stories, and understanding of what happened to us when we experienced abuse or trauma, were cheated on, lied to, hurt, or betrayed. Those stories carry emotional energy that gets locked in our bodies, cells, and our minds. Your ego or wounded inner-child can heal and experience relief when you release the emotional energy tied to those old events, good or bad.

Next, you need to nurture your inner child and allow it to grow. Then, as you heal the wounded inner-child from the past, you will naturally move beyond confusion, depression, anxiety, and fear, into a state of peace.

The "Dark Night of the soul" can last a night, a month, or years. Unfortunately, some people get stuck there and never come out. I've known people who have become so frightened and confused they just shut the door on all things spiritual. They chose not to move forward to grow in understanding and wisdom, refusing to face their shadows. It's unfortunate because that is just the beginning; it's simply the starting point. Our goal is not to merely awaken but to evolve toward enlightenment. The spiritual path is more than understanding concepts; we are to experience and live these truths to create change in the world by creating peace within ourselves.

> *"Out of suffering have emerged the strongest Souls; the most massive characters are seared with scars." – Khalil Gibran*

26

FINDING ALIGNMENT

Humans strive to connect at a deep level and create a union with God, our Creator. Science seeks understanding and proof of the existence of God and the Universal Laws, yet it seems science is always a step behind. Kabbalists, Yogis, and students of Spiritual Wisdom have obtained knowledge derived from intense study, contemplation, and meditation. I've made it a practice to study various spiritual texts and traditions. In my search for God and truth, I learned that there wasn't one religion or belief that had all the answers, recognizing the severe impediment to believing that any religion or belief system holds all the answers.

Universal wisdom is infinite, vast, and unknowable. The human ego is the veil of mind between physical form and Spirit, God. In yogic practice, it is said that it takes many incarnations to over-come the veil of the ego. Because of this truth, I continue to seek higher levels of understanding in my own life. Studying the teach-ings of the Master's like Jesus, Buddha, and Paramahansa

Yogananda and Kabbalistic teachings is humbling. I strive to grasp my ego better as I draw closer to God's infinite wisdom. Recognizing that I have much to learn and overcome keeps the practice alive, for when we think we know everything, we pinch off wisdom.

How can anyone be taught if they think there is nothing more for them to learn? It's absurd to believe that one teaching, one teacher, or one belief is the only way to God. Wisdom and understanding of the Infinite nature of our Universe can only be experienced by humbly approaching life as a student. Rather than striving, we must surrender our will, desires, and minds to a force greater than us. We must yield to the Infinite Intelligence that birthed us. As we seek the revelation of the mysteries of the Infinite during moments of surrender, we connect.

Raised Catholic and Christian, I was never satisfied with the limited teachings. There were many rules but not many experiences. For example, the Catholic practice of confession and communion were physical acts that held little in the way of actual "communion" with God/Goddess energy. Studying Pagan and Wiccan beliefs loosened the grip of my early prejudices and opened my mind to receive new teachings. Eastern religions like Taoism, Buddhism, and Hinduism not only intrigued me but fed me the necessary food of compassion, mindfulness, and love.

Spirituality has answers for the whole of society and life. When science can embrace the notion that we need to include true spiritual wisdom, we will evolve quickly. I believe we are heading in that direction. His Holiness, the Dalai Lama, has recently included scientists in discussions, seeking to unite both systems. We are on the precipice of a paradigm shift that will bring unification and holistic principles that lead to spiritual evolution. The Ego seeks to block expansion, closing our minds out of fear; it resists new information. Our work to identify and subdue egoic focus allows us greater revelation and union with our True Self.

Experience has taught me that even in my 50 plus years, I still have much to learn. While I've had many valuable experiences, I can never allow myself to think I know it all. Approaching life from humility, expecting daily to experience just a spark of Infinite Wisdom, makes it happen. However, when life becomes busy, when I allow it to distract from the vital practice of meditation and union with the Divine, my experience no longer reflects the miraculous. Honestly, I'm not always disciplined about long periods of meditation. Sometimes my practice consists of watching the sunrise, affirmative prayer, and thanksgiving. While daily reverence and conscious intention of the Divine are integrated into my routine, I am not always without distraction. Yet, I humbly continue in my practice, in my lessons, and in reflection. I know that no matter how much I think I know already, there are things that are far beyond my grasp that I long to experience.

Passion for knowing God in an intimate, visceral way drives me daily. Conscious of thoughts that hinder my growth, fearful things that want my attention are discarded continuously. What I do know for sure is this: fear is the opposite energy of love. Fear creates hate, defensiveness, resistance, and self-doubt. Love, however, drives us to share, help, forgive, accept and embrace others. Duality is a constant in life, a force of equals and opposites that we must overcome, override and balance. The most potent achievement in our lives is that of overcoming egotistic tendencies.

The bible says, "Seek first the Kingdom of Heaven, and all else will be added to you." When we focus first on union with the Divine, relinquishing worldly desires in favor of that union, everything is taken care of, including the manifestation of material desires. The Tao says, "In doing nothing, all is done." Both texts speak to the same thing. We must enter meditation, quieting the mind, ceasing all action, and seeking Divine guidance. As we do this, everything that needs to be done aligns in an easy, effortless way. However, when we choose to force things, letting Ego lead our lives, the effort and energy exerted are wasted. Ego leads solely to attainment and fulfillment of itself. Yet when ego gains achievement, it chases something else because there is always something else to do, to achieve. It's a treadmill of never-ending chasing. Yet when we seek Divine alignment, peace, contentment, and bliss are present in all we undertake.

Ego or the 'inner critic' constantly likes to insert fears and doubts into us. The ego is very subtle. For example, when you start to do something that you intend on succeeding at, the ego says, "You can't do that, or You shouldn't do that, and Who do you think you are?" Remember, there are two sides to the ego, the inner critic and bully on one side and the wounded inner child on the other. The bully tries to keep you protected, to keep you in the safe zone. Based on things that happened in the past, it created a fear-based program. The inner bully wants to protect you from experiencing that **past event** again. The wounded inner child is afraid of everything. This part of the ego repeats things like "Nobody likes You," trying to keep you safe yet sabotaging your efforts.

The wounded inner child wants to protect you by keeping you from experiencing **past emotional traumas**. Sometimes the ego is one-sided, but other times it's like your mind has a ping-pong match. Sometimes the bully becomes our voice, and we become arrogant. Arrogance and pride are a part of the bully side of the ego. The wounded inner child, however, can be very subtle. If what you are experiencing is super emotional, then it's typically the wounded inner child. We don't want to neglect our inner child. We want to silence the bully because the bully tends to get us spinning emotionally, putting us in fight or flight mode.

Whatever is consciously or unconsciously, emotionally energized is what manifests in our lives and circumstances. When we're hurting, angry, or confused, it's essential to calm down quickly. Otherwise, we emotionally energize the very things we don't want to experience. If you're emotionally or mentally triggered, identify the bully or the wounded inner-child, then quickly discharge the thoughts, feelings, and images.

Are you spinning yourself a different story than the one you want to be living? Words are **powerful,** and the stories we tell are compelling. We must be very aware of them. We can't operate at our highest level if we tell negative stories. Write down what the ego is trying to communicate to you. It's consciousness work, but it's also going to help in healing that thing. What are the words that it's saying? Now you can re-script it. Feed it back to the ego and tell it, "Here's your new script. This is what I want you to start repeating from now on instead of all this trash movie set on repeat".

When you become conscious of your ego and begin to quiet the bully and heal the wounded inner-child, you can stop the fight, flight, or freeze mode response as well. The ego reacts to things based on what is already known and experienced, and it hangs the past. It can create mind circling, where your mind circles over the same negative thought patterns repeatedly. To stop this, make a new routine to get out of mind-circling and break the cycle of madness you get into when you are in a place of anxiety. There is a metaphor I've used to help many people with this issue. It was an excellent lesson for me, and now I am going to share it with you.

When I used to train horses, I first put them in a round pen. Creating a safe place to train, a round pen is a fifty to sixty-foot diameter, enclosed pen. We use the round pen to teach horses to stop their fight or flight reactions and instead relax. When trying to ride them or work with them, the fight or flight response becomes very dangerous. Within the round pen, a horse is directed to run in a circle in one direction, then reversed on command. It can be nerve-wracking when a horse is not behaving or is in a full-blown fight or flight, coming toward you with hoofs and teeth. It takes on average twenty minutes when a horse is in that mode before they stop fighting and submit to instruction.

While horses typically last about 20 minutes in a fight or flight mode, humans can last much longer. Horses will shake, freaking out, appearing to listen to instruction while running, but still in a manner of resistance. I've trained horses in the round pen who foam themselves into a sweat from fear of things happening outside the arena. Sometimes they were triggered by past trauma, causing them to distrust humans. Nevertheless, it was necessary training for the horses, and it was an excellent lesson for me.

Throughout the years, I've found that we, as humans, have a very similar reaction to fear as horses. Human beings have that exact mechanism that kicks in when something triggers fear and makes us feel helpless, hopeless, or angry; and initiates the fight or flight response. Thus, when stuck in negative mind-circling, an anxiety response is created in the body. While we don't kick and fight with our bodies like horses, we certainly bite back with our mouths. We put others down, yell, scream, hide, run, and do all kinds of crazy, mad things to avoid feeling or facing what we are afraid of. Whether it's rejection, hurt, or abandonment, it can trigger fight or flight, and as with the horses – the unconscious is in full reaction mode. Horses will try to bite – humans use their words and bully behavior.

When stuck in mind chatter, you start to second guess yourself to the point of analysis paralysis. I like to do with humans; what I did with the horses; create safety in a circle, but not a mind circle. As human beings, we need to replace the mind circling, mind chatter with something positive. Using a tool or resource that discharges the emotional energy the ego is unconsciously reacting to will aid in that. Humans need to create a safety mechanism instead of using a defense mechanism. I use a combination of EFT/tapping and energy work with clients to discharge negative emotions immediately.

You can create 3 easy steps for yourself when you catch yourself in fight or flight mode

1. STOP - Stop talking, stop reacting, stop physically moving, stop all action.
2. You could take a nap, but if you're at work, that's not going to work, so if that means you have to go into the bathroom, go and if you know how to tap, tap, meditate, pray, if you have time, you can take a walk and walk it off.
3. Record yourself. Write down whatever you are reacting to or use the voice recorder on your phone and record it. You may not have a rational or clear enough head to process

all of it in the midst of it, but at least if you record it, you will have something to come back to later. And, when the ego knows something is stored, it releases the mind loop.

Three easy steps. Find something; it could be meditation, prayer, writing in a journal, something for when you find yourself in a state of fight or flight. Sit down and give yourself a good ten to twenty minutes to write it, record it on your phone, something to get that fear and emotional energy out of you in a safe way. You're creating a safety circle for yourself, not exploding and causing damage to your life. When you're finally calm, journal the answers to these questions: "Why was I reacting to that? What was it that I was reacting to?" **If you're an empath, "Is this my energy or thoughts?"**

The more you catch the places where your ego hooks you into this mind-circling madness, the quicker you're going to get out of fight or flight mode. As I said, human beings can stay in fight or flight a hell of a lot longer than twenty minutes. Your fight or flight mechanism can go days, weeks, or even years as a human being. The longer you stay in flight/flight, the more it affects your central nervous system, to the point of creating physical illness. If your mind gets stuck in a loop of negativity, you can easily slip into victim mode. Worst, you get defensive, and the arrogant asshole side of the ego goes on the attack. One defense the ego uses is to justify. It comes up with all the reasons why we should be mad.

If you REALLY start to lose it, take a walk. It's amazing how simple that little exercise is. Go for a walk to get your blood pumping. Walk for at least twenty-five minutes, more if possible. It's an excellent way to calm the mind and ease the tension. Walking while focusing on your breath can put you into a meditative state.

While your body is working on moving forward, your mind tends to quiet down, at which point you can begin to sort through your fears. After 25 minutes of walking, your endorphins kick in, dopamine and serotonin release, allowing the mind and body to calm. It's an easy way to get plugged back into spirit, process and release emotions and regain control. Sitting still doesn't allow you to get the ego voice to shut up, so go for a walk. While walking, your mind is focused on not tripping. So, keep your feet moving in a forward direction.

If time allows, commit to a twenty-five-minute walk, then walk for another thirty minutes. In the end, you will feel relief and release. You can also do an EFT/tapping round once home to release any leftover emotions. There are tons of free YouTube videos. If you do that instead of running to the refrigerator or running to the bottle, you are positively helping yourself.

Set a timer for fifteen minutes if your wounded inner child is unwilling to walk and would rather throw a pity party. Give yourself fifteen minutes to be depressed, to be angry, to be frustrated, to pitch a temper tantrum. Do it with all your might. Make a HUGE production out of it. Act like a two-year-old or a three-year-old having a temper tantrum. Get all that energy out. You can cry, you can snot on yourself, you can scream, you can roll around on the floor, but when that timer goes off, you are DONE! Get up and move on to something else. Set the intention "I'm going to feel this, I'm going to explore it, I'm going to express it for fifteen minutes with all of my attention and might, and when the timer goes off I'm done, I'll go find something else to do that feels better."

It is possible to reach a place with past wounds where there is no emotional trigger. Once healed, you will feel the emotions but not dwell there. It's okay to be sad, and I'm not saying you shouldn't have any emotional reactions because that's BULLSHIT. You should have emotional reactions, you are HUMAN, and emotions are part of the human journey. We aren't here only to experience positivity. We live on a planet of duality; anything less than experiencing both sides isn't a complete experience.

There is no magic wand to heal our wounds. Any healing is temporary until we clear the root issue. To find the root, we must identify our buried wounds. That's the work that most people don't want to do, but it's the work that sets us free. As you heal old wounds, you are creating a solid foundation to express who you are—allowing yourself to share your gifts and genius in the world. A foundation that will enable you to live in a loving, humble way, authentic, able to admit when you are having a hard time or a frustrating day. There will be times you slide back to old habits, like sliding down the mountain on your tail end, but you will be able to get back up. It's life work because no matter how much work we do, the ego is always there somewhere.

Humans can handle a lot more than we think we're capable of. Sometimes, healing requires Spirit to spoon-feed little triggers while peeling away small, surface layers, so we don't feel too vulnerable or exposed. That's the beauty of the ever-wise Universe, Source Energy, God. You will only be given what you can handle. However, if you tell Spirit to provide you with a huge heaping serving of truth, you might get a bucket dumped on you. Just remember you said you could handle it. How much can you take? Tell the Universe what you can handle. If you're ready to clear it all, tell Spirit to remove it all; but get ready because you might end up in trigger central.

The wounded inner child and the big bully part of your ego are active, so it's up to you to clear the energy and the past issues that trigger you. That doesn't mean you're never going to feel emotion again. Things people say and do that either remind you of a past event or don't align with your beliefs, judgments, and opinions may trigger new reactions. For example, if someone says something and you're all of a sudden flared up and offended, that's a trigger. We don't typically have big emotional triggers to something that just happened the first time, in the here and now. Usually, we're reacting to something that happened long ago, and it's uncovering something that wants to heal.

Life on this planet can be messy. It's not a simple, easy journey. It's an exciting journey with ups and downs, surprises, hurts, disappointments, victories, celebrations, and blessings. Still, the ego likes us to play small and be comfortable, sticking to the tried and true – BORING! I invite you to embrace the WHOLE ride, go beyond the illusion of the ego, and stand in your Divine Power.

27

PROTECTION AND ALIGNMENT

One of the reasons for writing this book was to share personal experiences that empowered me. It's my goal to share my journey and empower you to show you that it is possible to overcome anything. As an empath, I know how hard it is to navigate the many confusing energies you feel. Whether the energy and emotions from others are affecting you negatively or you are experiencing some form of spiritual or psychic attack, I want to teach you how to protect yourself. We have absolute authority and dominion over our lives.

Have you ever argued with someone you know is angry? You aren't face-to-face with them, yet you know that they're thinking about you because an image of them appears in your mind's eye and suddenly you become overwhelmed to the point where you feel very, very heavy? Maybe you feel a headache come on, or something goes wrong, and you know it isn't coming from you; it's something outside of you? That's a psychic attack. It can come from jealousy or someone being angry at you. A psychic attack can come from anyone, especially if you're tired, stressed, in fear, anger, or triggered -- these are all open doors. Abuse and trauma events can also bring on a psychic attack.

People can experience psychic attacks without realizing it. They can be used as tools for evil, even if someone is not evil themselves. If you know someone who is a narcissist, a psychopath, or just really selfish, maybe they don't believe in God or don't have a spiritual foundation, which can create an open door for them to be used as an agent or tool of evil. Narcissists, sociopaths, psychopaths, and people who are highly needy or manipulative are psychic vampires. Psychic vampires suck your life force energy; they plug in and drain you. Sometimes, it's because we've unknowingly given them an invitation to hook into our energy field. It doesn't mean they're evil, but without meaning to, people can become tools for evil, lowering our vibration.

Ephesians 6:12 says, "For we wrestle not against flesh and blood, but against principalities, against powers, against the rulers of the darkness of this world, against spiritual wickedness in high places." One of the versions says, "We wrestle not against flesh and blood, but against principalities, against powers of the air." In astrology, tarot, and symbology, air represents the mental - thoughts and words. So how do things travel? Communication is spoken into the air, or simply put, from what we say. When someone thinks or speaks ill of you, it creates an anger spear, a thought form that turns into energy directed from that person to you. You're the target. Do they mean to do it? No, but if their intention or thought is negative, it can create a psychic attack that manifests in physical form.

Lesser demons and psychic attacks can't necessarily hurt you physically, but the bigger ones can. Evil spirits will try to hurt you emotionally, mentally, and even physically. When under a psychic attack, it shifts your mood very quickly, causing things in your life to break down or fall apart, unexpected expenses come up, or drama from friends or family arise. People tend to think evil attacks or psychic attacks come from witchcraft or black magic. However, it can be caused by someone that is extremely angry at you or jealous. You can unknowingly absorb and react to that energy as if it was your own. Once you personalize the energy, thinking something is wrong with you, you unwittingly invite it into your energy field.

Negative spirits will look for an entry point or a weak link. Weak links are people in your life or situations in your life that create fear, attachment, or disconnection from Spirit and your Higher Self. Lower vibrational emotions create open doors that allow a spiritual attack. You need to be aware of where you have open doors so that you can close them.

Weak links and open doors are fears or judgments created by ego programs. When operating in ego, you are open to psychic or negative entity attacks because you are plugged into a lower frequency. Ego programs interfere with truth, creating fear, anger, even defensiveness. Those wounds and unhealed things in us can get activated or provoked by negative spirits. Sometimes, the attack comes from projections of judgmental people, full of ego, anger, and resentment. Negative or demonic spirits can use people in your life who are asleep, living in default mode; they are weak links that can provoke your ego.

Someone in your life that is jealous, angry, or resentful can create a lot of drama. If you're focused on or engaged in that drama, or you enter into fear (maybe you feel like you're going to lose something or lose them), you have opened the door for your ego to be used against you. Having pride in a particular issue when someone challenges you and tells you that you're wrong can draw you into an argument. When in defense mode, your emotional vibration lowers into the vibration of fear. When you are afraid of something, the ego or inner critic causes you to react by either defending yourself or mentally beating yourself up. Ego hooks are a doorway for lower energies. Unhealed trauma or wounds can create subtle ego hooks, causing you to attack others or your own worthiness, dropping into a lower vibration.

For the sake of simplicity and understanding, there is an emotional frequency scale. Fear is on the lower end of the scale; love is on the higher end. Fear holds a very low frequency, while love holds a high frequency. Each frequency within the emotional vibration scale is associated with a different dimension. The higher your frequency, the higher dimension you are plugged into. Physical reality is in the 3rd dimension. Hopes and fears reside in the 4th dimension. It's also where negative entities and disincarnate spirits reside, the riffraff of the Universe. When your emotional vibration lowers, your mind gets stuck in repetitive negative thinking, and you create adverse events.

Negative entities can use the people in your life that have not emotionally or spiritually grown. Someone without a spiritual foundation is the perfect candidate. It could be a past relationship. It could be a current friend or someone you thought was on your side. It could even be family. Negative entities will use whoever is a weak link in your inner circle. When people turn against you, you begin to doubt yourself. Self-doubt propels the inner critic, the ego. You lose clarity, faith in yourself, your energy drops, and you feel drained.

When operating in ego, we separate from God, Source Energy, no longer connected to our true self, we get sucked into the drama of trying to prove ourselves. Once in defense mode, we forget the truth of who we are, and we judge others as evil. They aren't evil! Even if others are used as a tool for evil through their words, thoughts, and actions, it's best to hold them in love. We judge psychopaths, sociopaths, narcissists as pure evil, but they're not. Because they are entirely in ego, they can quickly become tools for evil. You can dislike or disapprove of the behavior without judging the person.

Strong boundaries are essential to a sensitive person or an empath. Those closest to us, our partner, children, even friends, can be used as an entry point of attack. The dark side will use whatever is going on in their lives or any insecurities to create drama, confusion, or distraction. Remember, confusion IS NOT from God. Negative spirits or entities use the people you love as tools because it is an easy entry point into your emotions. Anything that distracts you from being in a state of love or state of abundance can create an opening, a hook for negative spirits and entities to attack. The point of the attacks is to lower your frequency and dim your light. The best line of defense is to stay in a state of LOVE!!

When I was young, I was super reactive. It took a long time to learn how to release my anger and not react to it. When anger is left alone, it returns to LOVE. Everything is created from love. You can't hate someone if you don't already love them. If there was no love for them, there would be no hatred, disappointment, or hurt; you would be indifferent. If you allow the energy of anger to run its course without engaging, that energy returns to love, and all is right in the world again. Rather than react or call the person out on their behavior, remain in a state of love. Jesus the Master said, "Love one another as I have loved you." When you choose to love, you not only fulfill Universal Law, God's Law, you hold yourself in the highest vibration. The energy of love allows you to remain connected to Source Energy, the creative energy of All That Is!

If you don't know who you are or what your energy feels like, alone and apart from everybody else, discernment is difficult. So first and foremost, you need to know yourself. Any kind of negative attack, be it psychic, demonic, a negative spirit, or an astral entity, uses fear, ignorance, the ego as an entry point.

Each dimension holds a vibrational frequency. 4th dimension is where your ego and hopes or fears are located. When you're plugged into the 4th dimension, you are open to attack, confusion, and chaos. If something bothers you mentally and you allow it to affect your energy, your emotional vibration lowers, making you more prone to psychic attacks. Therefore, it's vital that you consciously maintain a high vibration. The vibration of love, compassion, and joy is your best defense against negativity. Daily practice of faith in God, connection to Spirit, and conversation with Spirit keeps you in a circle of protection. Build that relationship, keep it going, clear away the things that block you from abundance, love, and connection to the Universe.

Intentional shielding is another powerful tool of psychic/ and spiritual self-defense. Sit in meditation, see or imagine a bubble around you that is two feet above your head, two feet below your feet, and two feet around your body. Fill the bubble with golden/white light from the Divine, from God. Know that you are protected, surrounded by angels, and always supported in the bubble of light. As you imagine the bubble, set the intention that this protection field will deflect all negativity from outside sources. Once in place, you may see or feel things coming at you, but you don't absorb them.

To clear energy, you can use sage to clear your space and body. When your mood or feelings shift unexpectedly, ask, "Is this mine?" If intuitively you feel it's not, release it, don't personalize or analyze it. If you're Christian or you have Christian beliefs, you can call upon the name of Jesus Christ and bind it. Matthew 18:18 instructed, "Whatsoever you bind on earth shall be bound in Heaven; and whatsoever you loose on earth shall be loosed in Heaven." Other traditions say, "As above so below." Whatever your beliefs, there is a way to clear the negativity and protect yourself. Do not respond with anger or with fear, but stand in your power with LOVE.

28

4TH DIMENSION SPIRITUAL HIERARCHY

There is a hierarchy in the higher spiritual dimensions, including Guides, Angels, Archangels, Teachers, Ascended Masters, and Healing Luminary Beings. There is also a hierarchy in the lower subtle and astral realms. There are legions of dark forces as well as legions of light forces. Thrones, lordships, legions, and principalities exist within the subtle realms. Principalities can significantly affect the governing bodies and territories on the earth plane. The average person isn't going to get attacked individually by principalities or legions of demons. However, if a gateway or portal opens, it can affect individuals. I've seen it in areas where battles have occurred, or a violent murder occurs—like Auschwitz, the Salem Witch Trials, and Native American Genocide locations. I've even seen it in old mental hospitals or places where torture took place.

In places of violence, gateways from the subtle realms into physical reality can be created, allowing territorial demons dominion of that area. When someone contacts me about repeating negativity at a particular property, house, or business, I consider the possibility of a territorial entity. Portals and gateways have been opened accidentally by those playing with a Ouija board. If protection isn't in place when opening a Ouija board session or the board isn't closed properly, portals can open. Locations, where dark magic has been practiced repeatedly are also prone to negative gateways and portals. When a physical location creates repeated illness, violence, or other negative patterns, these things must be considered and addressed immediately.

If you suspect there is an open portal or gateway, get help or advice from someone experienced. If there's been war, violent death, or murder, it can't always be cleared. Be willing to leave. Nothing is worth staying in that energy. Finances, health, and eventually your sanity are all at risk when entities have taken territorial dominion.

Spirits and entities can attach to families or an individual. Familial spirits and generational curses are real. These entities typically work through the weakest link in a family. Once attached to the individual, it spreads to different members until chaos reigns within the family. There are legions of spirits responsible for sexual abuse, physical abuse, drug abuse, and violence. Have you noticed there is a certain consciousness, behavior pattern, and emotional energy to people like Narcissists, Psychopaths, Sociopaths? The language, playbook, and thought patterns are the same. If you know someone in this consciousness, say a prayer for them but don't attempt to change them. It's not up to you to save people; it's up to you to protect yourself. When you experience trauma or abuse, your energy vibration drops, leaving you open to attack. Remember, you cannot combat hate and fear with more hate and fear. The only defense is LOVE. Love includes joy, faith, and compassion. Your energy will rise as you heal traumas and wounds.

The Bible talks about the seven deadly sins. They are deadly because they separate you from your Higher Self and God/Source, opening you to attack. It doesn't mean that you're going to go to hell, but it will take your life down a path of hell.

1. Pride
2. Greed
3. Lust
4. Envy
5. Gluttony
6. Wrath
7. Sloth

It's essential to recognize where these things are present in your life or the life of those close to you so that you can clear them. An excellent example of this is Wrath. When someone is angry at you or you are angry at someone, the angry energy projected creates an anger spear. This is why I say, "watch what you're saying" and "watch what you're thinking." If you're projecting anger toward someone, you're creating a negative thought form that can be charged up by a dark entity and attaches to people. When you send it out, you open yourself up for attack too.

The Ten Commandments are another excellent example of spiritual tenants meant to help us. The Ten Commandments were not created to crucify you, shame, or punish you. However, when you choose to lie, cheat, steal, kill, and so on, you create internal self-doubt, secrets, lies, and shame. Shame is one of the lowest vibrational frequencies. When you live in guilt or shame, you become a target for negativity. Since like attracts like, the only thing you can attract is that which matches that lower vibration.

Many people come to me after experiencing attacks in dreams. For this reason, I want to share one of the most common types of demonic attacks. Unfortunately, from lack of knowledge, many young people find these experiences intriguing. In my younger years, I experienced these attacks, even falling for them.

Incubus and Succubus are the male and female forms of a demon. The Incubus is the male and typically appears to women, where the Succubus are female and usually appear to men though they will certainly appear to the same sex if need be. Succubi are a bit craftier than Incubi, but neither is very smart. They feed off humans' sexual energy and orgasm energy by entering the dream realm, or the astral realm. When asleep, your psychic defenses are down.

Incubus and Succubus enter into the dreamscape, projecting an attractive, beautiful figure; this is the mask they have chosen to seduce you. They may even appear like someone you know and then try to engage you in an ongoing nightly connection that includes astral sex. It doesn't matter how good the mask they wear or the vision they portray and project; it's not of light. Even asleep, you can feel a different energy from them than the person they are copying. It doesn't feel like the person you know. They feed off the energy when you engage with them or have an orgasm, and this is the reason they want to lure you in and seduce you.

Some people have been raped or had dreams of being raped in the astral. Those are Incubi and Succubi. People who get attacked by Incubi and Succubi in their dreams may also experience sleep paralysis. Sleep paralysis is when you wake up from a dream or are in a dream, and you know you're dreaming, but you can't move your muscles. You may feel a heavyweight on your chest or may not be able to open your eyes, depending on how profound the sleep paralysis is; it's typically caused by demonic energy or negative entities. A psychic attack doesn't typically cause it.

When Incubus or Succubus appears, you can't move. They manipulate your thoughts and body to get you to orgasm or to emit a strong reaction of fear; then, they steal your energy. Once they do get you to orgasm, they return later to continue to feed off your energy. Suppose you do nothing to defend against it. In that case, it's like this light goes off in the astral realms where other lower-dimensional entities can come in, or more Incubi and Succubi, and they all feed on your defenseless energy. If they can create a link and plug into your energy field, they will continually call you back as a food source. Clearing, putting up boundaries, and protection is necessary to rid yourself of these forms of attack.

Children are sometimes easy prey when they watch scary movies or listen to violent things on TV or video games as violence creates openings. For that reason, we must educate ourselves to protect them. We don't want to scare them, but we want to teach them how to pray and defend against negative energies. Teach them that they don't need to be afraid, whether in their dream life or their waking life. Teach them that they have the power to get rid of these things, and they have ABSOLUTE authority in their sleep and lives.

During my incident with the carbon monoxide leak in my car, I was given Psalms 91 as I woke up. As I opened my eyes, I saw myself tucked under the wings of God. Large, white wings covered me. Then, in a loud voice, I heard, "This is the spiritual warfare prayer, and it's powerful!"

Psalm 91 King James Version (KJV)

He that dwelleth in the secret place of the most High shall abide under the shadow of the Almighty.

2 I will say of the Lord, He is my refuge and my fortress: my God; in him will I trust.

3 Surely, he shall deliver thee from the snare of the fowler, and from the noisome pestilence.

*4 **He shall cover thee with his feathers, and under his wings shalt thou trust:** his truth shall be thy shield and buckler.*

5 Thou shalt not be afraid for the terror by night; nor for the arrow that flieth by day;

6 Nor for the pestilence that walketh in darkness; nor for the destruction that wasteth at noonday.

7 A thousand shall fall at thy side, and ten thousand at thy right hand; but it shall not come nigh thee.

8 Only with thine eyes shalt thou behold and see the reward of the wicked.

9 Because thou hast made the Lord, which is my refuge, even the most High, thy habitation;

10 There shall no evil befall thee, neither shall any plague come nigh thy dwelling.

11 For he shall give his angels charge over thee, to keep thee in all thy ways.

12 They shall bear thee up in their hands, lest thou dash thy foot against a stone.

13 Thou shalt tread upon the lion and adder: the young lion and the dragon shalt thou trample under feet.

14 Because he hath set his love upon me, therefore will I deliver him: I will set him on high, because he hath known my name.

15 He shall call upon me, and I will answer him: I will be with him in trouble; I will deliver him and honor him.

16 With long life will I satisfy him and show him my salvation.

If you have resonated with this prayer and believe in the bible, you can use this prayer for protection. If you don't believe in the Bible, use chanting or other traditional beliefs that you've been taught. Chanting "OM" repeatedly raises your frequency. Apply spiritual principles, and don't be lazy about it. It takes consistent work to control your thoughts and energy. Smudging with sage in your space and around your body is another great tool. Ensure that you sage every part of your space, including cupboards, closets, and behind doors. Don't get sucked into believing that someone can burn candles for you, and that will clear it. You can do it yourself.

Gratitude is another powerful tool to stay in the higher frequencies. Write gratitude statements daily and state them aloud. Be grateful for everything, especially those things you take for granted every day. We take things like oxygen, trees, the rain for granted until it's not available.

Salt baths, the ocean, and protective stones like black tourmaline, black obsidian, or hematite are potent tools for clearing. I combine all these things to maintain my energy field and living space as a matter of prevention. By intention, call upon the higher powers, and know your place in this Universe that gives you power. It took me years to learn all this in an age with no internet or Google. Metaphysics were considered woo-woo or fringe, and books were hard to find. In this age of awakening and time of a great paradigm shift, those who have overcome trials by fire are leading the way for those newly awakened.

While I have faced the battles of the lower dimensions, I am grateful they don't affect me anymore. I've found that the lower astral have no effect once you've gone through the initiation of higher wisdom as if trial by fire. So, I won't say I "know" much of anything; I can only share what I've been taught or have experienced personally.

LOVE is the energy that will keep you connected to the higher levels of consciousness, vibrations, and energy. Love is always the answer, and it is the ONLY ANSWER.

29

CONTINUING THE JOURNEY

We never stop growing or learning. But, of course, as we grow, what we desire to create in our lives changes too. In 2016, after getting through colon cancer, I decided to move. Leaving my home in Colorado, which I spent 17 years building, was a huge but necessary decision. Hawaii has a strong pull for me. I thought I could move there and build a new life. But, while Kauai is a place of sanctuary and restoration for me, the Universe had other plans.

Brindi had moved to Seattle with her husband and my granddaughter. I wanted to have the ability to reach more people with my work. Missing my granddaughter and daughter, I decided to relocate. I had said that I would never move back to Washington after the traumas experienced there. But, more than twenty years later, signs and synchronicities led me back. In November 2016, Bela and I drove to Seattle to check it out and visit the girls, celebrating their belated birthdays. I tried to have an open mind even though I felt resistant. During our visit, I met a lot of people that were open to my work. The ability to reach the masses from Washington became clear. So, I ditched our plans to move to Kauai and set a target for Washington, making everyone in the family happy.

Before my 50th birthday, I declared to the Universe that I would have a buyer for the Colorado house by my birthday. The week of my birthday, I flew to Washington to celebrate with my foster daughter and Brindi. After arriving, I received a call from a young Colorado couple that was interested in my house. My girls planned a special dinner at Ivar's in Seattle and a comedy show. Just as we were heading out to celebrate, the young couple called, wanting to negotiate a deal. I explained I was on my way to celebrate and told them we would figure something out when I returned home. It was a special 50th birthday celebration.

Arriving home five days before Christmas, I met with the young couple to sign a lease/purchase agreement. During the negotiations, the couple was more than willing to provide a generous non-refundable deposit towards purchasing the house. Since I was carrying the loan for two years, I wanted them highly invested in the deal. They wanted to move in very quickly, which only gave us a few weeks to pack the house, find a rental in Washington and move out. Thankfully, my Dad and I work well under pressure. It only took a few days to find and secure the perfect rental in Washington. After that, things were quickly falling into place.

On January 6, 2017, we left Colorado, bound for Washington, in decent road and weather conditions. We made it to Moab, Utah, late that night just as the weather began to turn. Leaving Moab at first light on January 7th, we had no idea what we were about to drive into. As we slowly made our way into Idaho, we stopped at a Love's truck stop just over the state line. Road conditions and visibility were getting poor. We overheard some truckers heading to Washington say they closed the highway between Oregon and Washington due to ice and snowpack.

The weather reports said the ice storm impacting Idaho was the worst in 50 years. Truckers said we shouldn't risk trying to continue and to find a place to stay. We decided to find the closest motel in a small town called Burley to sit out the storm. It was 9 degrees Fahrenheit with blowing sleet. We passed several wrecks on our way to Burley, the worst one involved a horse trailer. The two horses were out of the trailer and looked alright except for the cold. When we checked into the hotel, we were told our dog was not allowed. Service animals were allowed, but Furby was only an E.S.A. We had to hustle to find somewhere else to stay. Luckily there was a motel just down the street. Exhausted and road-worn, we rented a room, grabbed dinner, and prayed for a break in the weather. I did everything I could to keep our stress down and spirits high. Dad was stressed since he was driving the big U-Haul towing his car on a trailer.

We woke up early and headed for Highway 84, hoping to get closer to our destination. Unfortunately, when we reached the highway, the high winds were making it impossible to see. It took us 5 hours to drive 165 miles from Burley to Boise. Playing it safe, we decided to get off the highway after passing several jack-knifed semi-trucks before the weather got any worse. Somehow, we kept our sense of humor intact and went with the flow. We were supposed to meet the property manager in Washington on the 10th to get our keys, but that wouldn't happen. Thankfully the manager was under-standing of the situation. Anytime I got worried about running over budget, I flipped my thoughts into gratitude. We were lucky that we made it to a motel safely and without incident despite the iced-over roads.

The following day, we checked the road reports before loading our bags into the truck and car, finding out that Highway 84 was closed just north of our location. We couldn't cross into Oregon the way we mapped it, so we detoured west onto Highway 20, a less-traveled pass. We didn't know a chain requirement was put in place until after we were well on our way. Burns, Oregon, is at 4,142 feet elevation. That didn't seem high, considering we were moving from an elevation of 6,500 feet. However, it is regarded as a high elevation, and the roads were a mess. Trucks were sliding and stuck as we passed them, climbing small hills. We were mostly alone on the trip from Idaho to Bend. The snow got worse as we got closer to Bend. Although it took close to 12 hours, we made it to Bend in one day. It was hard to navigate the moving truck and trailer with the amount of snow Bend had received. I called several hotels to find one we could pull in and park without getting stuck. The motel was accommodating, allowing us to wedge the truck and trailer next to a substantial 7-foot pile of plowed snow.

Thankfully there was a restaurant on the other side of the parking lot within walking distance from our room. We were tired of driving, hungry, and stressed. Checking the road conditions as we ate, the news was bleak; we were snowed in for the next two days, and chains were required to get from Bend to Portland. The doors on my 4Runner froze shut from the cold. Dad was tired from all the driving and delays. He accidentally locked the keys in the ignition of the U-Haul when he left it running to keep the battery charged. I could see his frustration and embarrassment. Quickly calling a tow truck for lock-out service, I tried to get him to let it go. The trip had turned into a stressful journey with unexpected expenses at every turn. We had to buy three sets of snow chains to continue the drive.

Without all the tools I have acquired throughout the years, I'm sure things would have been far worse. Dad had grown quite a bit in the years since moving in with me. He was agitated, but he was handling it like a trooper at 75 years old. Bela didn't have a choice. She went along for the ride and was excited to get to our new home. At first light on January 11th, we chained up the vehicles and headed for the mountain pass over Mt. Hood. We were the only cars on the road for most of the trip. It wasn't snowing, but the snowpack was deep. On top of the pass, before heading down to Gresham, I heard a loud, horrible rumbling sound. It sounded like my wheel well had ripped open. I signaled Dad to pull over so we could figure out what was going on. Ice was packed so deep in the wheel wells of my 4Runner that the chains and ice had torn part of the rear quarter panel and mud flaps. We quickly cut the mud flaps off and removed the broken panel, chipping as much of the built-up ice off as we could, then continued down the pass.

Since Dad was driving the 26' U-Haul and car hauler, I followed behind him in case he got into trouble. An hour outside Gresham, a rear tire from the car hauler blew, coming off the rim. With no cell service and on the deserted pass, I got through to 911 and explained our dilemma. The 911 operator connected us to U-Haul roadside assistance. It was dusk and getting extremely cold. U-Haul promised a tow truck would be there within an hour. Three hours passed with no tow truck in sight. We were getting worried and cold, using the car heaters off and on to stay warm. We were quickly running out of fuel. Finally, at 7 pm, I called 911 again and asked if they would patch me through to U-Haul again. U-Haul apologized for the delay but didn't know what happened to the tow truck. I told them it was dark, temperatures were dropping, and we weren't waiting anymore. I asked for their blessing to drive down the pass on the rim. Without any other option, they agreed that we needed to get off the pass for our safety. We drove five mph for 60 miles on a rim to Gresham, where U-Haul paid for a hotel room. In the morning, we were instructed to go to the nearest dealer to trade the trailer.

January 12th, six days after this planned "three-day trip" had begun, we sat in the parking lot at U-Haul as they shoveled a car hauler out of the snow to get us back on the road. All we could do was take pictures of the debacle and laugh. Thankfully, we were only 175 miles from our new home. Portland and Southern Washington were struggling with ice on the freeways and bridges. Chains were required until we entered Vancouver, WA. You have no idea how happy I was to get the chains off the 4Runner and moving truck. Our nerves were completely shot, but we were on the home stretch. We stocked up on junk food, filled the gas tanks, and headed to King County, WA.

As tired as we were, our excitement grew as we got closer. Movers were scheduled to unload the U-Haul on the 10th. I kept in contact with them the entire trip. It was a new company, so they were very flexible and understanding. They met us at our new house around 5 pm, unloading the truck in the dark. We had to return the U-haul the next day. Brindi, Addie, and Nick met us at the house with candy, wine, and flowers, the perfect housewarming gift. While things were super stressful, unexpected, and chaotic with circumstances beyond our control, everything worked out in the end. If I had let myself get upset or angry, things would have been so much worse during that trip.

So many things changed in the first few months we were there. Bela finally got to take ice skating lessons, something she had longed for since she was nine years old. She also got to take English riding lessons at a stable nearby. For the first time in her life, we lived near all sorts of activities. In Colorado, everything was 45 minutes away. When I say everything, I mean the town of Durango, Walmart, the seasonal ice rink, and the park. Seattle, Tacoma, mountains, and malls were all within 45 minutes now. The best part of moving was that my family was back together, and my granddaughter was close.

With the ability to upload videos and do live streams, my following multiplied. Charmed Life was in its 4th year online, and more students were transforming their lives. Everything was going great, but I began to have a growing concern about the couple leasing the Colorado house. They started calling me weekly with odd issues. At first, I thought it was just them getting acquainted with the property. However, problems progressed from burning fire in the woodstove using Duraflame logs instead of firewood to the disposal not working and finally flooding the laundry room, causing significant damage to the family room below. One of my friends who knew a relative of theirs went over to straighten things out. He told me they were fixing it all, calming down my concerns. He said they were young and learning. I trusted him and let it go until the neighbor across the street called with concerns.

Rent for August was late, and September was nothing but excuses. By the end of September, I had to go back to Colorado and evict them for defaulting on the agreement. Brindi, Nick, and I walked into a shocking scene. In nine months, this family destroyed the carpets, put holes in the walls, pulled doors off hinges, and left piles of trash. When I handed the house over to them, I deep cleaned it and replaced the blinds with new ones. Unfortunately, there were no mini blinds intact as I walked through the mess. I was in tears. We had planned on spending the night there, expecting a little clean-up but nothing on the scale it was going to take to get the house in order and up for sale. So rather than freaking out, I booked us a room at the Casino hotel 15 minutes away.

Sky Ute Casino was a favorite place for Dad and me to blow off steam and have some fun. After we checked in, we headed down to the restaurant for dinner. I said a little prayer and asked the Universe to give me the money to cover the unexpected hotel stay and repairs for the house. When we finished our meal, I walked over to one of my favorite machines, put less than $20 in, and won $360. Once again, the Universe delivered. Brindi knew I was able to manifest winning, but Nick couldn't believe it. I cashed the winnings, and we went to our room in a good mood despite the start of the night.

Properties and homes imprint the energy of those who live there. As a conscious creator, I set the intention for the property in love, peace, and serenity. Bela was born on that property, the placenta buried in the northwest corner of the pasture. During my final battle with Leukemia, Shasta was put down due to neck cancer, and she was buried on the property.

Returning to the house and feeling the change in the energy was hard emotionally. I couldn't allow myself to get attached to the home or be reactive about the damage. We had several days of clean-up and repairs ahead of us. Thankfully Nick is a hard worker, skilled at cleaning and painting. Both he and Brindi jumped right into the tasks at hand. Within four days, we put the house back in order and on the market as a "For Sale by Owner." Exhausted but not defeated, we drove straight through the 20-hour drive home.

Trying to sell the house on my own wasn't working from several states away. Although a couple of friends were willing to show the house, potential buyers were impatient. I signed with a realtor. I was hoping it would sell quickly. Months passed, and her inexperience, lack mentality, and attitude began to wear on me. Sure, the house wasn't as excellent shape as when we lived there, but it was a bargain. Trying to keep up with the mortgage for that house and the rent in Washington was overwhelming. By January, I had used most of my savings to keep up. For the first time in years, I wasn't able to pay all the bills on time. I had to stop making the mortgage payments and keep the faith that the Universe would deliver a buyer.

Spring came and went with no solid buyers. One deal fell through at the last minute because of the buyer's credit. I received the notice of foreclosure proceedings which weighed heavily on me. If I lost the house, I would have no choice but to file bankruptcy, an option I could barely digest. After speaking to a bankruptcy lawyer, I got all the paperwork ready but didn't feel right about giving up. I prayed for a solution and some Divine help to sell the house before it was foreclosed. Spirit led me to a short sale expert Leah, that was very friendly and optimistic. Her confidence and energy gave me a boost. I fired the first realtor and listed with her. Within two weeks, she had an offer on the house.

July quickly came to an end, and with it, that deal fell through. However, Leah wasn't discouraged; she and a colleague Andie at another agency were determined to sell it. Meanwhile, I meditated, wrote my intentions, and held gratitude that it was taken care of even though the mortgage company called weekly. Leah had a short sale offer come in that would at least get the house out of foreclosure if the bank agreed.

Short sales can take a year. Fortunately for us, the buyer was informed they only had a couple of months to leave their current home. Pressured, the buyer decided to offer full price. I accepted the offer, signed the paperwork, and returned it to the realtor. The following morning Andie called and said she received another full-price backup offer on the house. The backup offer came from a couple that was willing to wait. Things were finally working out. My faith was increasing. The first buyer backed out by the end of August, but the backup offer quickly proceeded forward. Everything lined up with this couple easily. The bank was set to auction the house off in November, but this deal would close by the end of September. Like clockwork, the house closed, exactly one year after going back to Colorado to evict the young family. Both realtors pitched in money from their commissions to make the numbers work. In the end, I received $58 at closing. I was free from the mortgage debt.

It took a couple of weeks to feel the weight of that burden release. Typically, I can manifest things quickly, but the energy wasn't supporting it. My astrological sign is Sagittarius with Jupiter, the planet of expansion as my ruler. Life was so stressful; I didn't even think to look at how the planetary aspects would affect the sale. Jupiter moved into Scorpio in October 2017, just after I took the house back. Jupiter in Scorpio isn't an easy placement. The "Me Too" movement made national headlines in October 2017, gaining global attention. Racial tensions, gun violence, and hate crimes were also spreading. I intuitively knew significant changes were taking place in 2018, but I didn't realize how much work would be involved individually to create breakthroughs.

It took a year to clear the emotional weight of the house and release 18 years of experience tied to that property. Living in one place, on one property for that many years, changed me on deep levels. For the first time in my life, I had roots, a place always to call home. In numerology, 1+8=9, which represents completion and endings opening to new beginnings. I could have waited to move until 2018 and not had to endure the financial loss in hindsight. I don't, however, believe in coincidences or mistakes. There is no value in questioning the "why" of circumstances or events that played out. The lesson and reminder for the entire year were to remember there is a season for everything. Whether I like the harvest season over the planting or growing season isn't the point. To each experience is an appointed season, an appointed hour. Infinite Intelligence makes no mistakes; therefore, I cannot question the timing.

Knowing that all things work for my highest good, even when they are challenging, allowed me to keep my faith as the months dragged on without a sale. It took great work to keep my ego in check as I opened notices and answered calls from the bank about my delinquent mortgage. I didn't run from it. I didn't avoid the communications. I faced it, holding my vision of a successful conclusion and sale.

I was conflicted when I contemplated bankruptcy. How could I teach on manifesting when I was in this horrible position? I chose to be transparent about it with my classes and clients. Instead of pretending to have a perfect life with no challenges, I shared my struggle to overcome the mind chatter that would seek to steal my peace. Knowing the human side of my life helped others relate to their own internal battles. My ego tried many times to tell me what a failure I had become.

Thoughts of "unworthiness, irresponsibility, and stupidity" bombarded me when I thought the house wouldn't sell. When I focused on the feeling of knowing it was sold, the negative, intrusive thoughts stopped. At one point, I noticed the bankruptcy paperwork on my filing cabinet. Spirit whispered, "Decide, declare, command your financial experience." I didn't want to file bankruptcy or accept that I would have to. I took that paperwork, put it in a manila envelope, and filed it away. "NO!" I vehemently declared, "I am not going to file bankruptcy; the Universe always guides me and provides solutions. I know Universal Law, and I know what I can co-create. The house is sold, the mortgage is released. And so it is done!"

Looking back at my journals, I reminded myself of all the obstacles and challenges I've overcome in life. Abuse, trauma, racism, loss, crisis, and cancer didn't beat me; this wouldn't either. "Remember who you are, Bernadette, remember what you are," I wrote in my journal. Life is a vast collection of experiences, growth, challenge, and victories. We would not appreciate the blessings if it weren't for the challenges. Throughout the year of financial challenge, I kept control over my thoughts as much as possible. Because I didn't speak about the bankruptcy or accept it, I was able to avoid it. I have no issue with bankruptcy, as I certainly could have benefitted from clearing credit card balances. It just didn't feel right for me. As soon as the loan closed, I burned the bankruptcy paperwork and thanked God for the 11th hour save.

30

COMPLETION, ENDINGS & NEW BEGINNINGS

2018 was a year of completion and endings on many fronts. This book, for one, is a project I've worked on and off for almost four years. Bela got her driver's license and is no longer dependent on me to take her everywhere. Our lives in Colorado and the growth cycle there have ended as I embark on a new way of life.

In November 2017, I sensed a spirit around but couldn't see it. The lights in my bathroom kept flickering when I went in. I changed the bulbs, and yet it kept happening. Bela felt the presence as well. She wanted me to take some time and figure out who it was. November was a busy time. I figured if a spirit wanted my attention, they could appear and make it more obvious. Bela was pretty freaked, so I quickly went into meditation and asked if someone wanted to speak to me. Brad, a man I dated in 2010, passed away when his body rejected his 2nd lung transplant. It didn't feel like his energy. It was familiar but nothing I could identify.

As I walked back to my office, I heard "Google Bryan Thomas." That was strange, considering I had been thinking about him for a year. He was the artist and runway hairstylist I dated back in the 90s. When we dated, he had relocated to the states leaving behind his hair salon after the economy in Mexico City crashed. I quickly googled "Bryan Thomas Hairstylist" and found an obituary from the Big Island of Hawaii. According to the obituary, the new boyfriend of an ex-girlfriend had shot him. It made sense why the energy was familiar but unidentifiable. It had been over 20 years since I last spoke to him. I sat back down in quiet and called his energy forward. Love and peace engulfed me. He was letting me know he cared. He popped in and out for several months, constantly blinking lights to let me know he was around.

Things had been quiet in the house with no flashing lights for a while. There was a spirit around, though, one that was having trouble communicating. Although it was faint, I could see the energy begin to materialize before it vanished. Then one day, as I put my contacts in, the light in the bathroom started to flicker. Out of 4 lights, only one was flickering. Immediately I saw a vision in my mind of Robbie, the love of my life. The flickering light and image shook me to the core. I ran to my computer and googled him. I didn't think I'd find anything since he didn't have social media. I was worried about him as I had been dreaming about him for almost a year. He had remarried and had a son, so we stopped talking not long before I moved to Seattle. I hadn't given him my forwarding information.

As I googled his full name and state of residence, my heart dropped at what I read. A short obituary with a recent photo of him stared at me through the computer screen. I ran back to the bathroom to see if he was still around me. The light began to flicker as I asked him questions. I knew instantly he didn't die of natural causes; he had taken his own life. I didn't want to believe it or accept it, but I had no choice. This man I had never gotten over, a man I compared every man to, was gone. I contacted his brother to offer my condolences and confirm what I was getting in Spirit. Sadly, the information I received was accurate. Never have I felt more loved by a man than I did by Robbie.

At 51, I had a hard time understanding how four people I had been romantically involved with were gone. Geo, a boyfriend from my junior year in high school, was the first. He died from a ruptured spleen caused by mono the week of Homecoming. Brad, Bryan, and now Robbie were on the other side. I'm still processing the impact each one had on my life. Robbie had the most significant effect for sure, but each one made an imprint on my heart. I knew I was reaching a new level of growth and understanding; I needed to let go of the past, which also meant letting him go. Although he appears from time to time, I don't idealize the relationship anymore, healing even deeper layers.

With the news of Robbie's passing, the urgency to finish writing this book was reignited. I could feel a major shift of energy on its way. I knew that to make the most of the lessons in my life to this point, I had to tell my story. This story of challenge, crisis, trauma and healing hopefully encourages you. My desire and intention are to empower you to face your challenges and keep going until you have overcome them.

Throughout the last few years, lighthouses have been very symbolic for me. A friend reminded me that I am a lighthouse to many. Lighthouses stand amidst crashing waves, offering light to guide the brave souls who travel the seas. Water represents emotions, the lighthouse symbolic of spiritual strength and guidance. Spiritual guidance is always available to us no matter how badly we get tossed by the waves of emotions. Lighthouses act as warnings to the sailors approaching the rocky shoreline. It can be a beacon that guides one to safety as well.

There have been many blessed souls that have acted as lighthouses for me during times of struggle. I am grateful for the lighthouses on my journey and equally thankful that I have been one for others. No matter how hard things become, our problems automatically get smaller if we are willing to shine our light on others. I have found the best therapy for me is to help others when I am struggling. In offering love and assistance to those in need, the perception of struggle in my own life dissipates.

Many people are experiencing their first spiritual awakening. There is a paradigm shift occurring. Historically, we have lived in a patriarchal, masculine-ruled society. Spirit has spoken many times to and through me, heralding the rise of the Divine Feminine. The Divine Feminine wants to be expressed in humanity, society, and our lives. Whether male or female, we each have masculine and feminine energy. For too long, these energies have been imbalanced, the feminine energy suppressed. In the coming age, we will witness the rise and freedom of the feminine energetic principle.

I've struggled with certain aspects of the feminine energy for much of my life until I became a mother. We see the growing pains already in our society as women take roles of leadership. I am constantly reminded that to express the Divine Feminine is to remain in a state of love, compassion, and nurturing. It is through the work of healing myself and life, in all that Spirit has taken me through, that has allowed the balance of the feminine in me.

It's time to liberate the Divine Feminine from years of repression and suppression to reach wholeness. I learned to embrace my empathic nature, psychic gifts, and sensitivities to express my true nature. Learning to feel my way through things instead of simply thinking through things allowed me the most significant shifts. Too many times, we try to avoid our feelings, especially when those feelings are painful. Yet, it is the very act of riding through painful feelings that bring us to wholeness.

As humanity shifts into the remembrance of the Divine Feminine, we connect to the force of love and creativity. As the feminine energy rises, our collective wounds heal, illusions fade, and our spiritual sight will be restored. Embodying wisdom, compassion, kindness, and intuitive guidance, the Divine Feminine is the lighthouse in the storms of life. Humanity seeks to restore balance to nature and the flow of energy to evolve beyond our current limitations. We must strive to hold the vibration of love in the 5th-dimensional consciousness and beyond, where unity and harmony reside.

Changing my thoughts, replacing outdated beliefs and programs, and releasing stuck emotions opened the doorway to freedom and connection to God/Source. Creating a relationship with my Creator that moved beyond rules and limitations has allowed me to experience a magical, charmed life. Working on myself is an ever-changing journey of discovery and experience. As I get older, the one thing I know for sure is that I don't know much. There are infinite possibilities, realities, and dimensions available if we are open to the experience.

I have no doubt there will be many new adventures in my life. Life is like climbing to the peak of a mountain. As we reach the top of the peak, another mountain with a higher peak appears. Thus, with each lesson, challenge, and season of growth, we evolve and ascend to higher states of consciousness.

Growing up as an empath with psychic gifts was not easy. It was made worse by family dysfunction. I have no anger at what I've gone through. Working to heal on a deep level has afforded me an appreciation for all my experiences. From where I stand now, I am glad I never gave up. Grateful I failed at suicide and grateful illness didn't end my life. Once I learned how to control my empathic and psychic gifts, life got easier.

Know that life leads you to greater awareness and true inner strength no matter where you are on your path. Learn from the lessons of the past, but don't let them define you. Don't let the inexperience or misunderstanding of others deflate you. Instead, set your intention for the course of your life and follow your heart. Your heart and intuition are your internal GPS, your personal guidance system. Learn to trust yourself, embrace and receive help from others, knowing that you are never alone.

Peeking into people's lives and living a full life myself has allowed me a view many don't get. I've learned repeatedly we never really know what people are honestly thinking or feeling. People wear masks, and they hide their pain, fear, and insecurities. Either for the sake of approval or to seemingly spare their loved one's worry. Some are lost and in search of who they are. As they journey along their paths, it's a series of trial and error, each choice creating a different outcome. Some people live colorful inner lives yet never project that to the outer world. Others live colorful lives in the external world, but their inner world is dull, numb, and colorless. Can we really ever know someone? Some things defy human language and understanding.

As souls, we have lived many lives and experienced various cultures. Things we have excelled at in one lifetime may never be expressed in this one. Something we were horrible at in a past life may achieve greatness in this life. My life has been an adventure spent bridging the subtle realms and 3rd dimension. Some parts of the adventure are heartbreaking, others exhilarating, none of it boring.

As I reflect on the vast knowledge of people's lives, their feelings, and their innermost thoughts, sometimes unexpressed, I am in awe. We are exposed to 20,000 bits of information a second. Yet, most of those bits are missed by our busy minds, occupied by mundane activities. On average, we use one-tenth of our brain's capacity to process. I continually wonder when we will evolve and use the other 90 percent. There is so much to learn and experience, but we must be fully present in each moment to get the most out of it.

I've learned that no one experiences things at the same level, with the same feeling or even the same perception. What I see and feel can't be compared to what you see and feel. The level at which I feel one thing might pale in comparison to your experience of the same thing. Preferences, desires, beliefs, and history all create a different reality in each person. We are all alive in this moment and yet living multiple realities simultaneously.

When I communicate with souls who have crossed over, each one is still learning, growing, and evolving. Even beyond physical death, our souls, our spirit continues to expand. We live in an infinite universe, so it only makes sense that we continue to evolve even in spirit form. I've had the great honor of delivering messages from those on the other side. They always have wisdom that they admit to not having while living their 3rd dimensional, physical lives. Yet, no matter how they lived, they are happy, filled with love and compassion. It's always amazed me how they choose light bodies that reflect a time when they were happiest with their body image and physical abilities. Sometimes 70-year old's come through as they appeared in their 30's. Having access beyond the veil has allowed me to broaden my perspective. I know one thing for sure, there is more to learn and understand than can be done in one lifetime.

It is approaching the end of summer 2021 as I complete the final edits, releasing this to the world. With great vulnerability from my new home in Texas, I entrust you with my journey. May it encourage you and inspire you to trust your intuition wherever it may lead.

AFTERWORD

This journey has been exciting, expansive, and full of every emotion. I don't' know what the next leg of my journey will look like, but I'm finally sure I'm up to the task.

May your journey be filled with insights, joy, and the light of Spirit. Please review the free resources at the end of the book to receive access to meditations, tools and tips for success, and more.

Be Blessed and be a blessing!

ACKNOWLEDGMENTS

I dedicate this book to my girls, Brindi, Bela, Alissa, and of course, Addie. It wouldn't be possible without the support and love of my Dad, my cousin Grant, and all the unnamed heroes who were there to hold me up. I LOVE YOU!

Thank you to the family and friends who have witnessed my life, out of the ordinary as it is, and still believed in me and loved me.

With special thanks to Brindi, my firstborn, first love, and the reason I made it beyond my twenties. You helped me grow up. I'll love you forever and like you for always, forever you'll be a sweet baby to me.

A special thanks to a successful, talented Young Adult Fantasy Author, Tessonja Odette, for formatting the book multiple times.

May you be blessed with a hundred-fold return. Check out her books: www.tessonjaodette.com

Thank you, Miss Lane (Valkyrie), for being an amazing assistant and friend.

Thank you, Megs, for cheering me on through the spirit craziness of the last edits. You are a warrior through and through.

Thank you Laura @govirtualnowinc.com for all the help with the launch!!

And to my Charmed Life crew, past, present, and future - I LOVE YOU!

BERNADETTE'S BIO

Bernadette Gold is a no-nonsense, Clairvoyant, Spiritual Teacher, Master Healer, Consciousness Leader, and Success Coach facilitating rapid breakthroughs that create insights leading to quantum leaps in health, happiness, and prosperity. She runs a successful practice, using her skills and spiritual gifts to guide successful, high-achievers to their highest path and purpose, connected to Spirit. Bernadette also facilitates group coaching programs where she helps clients clear old wounds, beliefs, and trauma, creating a new energetic paradigm that leads to elevated income, increased impact, and fulfillment in all areas of life.

She has a vision and mission to create a movement and paradigm shift within humanity to activate the intuitive intelligence of our current leaders and the next generation of leaders. Bernadette envisions a world led by heart-centered, intuitive leaders that celebrate each person's Divine gifts and genius.

Bernadette has helped tens of thousands of clients worldwide since 2000, and has been a successful entrepreneur since 1998. She has never settled for the ordinary. She demands excellence in work, life and has created an extraordinary life for herself and her clients.

Sarvatva Healing™ is an original healing modality to bring "wholeness, completeness, totality" to the mental, emotional, and physical bodies, using a combination of psychology, spirituality, and energy to create rapid healing.

We live in an INFINITE, BENEVOLENT UNIVERSE where everything you want is already here. You just need to align to your highest-level frequency to express it fully. I'm best known for my no-b.s. approach to simplifying spiritual principles, delivering practical tools, and energetic keys for transformation. I am so glad you were guided here, I invite you to explore the possibilities available for your expansion, to create powerful solutions to everyday issues of the heart, mind, and soul. ~Bernadette

FREE RESOURCES

FREE meditations, high vibe tips and more:

https://www.bernadettegold.com/successrituals

Join our Community of Empaths, Sensitives, and Spiritual Seekers:

https://www.facebook.com/burninggold

Follow on FB:

https://www.facebook.com/enchantedwealth

**Follow on Youtube:

https://www.youtube.com/c/bernadettegold

** Scan the QR Code to listen to the Intuitive Intelligence Podcast on Apple Podcast: